The Eighth Sacrament

How God Transforms Our Lives by the Sacraments of the Church

God bless you.

Fr. Mathew

MATHEW C. JOHN

ISBN 978-1-64028-064-9 (Paperback)
ISBN 978-1-64028-065-6 (Digital)

Christian Faith Publishing, Inc.
296 Chestnut Street
Meadville, PA 16335
www.christianfaithpublishing.com

Scripture quotations are from the New American Bible – Revised Edition published by American Bible Society, 1865 Broadway, New York, NY 10023.

Printed in the United States of America

Contents

To Be Kept in Mind

I am not a writer. You might even question the validity of the situations and events that I am going to describe in this book. My explanation is that these are personal moments and events that just happen. I wrote this down, just because I was inspired to do it this way.

Sometimes I ask myself, "Why do we have all the sacraments of the Church?" The answer is that they confer on us supernatural graces. God gives us supernatural graces for a higher purpose. I have been reflecting on what that purpose would be for quite some time now. I humbly realize that the purpose of all the supernatural graces God showers upon us in this earthly life is for us to become another "sacrament," to become the masterpiece of God, to be a blessing to other people. I call it the *eighth sacrament*. This work is a humble effort to tell you how I look at the seven sacraments of the Church as transforming a Catholic into God's masterpiece and another sacrament in this world.

If you ask me about my qualifications to write this book, my only qualification is being a priest of the Lord for just thirteen years. Nothing else. If you ask me about the tools I used for gathering information, it is mostly observation, discussion with other people, and personal reflection. I observe my life and your life and reflect on it and around it. I try to analyze our faith-life in the light of the sacraments of the Church. I find deficiencies in how we live our lives and what we consider important in our cultural setting. They seem to contradict the faith that we profess and the kind of life God wants us to lead. I criticize the way we live our lives and in particular some of our practices in our cultural context. To question our social and cultural practices that have crept into one's Catholic life might become painful, might hurt our feelings, or might go against our practices. Well, truth can be hurtful at times.

This book is my prayer, my praise, my cry, my frustrations.

One thing you might notice is the lack of references. I didn't want to borrow someone's opinion to support mine. I told you already that these are my own convictions and conclusions that I have come to by observations and reflections. But everything that I have written has been written in the light of Scripture; so it is also a journey through Scripture, both Old Testament and New Testament.

This book is not meant for people who are well-grounded in Catholic theology, but rather for men and women in everyday life who would like to find more meaning in their faith-journey. For a Catholic, there is no faith-life without the sacraments of the Church. The sacraments are the lifeblood of a Catholic. Trying to understand one's life from the sacramental point of view, and analyzing it in the light of the sacraments, will definitely help one to reevaluate one's life. That might help the person to appreciate more the immeasurable value and beauty of each sacrament and the worth and beauty of his/her life. This may lead a person to consider how God transforms him/her into another sacrament by the supernatural power of the sacraments of the Church.

My sole intention is to make you rediscover the beauty of our Catholic life that has been embedded in the sacraments of the Church. The sacraments are furnaces in which we are refined. Try to purify your life in the fire of each sacrament. As you continue to read through these pages, it is my hope that you will see what it means to be a Catholic.

Foreword

Harry S. Truman was president when I first learned about the Seven Sacraments. My *Baltimore Catechism* defined *sacrament* as "a visible sign instituted by Christ to give grace." In his book, Father Mathew tells us that we are the *eighth sacrament*. Some traditionalists might find this incredulous while others may even be shocked.

I first encountered this novel idea well over fifty years ago during my orientation for the Catholic Lay Extension Volunteers in 1965 at Barat College in Chicago. One day we attended a lecture by Sister Charles Borromeo. She said that the eighth sacrament was "the human person, and it was the only sacrament that everyone in the world could receive, no matter if they were Catholic or not." Since then I have tried to identify the people who have acted as *messengers of grace* in my life.

Since then I have been surprised that it has taken this long for someone to tap into this profound expression of what the late Fr. Andrew Greeley called the *Catholic imagination*. Father Mathew's book fills the dark void that is much more than timely. It is very much in line with what late Hall of Famer Yogi Berra once said at a celebration of his career by his hometown,

St. Louis Browns, in 1947. Before a large throng, Berra thanked all those "who made this award necessary."

Father Mathew writes that his main intention in writing this book was to make Catholics "rediscover the beauty of our Catholic life that has been embedded in the sacraments of the Church." He sees the sacraments as furnaces that can purify one's life in their redemptive fires. He firmly believes that the purpose of "all the supernatural graces God showers upon us in this earthly life is for us to become another sacrament," that is, to become "the masterpiece of God" and a "blessing to other people."

While the *Eighth Sacrament* is one for the ages—all ages, Father Mathew has written it, primarily with the ordinary Catholic layman in mind. I believe their numbers are legion. When I graduated from Holy Cross in 1965, I had sixteen credits in theology and twelve in philosophy. That is hardly the case today as many Catholic institutions have all but eliminated the study of the faith as part of its core curriculum.

I think it is also true because the Church is a very human institution—a living contradiction. I once asked a priest during a Christmas Mission in my parish if he had any advice for someone who had been born into the pre-Vatican Church but came to his full religious maturity during the inchoate reforms of the Second Vatican Council called by Pope John XXIII. I do not think he answered my question nor did anyone else seem to understand my dilemma.

Since Vatican II, I have felt caught twixt and tween the old and new Church. It is as if I had one foot anchored in the traditional Church and the other foot desperately trying to maintain my religious equilibrium in the reformed Church. There are many things about the old Church of my youth, which I still relish. As a child, the many rules, moral laws, and order of the faith were deeply ingrained in me by habited nuns and humorless priests. Along with the *Baltimore Catechism*, they laid the foundation for my adult faith.

Catholics then all learned the dogmas of the faith by rote memory with a diligence and certitude that armed us to face the three major enemies, who competed for our immortal souls— *the world, the flesh, and the devil.* To paraphrase TV's *Dragnet's* Sergeant Joe Friday in the 1950s, "we knew the facts." The rules worked! I have kept the faith all these years. I have avoided most of the near occasions of sins. However, the Church's abject legalism did take a toll on my understanding of God's divine mercy and the agape reflection of His unlimited personality.

For most of my life, I have been a habitual worrier who is relieved when things are over, instead of capturing the many joyful moments of grace in my life. The new Church is much different. The Church of love and forgiveness has replaced the Church of law and order. In the Church of divine rules, I had tried to micromanage everything and had left nothing up to God. But the freedoms of the modern Church can also be the worst nightmare of the Grand Inquisitor, in Fyodor Dostoevsky's classic *The Brothers Karamazov*, who cursed God for making men with a free will.

For me, the bifurcated Church poses a stark contrast between the vertical of the old Church with its individual approach to God versus the new Church, where the horizontal plane of community reigns unfettered. When joined in perfect union, they form the Cross of Christ, which is the essence of the Church's role. However, being human, its leaders over the years have inclined to overemphasize one direction over the other.

It is into this landscape that Father Mathew has introduced an *old idea* that never found its footing in the 1960s. Father is well aware that the modern ideas of relativism and secularism have permeated our culture. These treacherous ideas have infiltrated Church thinking on many levels. The modern Church has in some respects thrown the Christ child out with the bathwater. Scandal, indifference, and moral confusion have been woefully present. Unfortunately, too many of my fellow Catholics do not have the double grounding in the faith that I have.

To help remedy this situation, Father Mathew has put the sacraments, especially Holy Matrimony, at the forefront of the culture war. Unlike too many priests who have conveniently ignored the decline of family, Father clearly and rightfully identifies the marriage of a man and a woman as the cornerstone of our civilization. I picture *Eighth Sacrament* in the context of the Augustinian tradition of the *City of God* as it engages in an eternal battle with the *City of Man*. In the last half century, it has become apparent that man's secular city is winning. A full appreciation and application of the *eighth sacrament* just may help turn the tide.

Father Mathew's approach to the gospel of marriage is more communal than the vertical approach of the venerable bishop Fulton J. Sheen's 1951 Classic *Three to Get Married*. A source no greater than Pope Francis stands in agreement with Father Mathew's emphasis on the importance of focusing on marriage.

In his 2015 book, *The Joy of Love: On Love in the Family*, the pope writes, "Just as God dwells in the praises of the of his people, so he dwells within the married love that gives him glory."

Father Mathew imagines God as the master artist. We all existed in the mind of God long before our birth. He loved the perfect design of us so much that He wanted to give life to it by creating us in his image and likeness. But all artists need a canvas to realize or capture the design that exists in their minds. The sacrament of Matrimony provides the flesh-and-blood canvas God chose to give expression to his design. But He chose to rely on us to help bring His human design into perfection. The sacraments are the oils God fashioned to give us the graces we needed to effect his design. Each sacrament invites us to make our own the favorable time of the Lord that the Church proclaims. One need only study Saint John Paul II's idea of the *spousal meaning of the body* in his *Theology of the Body* to fully understand the importance of Christian marriage.

During the course of his sacred narrative, Father Mathew writes about all the sacraments in great detail. Simply stated, *Baptism* brings us into the life of God with the Church! The *sacrament of Reconciliation* is a continuous process of cleansing souls. The *Eucharist* is the divine food and the drink of life. *Confirmation* shapes our *real person*, the spiritual person within us. The *Anointing of the Sick* is God's final touch on our souls before He calls us to Himself. *Holy Orders* is that sacrament which facilitates all the other sacraments that help us become a blessing to other people in this world.

In summary, the *Eighth Sacrament* is a biblically focused book, written in a lyrical style that corresponds perfectly with the Catholic imagination. For those who are obliviously to most of the above or see their Catholic faith as purely cultural or ornamental, this book could be a lifesaver. More importantly, it could be a soul saver.

William A. Borst, PhD

Introduction

One of my friends, who could not receive the sacraments because he had divorced and remarried outside the Church, said with tears that we do not realize the importance of the sacraments until we are deprived of them. That made me reflect upon the significance of the sacraments of the Church in the life of a Catholic.

The sacraments of the Church, as you know, are visible signs of invisible but supernatural powers that come forth from God by the working of the Holy Spirit, flowing into a Catholic who receives them in good faith. They are instituted by Christ, but entrusted to the Church, the mystical body of Christ, for the sanctification of our lives. We are, as you know, born sinful, as the Prophet David says in Psalm 51: "Behold, I was born in guilt, in sin my mother conceived me" (7). The Lord wills that we be guided continuously in our earthly life through the sacraments of the Church so that by receiving the sacraments, we will become spiritually perfect to stand in the presence of the Lord at the end of our earthly lives.

I do feel that even many practicing Catholics fail to realize the importance of the sacraments. If we observe the general reactions of our Catholic population to the sacraments of the

Church, and the manner with which they receive some of the sacraments, we will realize this. There are many Catholic parents who do not care to baptize their children in the right time; some do it for social reasons. Many Catholic parents don't encourage their children to receive the sacrament of Reconciliation on a regular basis; so many, as you are aware, do not go to this wonderful sacrament of God's mercy anymore, or go to it very rarely.

Haven't you observed how careless and casual many people are these days at the Eucharist? For a number of people, Sunday Mass is just an obligation. Many young people have told me that they feel bored at the Eucharistic celebration! This makes me sick and sad. Talking to many eighth graders who are preparing for the sacrament of Confirmation, I realize that many of them do not know what this sacrament is all about. Many of them, though they are old enough to receive this sacrament, do not seem mature enough for it. But it is given to them anyway when they reach the eighth grade. The sacrament of the Anointing of the Sick, of course, is sought by many people with enthusiasm, as they know it will help them get better; some are scared that the reception of this sacrament means that they are going to die! The sacrament of Matrimony, in my observation, is not given enough consideration. This sacrament, in my opinion, should be given the utmost importance because this sacrament, which forms a family, is the cornerstone of society. If our society is bad today, it is because many families are not places of virtues anymore; it is because we don't place due weight on the sacrament of Matrimony that forms families. I also dare to say that without this wonderful sacrament, there is no other sacrament! That is the reason the first chapter of this book deals not with Baptism, but Matrimony. What kind of preparation do our young people go through to enter into such an important sacrament? A few hours of a marriage preparation course, family planning, and a few sessions with the minister who witnesses the sacrament!

The Church is proclaiming a favorable time of the Lord to us through the Seven Sacraments. The Seven Sacraments are seven marvels of the Lord in our lives. Each sacrament invites us to make our own the favorable time of the Lord that the Church proclaims. The Church continues to invite us to immerse ourselves in the ocean of supernatural graces and to come out as better human beings, in short, to become closer to the image of Christ!

I like to consider God as the master artist. We existed in the mind of God before our birth. The design He had in His mind was perfect. He loved the design of us so much that He wanted to give life to it by creating us. An artist who has an image or a design in mind needs a canvas to realize or capture the design that exists in his mind. The sacrament of Matrimony is the canvas God uses to give expression to his designs: you and me. God works through people as coartists to realize the design that exists in His mind and to bring His design into reality.

Although we are "wonderfully made" (Psalm 139:14), we lack inner perfection, since we have been procreated by our parents as God's coartists. Therefore, God, the master artist, gives us ongoing touches throughout life from time to time with the other six sacraments of the Church so that we will become perfect, a real masterpiece; we will become the "eighth sacrament" in this world.

Once a human life takes shape on the canvas of matrimony, God calls each by name. The prophet Isaiah says, "I have called you by name: You are mine" (Isaiah 43:1). The act of calling us by name is done through the sacrament of Baptism. Baptism brings us into the Church, the Eucharistic community: into the life of God.

The sacrament of Reconciliation is a continuous process of cleansing souls. This sacrament gives us hope of salvation on a day-to-day basis, or we would have to carry around the burden of our sins. The Lord, in his mercy, polishes us in this sacrament so that our souls will shine like gold.

The Sacrament of the Eucharist is the symbol of the eternal love of the Lord by which He is present among His people. The Eucharist is the divine food and the drink of life. The Lord said to the prophet Elijah, "Get up and eat, or the journey will be too much for you!" (1 Kings 19:7). The Eucharist strengthens us in this world to carry on our earthly pilgrimage. Jesus said to His disciples, "Unless you eat the flesh of the Son of Man and drink his blood, you do not have life within you" (John 6:53).

The sacrament of Confirmation is God's seal of ownership and love of the Holy Spirit. This sacrament gives us power from on high. By pouring out the Holy Spirit, God continues to shape our *real person*, the spiritual person within us. We become spiritual people by producing the fruits of the Spirit. Life in the Spirit makes us the "eighth sacrament" in the world.

The Anointing of the Sick, if received in good faith as part of the last rites, is God's final touch on our souls before He calls us to Himself. It is a moment of God's reassuring smile before we make our final journey. I like to consider this sacrament as the final preparation of the masterpiece of God to return to the master craftsman or artist Himself. It is the final touch of God on His art; it is the last touch that makes us ready to present ourselves before our maker.

The sacrament of Holy Orders is the fulfillment of God's promise: "I will appoint for you shepherds after my own heart, who will shepherd you wisely and prudently." (Jeremiah 3:15). The sacrament of Holy Orders is that sacrament which facilitates all other sacraments that help us become perfect, that help us become a blessing to other people in this world, and make us worthy to stand in the presence of the Lord when our earthly journey is complete.

To create us, God used the instrumentality of our parents in the sacrament of Matrimony; to perfect us, He calls men to Holy Orders who will perfect His people with the sacraments of the Church. Nourished and strengthened by the sacraments of the Church, we become the perfect image of the design God conceived in His mind before He formed us in our mother's womb.

CHAPTER 1

The Canvas for God's Masterpiece

You formed my inmost being; you knit me in my mother's womb.
—Psalm 139:13

I consider God as the master artist and myself as a masterpiece of God. He knit me in my mother's womb like a great weaver, like a craftsman, without any defect, but with accuracy and perfection. Like a renowned artist or a painter or a sculptor, God formed me in my mother's womb. I like the word *formed* because it sounds as if God is a great artist, a painter, a sculptor, or a potter. God is a potter; Scripture says so (cf. Jeremiah 18). Yes, God is a wonderful artist; that is why I am so perfect! I like to think that God made many attempts, like sculptors and artists do, before He gave me a final form, the best shape in the womb of my mother! God must have refashioned me over and over again to make me perfect. Like a potter, He must have remodeled me. As God Almighty, He didn't have to reshape His creation; He didn't have to remold His works. He could certainly bring out the best shape with one touch at the first attempt. But since He sounds like a sculptor or even a potter, I think, God must have reshaped His creation to give it the best look. That is not a sign of any bit of inefficiency, but instead it tells me how important His work is to Him, how concerned and meticulous He is about His creation, how precious I am to Him! Isaiah, the prophet, tells us that we are precious in the eyes of the Lord, honored and loved by Him (43:4). It simply means that God did not make you and me casually or carelessly, but with utmost attention. This is yet another sign of His uncompromising love for us even as we're being fashioned in the secret of the earth by His divine fingers.

The design of each of us existed in the mind of God before we were born. It means that we were born first in the mind of God before we were conceived in our mother's womb. God needs a canvas to give shape to the idea, the image, or the design that He has in mind. Every artist, I believe, conceives his/her masterpiece first in his/her mind. Then he/she realizes that design on a canvas. God, as the master artist, chooses to portray His masterpiece on a canvas. The canvas He uses to portray you and me in this world is the sacrament of Matrimony. I would like to think that God, though He conceives the idea of you and me in His mind, does not portray us all by Himself; He makes use of men and women as His coartists to realize the design He has in His mind. Our parents were His coartists who cooperated with God to bring us into this world. In other words, God used the sacrament of Matrimony as the canvas and our parents as the coartists who cooperated with God to realize the image that He conceived in His mind. Try to recall our preexistence in the mind of the Almighty: "Before I formed you in the womb I knew you, before you were born, I dedicated you, a prophet to the nations I appointed you" (Jeremiah 1:5).

I firmly believe that the image God conceived of us in His mind was executed through the instrumentality of our parents. We were brought into being through the cooperation of our parents. God forged a wonderful sacrament to execute His plan, to give life and shape to the image of us that He conceived in His mind, to bring us into this world. The sacrament of Matrimony must be the most wonderful sacrament of all, because without this sacrament, we would not be what we are now.

Catholics, as you know, speak of seven sacraments. What comes first in our Catechism is the sacrament of Baptism. At least, that is how I was taught. I am sure if someone asks us to list the seven sacraments of the Church, we will start with Baptism. But for me, there is another way to approach it. The sacrament of Matrimony should be the first one, because without this wonderful sacrament, no other sacrament would be possible. A priest can baptize a child, hear confessions, give Holy Communion, or anoint the sick, only if a person has been brought forth in the first place; and that is done through the sacrament of Matrimony. A bishop can administer the sacrament of Confirmation or Holy Orders only if there is a person present. And life should only be generated in the context of marriage. Marriage means "matrix of life"! The Pope and bishops wear rings as a symbol of their authority, but their position would not be possible if their parents had not first entered into the sacrament of Matrimony, which is also symbolized by rings. In that sense, it is the wedding ring that is more important than the ring of the Pope or a bishop. That is the reason I say we must place the sacrament of Matrimony first.

Other religions may not consider marriage as a sacrament, as Catholics do; but it is sacred in every religion and culture across the world. The other sacraments we speak of may be unfamiliar or even unheard-of in other religions and cultures, but marriage is honored everywhere. It is familiar to all religions and cultures. Even primitive peoples who live away from mainstream society consider the union between a man and a woman sacred. This shows the importance of this act. That is the reason I thought of speaking about the sacrament of Matrimony before all other sacraments. For me, the other six sacraments are the outcome of this single sacrament, Matrimony. Though we speak highly of this sacrament, we usually place it as the last of the sacraments in their order. Honestly, I do not know why!

The Church father Tertullian wrote: "How can I ever express the happiness of the marriage that is joined together by the Church, strengthened by an offering, sealed by a blessing, announced by angels and ratified by the Father... How wonderful the bond between two believers with a single hope, a single desire, a single observance; there is no separation between them in spirit or flesh; in fact they are truly two in one flesh and when the flesh is one, one is the spirit."

How could God love us with an everlasting love if we were not brought forth by our parents? How could God call us by name if we were not born into this world? How would God appoint us over nations and kingdoms to pluck and to uproot, to destroy and to overthrow, to plant and to build? How could we have been born into this life if our mothers did not conceive us in their wombs? How could we praise God's name or glorify His name when looking at ourselves, at our marvelous being! How would God feed us with milk and honey as a mother would feed her baby? How would God engrave our names upon the palm of His hand?

God knew that we had to be created first to shower us with His love. His plans for us could be realized only through the sacrament of Matrimony. That is the reason God forged the covenant between a man and a woman. Actually, marriage was behind God's entire scheme for humanity. In the book of Genesis, the Lord blessed Adam and Eve, our first parents, with the words, "Be fertile and multiply; fill the earth and subdue it" (1:28). We call Adam and Eve our First Parents. For me, that points to a family, which takes shape through the sacrament of Matrimony. God blessed them only after bringing them together in a wonderful union. Humanity proceeded from them as a result of a life together, which the Lord blessed. The destiny of the world would have been different if God hadn't forged a covenant for men and women to enter into a permanent union. This points to the importance of marriage and family life in the world.

Importance of Marriage

Marriage is a universal act that exists in every culture and religion. Every religion considers marriage as a sacred act; there is a supernatural coloring given to it. It is nothing unique to our times that some people oppose and destroy marriage; it has been there from time immemorial. We find marriages in the Old Testament. Though we know that God created woman as a helpmate to man, and we consider them our First Parents, we don't have the word *marriage* mentioned when it speaks about Adam and Eve. But we have many places where it is said, "the man had intercourse with his wife Eve" (Genesis 4:1). In the same chapter, we read, "Cain had intercourse with his wife, and she conceived and bore Enoch" (Genesis 4:17). Even today, in our common language, men and women who are not married but staying together are addressed as boyfriends and girlfriends or partners, not husband and wife. "Husband and wife" is used only when people actually get married.

But as we move from Genesis to other books of the Old Testament, we find the word *marriage* used. For example, Genesis 29 speaks of Jacob's marriage to Leah and Rachel. I think this is the earliest mention of the word *marriage* in Scripture. Verse 21 says, "Then Jacob said to Laban, give me my wife, that I may consummate my marriage with her, for my term is now complete" (Genesis 29:21). In the book of Tobit, the word *marriage* is mentioned more than once. The angel Raphael says to Tobiah, "Since you are Sarah's closest relative, you more than any other have the right to marry her" (Tobit 6:12). Chapter 7 speaks about the marriage of Tobiah and Sarah. The prophet Isaiah uses marriage imagery to show God's love for his people, Israel: "For as a young man marries a virgin, your Builder shall marry you" (Isaiah 62:5). Of course, the New Testament mentions the word *marriage* many times. I hope no one will have any room for doubt about that.

I am trying to tell you that marriage is not something we invented just this morning or last night; it's not something invented by my grandparents or yours, at the beginning of this century or at the end of the last. It was willed by the Lord from time immemorial, from the foundation of the world.

If you look into various religions, we find that marriage is considered sacred. Most Hindus get married in temples. They can also do it in some other place, away from temples, but it is done in a religious context; the one who officiates the ceremony is a qualified person, a Hindu priest. Muslims get married in a religious environment in the presence of their religious leader, though not necessarily in mosques. I have seen many marriages among the aboriginal peoples of India; all of them were done within a sacred, religious belief system of their own. I do not think there is any culture or people or nation that considers marriage as not sacred or important. Even people who do not believe in or belong to any religion get married in the presence of a registrar in a civil ceremony; it is official and formal. There must be an *authority* that allows a man and a woman to live together as husband and wife.

A clay pot can be made only at a wheel. I do not know, neither have I seen, any potter making a pot without a wheel. So too is the sacrament of Matrimony. To give the best shape to their children, parents need the sacrament of Matrimony. Let us call that the "potter's wheel." If they try to bear children without marriage, most likely the children will be "disfigured," as a pot will be disfigured without a wheel. I am not speaking about physical deformity, but of moral deformity. That is one of the major concerns of the present situation, of our present culture.

People are unwilling to get married, but they happen to generate children. This poses two problems. First of all, since they do not have the potter's wheel of marriage to function with, they fail to work properly and sincerely. The children they bear may not be the best of shape. Secondly, the parents may fail, as in many cases, to give continuous touches to remold their children. This means that those who do not get married but bring forth children anyway are not the kind of parents God is looking for as His coworkers in giving shape to the world. They are not working to perfect the world, but they work with the devil to disfigure the face of humanity and human dignity. Our society and culture have been so infected, largely because of this factor.

Canvas and Studio

I like to consider the sacrament of Matrimony as the canvas on which God, the master artist, portrays His masterpiece, man, and a family as the studio wherein the artist continues to work at his artwork until he finishes with his artwork. Every family should be like a studio wherein God's coartists, parents, continue to work at their children, God's images, into His masterpieces.

Haven't you seen how an artist works at his/her painting in his/her studio? He/she, after doing some work at the image, may step back a few yards and gaze at the work for a few seconds from different angles. Then he/she may step in and give one or two touches here and there, may step back again and look at the image, may step in and touch here or there. This might go on for several times until the artist is satisfied with the image, until the image assumes the exact shape of the design he/she had in mind before he/she started out to portray the image on the canvas.

I was visiting a friend of mine, a great artist. He took me down to his vast studio where he spent most of his time, working on different themes. There were many finished and unfinished works. He told me that the studio was everything to him! He said he would simply sit, sometimes many hours, staring at the image he is trying to complete, trying to make sure the image he is working on perfectly conforms to the theme he has in mind.

This reminds me once again the potter and clay passage in Jeremiah 18:3–4: "I went down to the potter's house and there he was, working at the wheel. Whenever the vessel of clay he was making turned out badly in his hands, he tried again, making another vessel of whatever sort he pleased." The sacrament of Matrimony is the " wheel" and family is the "potter's house." Children are like clay in the hands of their parents. God wants the parents to reshape the lives of their children constantly, until they are pleasing to the Lord.

Now, everyone cannot create a masterpiece. For example, I can give talks, sing a little bit, write on certain subjects. But I cannot do any painting or sculpturing. I am not simply talented to do painting or any kind of artworks. If I try to paint, well, that may not be impressive to others. If a person who is not talented in music tries to sing before an audience, he/she may make himself/herself a fool in front of them. We need some "qualification" to do certain things. For example, if a priest ordains a person to priesthood, that will not be a valid ordination because the one ordaining is not qualified for the job.

Every artist works strenuously at the artwork in his/her studio. A masterpiece is the result of passion for the profession and hard work and commitment. Married people should have a passion for their vocation and commitment in forming their children into masterpieces for God.

Making a Catholic Home

The Syro-Malabar Catholic diocese of Chicago brought out a document a few months ago with the view of strengthening Catholic families. Syro-Malabar Church, or Church of Malabar Syrian Catholics, is an Eastern Catholic Major Archiepiscopal Church in full communion with the Bishop of Rome, the Pope. This Church focuses very much on families as it knows that there is no future for any Church without great families. The document suggested eight points for the families to consider. Though these eight points might seem simple and even silly, I think they are of great importance.

Pictures of the Sacred Heart and Holy Family

This is one of the distinguishing marks of a Catholic family back in my place. Every Catholic family has these pictures. To be honest, there will be at least one holy picture in every room! Every home has a crucifix, a Bible, rosaries, scapulars, and many prayer books. Every child grows up amid all these religious articles. A mother who feeds her child takes it to one of these pictures and points it out to the child, tells stories about the pictures, might even say, to make the child eat, that "Jesus will get angry." Children get used to these sacred pictures and what these pictures stand for.

In addition to these sacred pictures on walls, most of the houses would have a prayer room with a small altar. The family gathers in this room for family prayer every evening. Children, before they leave for school, go there to make a small prayer. Their day is blessed! I wish our families here gather around some sacred pictures in the evenings; I wish our mothers here told stories of saints to their children. I am sure, our children will grow up loving God and their religion.

When I am invited to bless a house here, I look for a sacred picture or a crucifix, facing which I could start the prayer. In many cases, I wouldn't find one. I stand in the kitchen or else-where to do what I am called to do. I would then think of my home with a prayer room where the priest would stand and lead the prayers. I wish our families here had more signs of being Catholic. Not having any religious articles around our homes is a sign of the presence of God leaving our homes, our society, and our culture. Maybe we are slowly slipping into religious sloth.

Sacred pictures sanctify our homes; they bring to us the presence of the Lord. Children grow in the company of the Sacred Heart, the Holy Family, and other saints. Our families grow in the shadow of God's grace.

Renewal of Marriage Vows

This is yet another important point to consider. I am sure every Catholic couple, who got married in the Catholic Church, would remember their wedding promise they made before God and the community on the day of their wedding. Some of you may have forgotten this vow by now. I am writing this down here for you:

> I, n., take you, n., to be my husband/wife. I
> promise to be true to you in good times and
> in bad, in sickness and in health. I will love
> you and honor you all the days of my life.

Try to renew it every day, if possible before your children. If couple can find time to repeat this every day, I believe the divorce rate among our Catholic population will probably be nil! The reasons or rather excuses couples level against each other will certainly melt away if they can say this promise from the depth of their heart.

By Heart 1 Corinthians 13:4–8

> Love is patient, love is kind. It is not jealous,
> [love] is not pompous, it is not inflated, it is
> not rude, it does not seek its own interests,
> it is not quick-tempered, it does not brood
> over injury, it does not rejoice over wrong-

> doing but rejoices with the truth. It bears
> all things, believes all things, hope all this,
> endures all things. Love never fails. If there
> are prophecies, they will be brought to noth-
> ing; if tongues, they will cease; if knowledge,
> it will be brought to nothing.

This scripture passage can work miracles in a family. Try to examine from time to time if your love for your spouse has all the qualities listed above.

Daily Family Prayer

This is one of the most important characteristics of a Catholic household. Remember the famous saying: "The family that prays together stays together." The family of Nazareth became a *holy* family because there was the presence of the Lord Jesus in the life of Joseph and Mary. Our families become sacred and holy in the same way, with the presence of the Lord. It is family prayer that sanctifies our homes; it is when we pray together as one family that the Lord comes to dwell in our families. The Lord said, "Again, [amen,] I say to you, if two of you agree on earth about anything for which they are to pray, it shall be granted to them by my heavenly Father. For where two or three are gathered together in my name, there am I in the midst of them" (Matthew 18:19–20).

By talking to both young and old, I have come to learn that many of our Catholic families have no family prayer at home. By family prayer, what I mean is not individual prayers. Certainly, people may be men and women of prayer. Many people pray the rosary, but they do it all by themselves. But individual prayers don't become family prayer. The same rosary prayer, when the members pray together, becomes family prayer. Family prayer means father, mother, and children sitting down to pray together every day, at least for a few minutes. If you ask older people about family prayer, they might say the family prayer they have is grace before meals.

Whether at home or outside, saying grace before meals is wonderful. Once I was with two of my friends at a restaurant for breakfast. There was a man in his early fifties working on his laptop computer two tables down from us. When the order arrived, we folded our hands and said the grace. The man looked at me and nodded and smiled. Later on, he left. When it was time to pay the bill, my friend who invited me and the other person pulled out his credit card. The waitress came back with a paid bill saying that the man who sat behind us paid our bill! I looked at the bill she left on the table. On the reverse side, it read, "God bless you today and every day"!

When I go around our school, I ask the kids if they have family prayer, that is, if they sit down with their parents to pray together. The answer, unfortunately, is often no. One reason for not having the family prayer in our society is that the parents may not be of same faith. That of course makes family prayer somewhat difficult, if not impossible.

I have sweet memories of my childhood. I grew up under the strict discipline of my parents, who taught me to distinguish between right and wrong. They enforced the home rules, sometimes very sternly, which of course was not very pleasant at that time. If I have any convictions of life, any moral values, it all came through my parents. I grew up in a family who was God-oriented, God-fearing, Church-oriented, and prayer-oriented. My family had clear priorities of life. God, religion, family, friends, etc. took priority in my family; everything else was secondary.

My parents did not compromise on God and religion by an inch. They did not let the children do so either; neither did we want to disappoint the good examples of our parents, the many sacrifices and hardships they went through in the process of our growth. I can still remember the prayers they raised before God for me and my two other siblings. Seven o'clock was for family prayer every day without fail. The picture of us all sitting down on the floor of the house in front of the pictures of the Holy Family, Sacred Heart, and Divine Mercy is still an evergreen memory. Our family prayer was for thirty minutes. We started with a hymn to the Holy Spirit, invoking to fill us with His life. Then my mom led the prayer with the Angelus. (In all my life here in the United States, I haven't heard anyone praying the Angelus!) Then my dad took over with one Our Father, one Hail Mary, one Glory Be, and the "Eternal rest grant unto them O, Lord." He repeated them five times. Later, my older brother would lead us with the Rosary and the Litany. After he concluded it with Hail, Holy Queen, Mom would catch up with a prayer to St. Joseph. Later on, we would pray for all priests. That prayer is said in all families. At the end, my sister would say her most favorite prayer, the Memorare, which marks the end of the prayer. But still we would have a passage from the

Bible, which was my contribution. We would conclude with a hymn to Our Lady. We would, then, spend a few minutes in silent prayer before each of us got up to greet one another with the greeting, "Praise be to the Lord Jesus Christ" and to kiss each other's cheek. That was the basic structure of our family prayer, every day. We would cut short only if we were late for prayer due to some unavoidable circumstances. Otherwise, there was no compromise. By the time we were ten years old, we knew by heart the entire prayer that I mentioned!

The family dinner followed the family prayer. If you asked my little sister what prayer was the dearest to her, she would say it was the Memorare. Ask her why. She would say the Memorare marked the end of the family prayer; then would follow the family dinner! After sitting down together for prayer, we all sat down at the same table for dinner. That was a wonderful time. Even now, that is the custom of our family, no matter how grown up the children are, regardless the fact that one of them is a priest.

As children, the first sight we saw when we woke up in the morning was our parents on their knees with their hands raised in prayer. As we slept under the black blankets, lulled by the "songs" of crickets on our mango trees, they rose early to make their morning prayers before they set out for their respective jobs. Their life of witness was a lamp for our feet; their prayers were food for our life. The strength we received through their prayers, I am sure, made us what we are today. Hear what the book of Ecclesiasticus says: "Trust in God, and he will help you; make your ways straight and hope in him. You that fear the Lord, wait for his mercy, do not stray lest you fall. You that fear the Lord, trust in him, and your reward will not be lost. You that fear the Lord, hope for good things, for lasting joy and mercy" (2:6–9). From the life of my family, and from the examples of my parents, I can tell with utmost conviction, marriage and family life are much bigger than what most of us think in this land.

I wish all families had family prayer; I wish all parents had great memories of praying together with their children; I wish our children loved those memories and retained them for the rest of their lives.

Encouragement and Corrections

This is of supreme importance in family life. If everyone in the family should grow strong with positive attitudes, we need positive stokes—I mean, encouragement and appreciation. Individuals who get positive strokes from families, in my understanding, are much better individuals with self-confidence and positive outlook toward life than individuals who get negative stokes or no stokes at all from their families. "Therefore, encourage one another and build one another up, as indeed you do" (1 Thessalonians 5:11).

I can still visualize my mom standing close to my dad after serving meals for all of us. She would keep standing by dad's side until he would say, licking his fingers, "Mmm, fish curry is wonderful." Later on I understood that my mom was waiting to hear that compliment from my dad. It was a simple comment, but it made my mom so happy.

My parents not only encouraged and appreciated us, their children, but also corrected us lovingly, but with firmness, each time we failed to conduct ourselves the way we should. This is what St. Paul advises parents: "Fathers, do not provoke your children to anger, but bring them up with the training and instruction of the Lord" (Ephesians 5:5). Today I find lack of corrections not only in families, but also in our Catholic life. Nobody seems to be responsible for anything or anybody. We all like to live as we please. Parents seem to be afraid of their children; priests seem to be afraid of speaking the truth; teachers are reluctant to correct their students. Society seems to encourage anything and everything. When we fail to correct the flock entrusted to our care, we fail the master design of God that He had in His mind. We must not forget the fact that we are coartists with God in creating masterpieces.

One reason there is comparatively more sexual morality where originally I come from is that there is a combined discipline from the part of Church and society. Society includes parents, teachers, and, to a great extent, every individual in one neighborhood. For example, if an adult sees a boy or a girl wandering around on a school day, without going to school, he/she would certainly ask him/her the reason. He/she would even inform his/her parents. If a cop finds a boy and a girl hanging around, when they are expected to be in school or college, he would interrogate them! He would inform their parents. They would be in trouble! Sometimes cops might even stop by a school and ask for the attendance register; if they find many absentees, they would call each family and ask if their son/daughter is at home to make sure that they are not in any unwanted company.

On the whole, the society exercises discipline on an individual. Parents correct their children, regardless their age; teachers correct their students regardless their social status; priests are not afraid to speak the truth. The result is that there is a better discipline particularly in the area of sexual morality.

Because the Church, families, and the society supervise individuals, especially when they are young, they are not "free" to do whatever they like. In some sense, people are "afraid" of their society. In other words, they are not able to challenge an existing system. That contributes to moral discipline in society.

If parents can exercise this kind of a check on their children, I am sure there will be much less irresponsible and undisciplined dating, premarital sex, cohabitating, unwanted pregnancies, and abortions. Lack of genuine supervision and timely corrections from the part of the parents and general laxity from the part of the Church and society leads to lack of moral discipline.

Invite the Lord into Family Celebrations

I am very proud of some of the practices that Syro-Malabar Church enforces on its members. The Church strongly encourages families to make sure that their celebrations like weddings, Baptisms, First Holy Communion, Confirmation, jubilees, and anniversaries be celebrated with appropriate spiritual preparations. For instance, when there is a wedding in a family, it is mandatory that not only the bride and the groom receive the sacrament of Reconciliation, but also their parents. Actually, the priest does not even have to remind them to do that. They know what to do and how to do it. I am not sure how many of our couples getting married, and their parents, go to the sacrament of Reconciliation. That is for you to consider. When there is a baptism in a family, the parents and godparents go to the sacrament of Reconciliation and Mass; when there is a First Holy Communion, parents and other members of the family are spiritually prepared as well by going to the sacrament of Penance and Mass.

Back in India, no Catholic family will ever move into a new home, be it a hovel or a mansion, without a house blessing. Housewarming, as we call it, is a big celebration. But the most important part of it is the blessing of the house by the priest.

The priest blesses each Syro-Malabar family—I am not sure if this is strictly done in Latin Church in India—after Easter, every year, with the newly blessed water. Well, that is not a big event as is the case of blessing a new home, but a custom that has very important significance. That shows how carefully the families stay blessed, how committed the Church is in making sure that her families stay strong and committed to the Lord.

Avoid Unhealthy and Unfair Criticisms

Parents are to make sure that they do not make unhealthy comments and criticisms about the Church and her leaders around their house, especially if their children are not mature enough to understand. This will only create negative attitudes in the young minds. I am sure there are many things that are not up to your expectations in your parish, diocese, and the Church at large. But your comments and negative talks about the Church and her leaders are not going to help rectify the problem. Feel free to talk to your pastor directly, or write to your bishop how you feel about a particular issue. That is much more helpful than your private talk.

Good Catholic Publications

Let your children grow up with great Catholic publications, which will help season the attitude of your children toward the Church, the sacraments, the saints; that will certainly help them appreciate priesthood and religious life. That might, of course, inspire some of them to consider a call to priesthood and religious life.

I remember my childhood. We had many books on the lives of saints; we had various Catholic publications like *Shalom*, *Little Missionary*, and *The True Light*. They receive this input mostly from Catholic publications. Most of the children, very particularly of the Syro-Malabar Church, are well informed on the Church-related matters. They remain loyal to the Church, her leaders, and their teachings all their life. Although it is the result of a combined religious formation, the role the Catholic publications play in a family is much bigger than what we think. While the secular newspapers bring half-truth and falsehood, Catholic publications bring the truth.

You might say that these are not anything big. But these are the few ways the Syro-Malabar Church of the Syrian Rite remains powerful and strong. Here are some things I have learned, and I think they are valuable, and I offer them for your consideration: Syro-Malabar Church is one of the strongest churches in the world with vocations that can support the rest of the Church in need. Don't be surprised to hear that wherever you go in the world, and if there is a Catholic population, you will certainly find a priest or a nun from the Syro-Malabar Church! I am one of them.

Try these points at home with all other efforts you are taking now. You will see the difference.

Being Responsible Parents

Try to be a bit more responsible as coworkers of the Master Artist in touching and shaping the life of your children. Remember, the Lord wants you to create masterpieces in your studio, home. That is the most important job description.

Being responsible parents means walking every step with your children, feeding them with "right food" that is appropriate their age, knowing what they need for each stage of life. As children, they might *want* so many things that they find in the market. But they may not *need* them at their age level. As parents, you should decide for them because they are not mature enough to decide for themselves.

Let me suggest a few examples. Children may ask for an iPhone or iPad. But does a ten-year-old need an iPhone, Apple watch, laptop, or iPad? That is for you to decide. Being able to buy one does not mean that you should buy everything your children ask for; neither is it a sign of love. If you succumb to the pressure of your children and get something like these, you may be leading them to danger. Hear this story: A parent comes up to me with his eleven-/twelve-year-old son. He was in deep trouble. He bought an iPad for his son a few days ago with Internet access. The son sent his own naked pictures to his girlfriend who sent them to her friends. After talking to the boy, I called aside the parent and told him that buying an iPad for his eleven-/twelve-year-old son was not an appropriate gift; that was irresponsible parenting. Sometimes, some touches disfigure the art; not giving inappropriate touches on your art might be the means of turning it into a masterpiece.

As responsible parents, you have to know what they do, where they go, or who their friends are. You may have to ask them, "Why are you late today?" or "Where did you go with your friends?" Try to read the story of the Child Jesus being lost in the temple. Joseph and Mary went back three days' journey to find Jesus in the temple. The question they asked their son is very important for all parents to remember: "Son, why have you done this to us?" (Luke 2:48). This going back and asking the reason for doing certain things are what I mean by responsible parenting. Maybe our children are lost these days because parents don't take the trouble of going in search of their children; they don't bother to ask for an explanation for certain behaviors.

Use of electronics like iPhones, iPads, and laptop/computers at an inappropriate age and time has much to do with addictions like pornography. To avoid this malady, parents have to take their gadgets to know who they are contacting, the content of the messages they send, the site they are visiting, and the time of it. As a good parent, to save the life and soul of your children, you may have to block certain networks; you may have to lay down certain rules such as disallowing your children to use computers in their rooms. Make sure that they do their works on the computer in an open area like the sitting room. That might restrict their browsing options. This is what I mean by responsible parenting.

Encourage your children to watch value-based movies. The content of many of the movies and shows are not appropriate even for older people. Many of you must have taken your children to watch the movie *Hunger Games.* How many of you took them to *Letters to God, God Is Not Dead, Son of God, Heaven Is for Real,* or something like it?

It is tough to make a masterpiece.

When the Lord gives a canvas in the sacrament of Matrimony, He also attaches an oblation to it, to work tirelessly in the studio, family, to form their children into masterpieces for the Lord.

Family is the place of character formation. Children learn virtues and vices from this place of formation. If you plant a tree in a fertile ground, that will grow rich and green. If you don't cultivate the ground, eventually the tree might die out.

When a man and a woman decide to enter into the sacrament of Matrimony, the Lord rejoices. He has high expectations of them, that they will collaborate with Him to turn this world into a more beautiful place.

Parents should touch the lives of their children constantly, until they think that their children are what God wants them to be like.

Save the World by Saving Families

The devil tries to attack our families because he knows that that is the easiest way to destroy the world. There are many problems that have crept into our culture and society that undermine our families. It is high time that we identify those problems and eradicate them so that we will have a stronger society and a stronger Church.

Everyone, I believe, knows the so-called big threats to marriage and family that the West faces. Some of the major dangers, of course, are premarital sex, cohabiting, abortion, gay marriage, divorce, and horror pornography. But what surprises me is that most people, and even the Church, do not want to talk about these big issues. We are afraid to talk about them and to address them. Everyone knows that these are the "big issues" of our time, but nobody wants to acknowledge them as cancerous growth in our time. Many people like to talk about terrorism and poverty that exist elsewhere, because they are not our problems here in our country. But sadly, many people get upset when someone challenges our practices or when someone says that irresponsible and undisciplined dating, premarital sex, cohabiting, abortion, gay marriage, divorce, sexual anarchy, and horror of pornography are threats to our culture and society.

Society is built on families. When family is threatened, society is threatened. Fabrics of a nation can unravel when families are broken.

Those who are responsible for families are people who get into the sacred covenant of marriage.

Why does the world—West more than the East—suffer so much morally along the areas of marriage, family, and life? Why does the West have divorce, cohabitating, premarital sex, etc. more than other parts of the world? Why does the Western world compromise God, religion, and religious values to a great extent? Other parts of the world have problems like terrorism, corruption, poverty, etc. But I see a difference here. Terrorism or corruption or poverty, or anything like it, is inflicted upon the people by force. People do not choose them. People become helpless when faced with these problems. But they do not compromise God, religion, or religious values. The moral issues the Western world suffers today are all due to personal choices. They are not forced upon by anybody. Therefore, the crises that surround the Western world are all brought about by free choice of individuals. Maybe it is all due to a vitiated philosophy of the West; a philosophy that helped people to break away everything that is perceived to be binding people; a philosophy that encouraged people to follow passions of their life; an estranged philosophy that upheld materialism and liberalism, which are contrary to spiritualism.

As I try to probe into the present moral problems like premarital sex, wide use of contraception, cohabitating, abortions, and lack of a religion and religious practices, the root cause that appears to me is the culture of irresponsible and undisciplined dating, as we have it now in many cases. Dating is something that everyone speaks of proudly. Parents proudly say, "My daughter is dating a guy now"; "My son is going out with a girl these days"; "My son dated a girl for three years, but that did not work, and now he is hanging out with another girl. Hope that will work"; "She is dating her childhood sweetheart"; etc. Good to hear. But have you ever considered or thought about the potential dangers of irresponsible and undisciplined dating?

When I say dangers, there is yet another clarification needed. For a good many people, most of the dangers are no longer dangers at all; problems are not problems! A problem becomes a problem only when we consider it as a problem; otherwise, it is not a problem. This is what our society precisely does: many people do not want to admit that the present moral problems are problems. Therefore, all these moral confusions that stand in the way of a civilized society are no longer confusing to many men and women. In other words, wrongs have become right because "many do it." When everyone does wrong, naturally, wrong becomes "right" for the society. As times goes by, people's attitude gets adjusted to it. That is the reason most people do not have any problem with undisciplined and irresponsible dating, premarital sex, contraception, cohabitation, divorce, and even abortion. Remember, we live in a situation in which people protest in our streets to legalize abortion! An act that used to be a horrible crime becomes a lawful act in our society. Why? Because many people seem to support it. This can be called a widespread corruption of moral values. See what Psalm 14 says. The title itself is "A Lament over Widespread Corruption." "The fool has said in his heart, 'There is no God.' Their deeds are loathsome and corrupt, not one does what is good… All have gone astray; all alike are perverse. Not one does what is good, not even one" (Psalm 14:13).

Dating, though it appears to be a great way of finding one's future life partner, leads to so many moral issues in our society.

Everyone knows that our society faces problems like premarital sex, sexual anarchy, widespread use of contraceptives, cohabitating, abortion, etc. Perhaps the single factor that triggers all these moral issues in the society is the culture of dating as we have it today. Many will not agree with me on this statement. But when we scratch beneath the surface looking for the real cause of "big issues" in the society, the underlying issue is the present culture of dating as we have it today.

Irresponsible and undisciplined dating triggers the use of contraception even among teenagers; it leads to premarital sex. The society, as we see it today, encourages sexual anarchy by promoting contraceptive methods. Irresponsible and undisciplined dating promotes cohabitating and, to a certain extent, contribute to abortions. See what the Scripture says: "Then desire conceives and brings forth sin, and when sin reaches maturity it gives birth to death" (James 1:15). In a more simple term, sin begets sin. That is why I said above that these are all correlated.

Premarital Sex

It appears to be a "nice" thing to have a friend of the opposite sex. Having a friend is very good, there is no doubt about it. But we need to consider many other things when we give a waiver to a thing like this. It is very common that young people find friends of the opposite sex. When I say "young," I mean individuals who are not mature enough to date a person of the opposite sex—like teenagers. That age itself is a "dangerous" age; it is a time of stress and storms; it is a time of experiments, trials and errors in life; it is a time of curiosities. When a young man and a woman get together as boyfriend and girlfriend, they might cross the boundaries of moral life. I can tell you this because I have interviewed youngsters to know the reality. As a priest, I also hear stories of people that you don't hear. Many of them admit to the fact that they do cross personal boundaries, of course, with mutual consent, when they get a chance. I don't mean to say every boyfriend and girlfriend have premarital sex. But many of them engage in premarital sex. Even if they don't engage in "real sex," they engage in many other sexual activities.

Well, one may ask what is wrong in engaging in premarital sex. If we say that there is nothing wrong with people engaging in sex before getting married, then we will have to say that there is nothing wrong with transitional deacons celebrating Mass and other sacraments, which only ordained priests are allowed to do. A transitional deacon is not "qualified" to celebrate sacraments such as Reconciliation, Eucharist, Confirmation, and Anointing of the Sick. If any deacon attempts to do them, the Church will not approve of it. So too we cannot approve of premarital sex because unmarried people are simply not "qualified."

Now, it is not a sin to feel attracted to the opposite sex; it is quite possible that a young person wishes to be with the opposite sex, and to have sex with his/her boy/girlfriend. That, I think is a part of being human. But the society should place some norms by which that natural desire is controlled and the person remains disciplined. I hope you know the reason smoking is not permitted around gas stations! I know of some girls who are single because they refused to have sex with their boyfriends. They said they were perfectly happy to remain single and to hold up their convictions! One of the parents once told me that they were proud of their girls, though their girls may have to remain single for the rest of their lives. That is called a value system; that is called the convictions of life. When parents allow their children to hang out with their boy/girlfriends unsupervised, they are actually creating a situation for them to indulge in all types of moral problems, especially with sex-related issues. Eleven-year-old girls giving birth or twelve-year-old boys becoming dads is not anything to be proud of. We must not forget that this situation continues with the knowledge and consent of our society.

Cohabiting

Cohabiting is one of the worst infections, like premarital sex and pornography, that chews up family life in our society. Cohabiting couples live together because of the culture of dating as we have it today. This is yet another very serious problem that we must consider as we reflect on the sacredness of the sacrament of Matrimony. This is an infectious disease that eats up the moral fabric of society.

I wonder if there is no distinction between a human life and an animal life! If people can meet and mate and procreate, and later leave, how is it different from being an animal that mates with another of its kind and then later goes away to another of its kind? One of the most serious problems of cohabiting is the lack of stability of family life, lack of responsibility for each other and one's actions. Family life is not just companionship; it is much more knitting the fabric of a strong and permanent web under which the man, the woman, and their children live safely and securely, for their well-being and the well-being of society.

Many of the young couples who come to make their wedding arrangements these days are cohabiting. Now, people who cohabitate can ask, "Why can't we make a strong and permanent web without so-called formal marriage?" Or they can say that it is not essential to make a solemn vow before some authorized person to make a family. Some people claim that although they are not married, they are happily staying together like a family. My question is, "If you are happily staying together 'like a family', what prevents you from getting married and *being a family?*" Most cohabiting people are now happy, but they expect a time of unhappiness and dissatisfaction. If that happens, breaking away from the web and getting away from the present partner is easier than if they are legally married. It is less expensive and avoids all the hassles of a formal divorce. So even when they say they are happy, they are leaving a margin; they are foreseeing a time of turmoil. This shows that they are unwilling to be committed to the many hardships of married life. Most of these people are only looking for their emotional and physical satisfaction. Though they say they live together to test compatibility, they never seem to finish their period of testing!

As far as my understanding goes, cohabiting is a fashion of the Western world only. I do not mean to say that there is no cohabiting at all in other parts of the world. But it is nothing like in the Western world. For example, you cannot find many cohabiting couples in India. There may be a few here and there, maybe among celebrities. If someone does, society frowns on them and never supports them. People have respect for the society and the social structure. This is the case in most of the Asian countries. I do not think the society allows cohabiting in Islamic countries anywhere in the world.

Cohabiting culture tells us that those who choose this style of life have no regard for the importance of marriage. If they have no regard for this basic value system, they are unlikely to have other values in life. If one partner happens to become pregnant, and if the pregnancy was unexpected or unwanted, then abortion becomes the first choice. One of the reasons for the increase of abortions in this culture must be attributed to cohabitation, which in turn is one of the many evils of irresponsible and undisciplined dating.

The world will be much stronger and will work according to the plan of God if people had a stronger respect for the sacrament of Matrimony. When cohabiting becomes the fashion of the world, and when even practicing Catholics say it is okay, saying it is part of our culture, kindly keep in mind that it is an infected culture. The rate of abortions would have been much less in our country if we had greater appreciation for the sacredness of marriage. Most abortions, I believe, are the result of unwanted or unexpected pregnancies, which happen mainly because the couples engaging in the act of sex do not have the appropriate context, the "potter's wheel."

Couples who cohabitate or couples who "live like a family" without getting married are the foolish people who try to build their homes on sand, of which the Lord speaks in the Gospels: "And everyone who listens to these words of mine but does not act on them will be like a fool who built his house on sand. The rain fell, the floods came, and the winds blew and buffeted the house. And it collapsed and was ruined completely" (Matthew 7:26–27). When trials come their way, they wither and fade, because they have no strong foundation. Christian families will be strong if we can build them on the teachings of Christ and the sacraments.

It is quite sad to see what is happening to our society today. People seem to complain all the time about our current situation, particularly about the decline of family life. While everyone knows that we are sailing on a sinking ship, no one does anything to save the vessel. How many of you have seriously thought about the reasons for the present challenges? How many of you have come up with any answer to the problems? Your answers may be right or wrong, but the basic question is, have you seriously reflected upon these crises? Or are you one of the many who lament the present situation but does nothing to improve the situation? If you are really serious about resolving or contributing toward solving some of the problems, what was/is your contribution?

We live in a culture that is unraveling very quickly. One of the main reasons, as every one of us knows, is the breakup of family life. Family is the core unit of any society; that is, a strong society is based on strong families. If our society is so infected, it is because our families are infected. Our time tells us that to destroy a nation morally, it is enough to infect our families. The devil so cunningly crept into our families to destroy our society, and thus to destroy the nation.

Abortion

This reminds me of a story that I found on Facebook. A lady goes to a doctor, seeking an abortion. Her excuse was that she already has an eighteen-month-old baby. The doctor tries to persuade the lady to continue her pregnancy. She explains to her the evils and ill effects that can endanger her health and, sometimes, her life itself. But the lady was persistent. At the end, the doctor said that if her problem was that she cannot afford to have two babies, she can kill the baby that is already outside, and that would be a much better solution; she would not have to bear the risks of the abortion. The lady was outraged. "How dare you say that!" she screamed at the top of her voice. But the doctor said, "Well, if you can kill a baby inside, you can kill a baby outside."

Sixty million babies have been aborted in the United States alone. That is an appalling figure. We killed sixty million possibilities. They would have, perhaps, changed the course of this land, of this world, had we given them a chance to live. What would the world have been like if great people like Mother Teresa, John Paul II, Abraham Lincoln, Martin Luther King Jr., Gandhi, Nelson Mandela, etc., who redirected the course of the world, never had a chance in this world? That is why I said we killed sixty million possibilities in this country alone. This world, this garden, would have been much more beautiful if the unkindest hands hadn't nipped them before they blossomed.

I like to believe that you are angels in heaven; sixty million little stars twinkling up in the sky. You need to intercede for this world that didn't let you see light, for this murderous generation, for this wicked generation that seeks convenience.

One of the reasons for the high rates of abortions in this land, I think, is due to a lack of a strong family life; that is, a strong foundation and a platform for well-prayed and premeditated pregnancies. What really leads to the moral problem of abortion, in my understanding, are premarital sex and cohabiting. According to some statistics, 85 percent of people who seek abortion are unmarried people, of which about 29 percent are cohabiting. When we say abortion is morally wrong, and it is murder, we should also say that premarital sex and cohabiting, which lead to 85 percent of abortions, are wrong too. In other words, if we can eradicate these two evils from our society, we can easily eradicate 85 percent of abortions; what remains is 15 percent.

But how many of us have the real courage to speak against these two evils? Or how many of us really think that these are real issues of our times? How many times do we really look into what leads to abortion? If we had dedicated half the time, energy, and resources we spend on the issue of abortion to look into what leads to this evil, and to correct it, abortion would have been reduced by 85 percent! I am sure you are aware of premarital sex and cohabiting and that they are rampant in our society. We are not diagnosing and treating the causes of abortion. We are just trying to treat the malady of abortion, which is the aftermath of two other serious problems that we conveniently ignore. On the one hand, society encourages or supports premarital sex and cohabiting, which are largely responsible for unwanted pregnancies and thus abortions; on the other hand, we shed tears for killed babies.

I happened to meet a young unmarried man of twenty-four who was living with his girlfriend. He obviously had screwed up his life: he was addicted to drugs, stole money from his father's business and spoiled his career, and ended up in a rehabilitation center. During our conversation, he told me that he and his girlfriend had obtained abortions twice already. When we say "respect for life," do we mean just abortion? If we do, I think it is a very narrow interpretation. These kinds of fake interpretations and hypocritical morality of society lead us nowhere. We conveniently ignore or even silently consent to premarital sex and cohabiting; then we shed tears for aborted babies, which are the results of the other two evils!

Pregnancies must come about by prayerful deliberation, not by chance. "By chance" pregnancies can occur even in a family setup, but that is a better platform for turning it into a wanted pregnancy. Among cohabiting couples, pregnancies can easily become unwanted, and because they have no real commitment to life, their first choice would be abortion. This is also true with premarital sex. When a woman becomes pregnant out of wedlock, the first and the most immediate thought would be to get out of the "problem." Every pregnancy is the result of a sexual act between a couple; responsible and disciplined sex is possible only under the umbrella of marriage. When people engage in sex without the protection and approval of marriage, undisciplined like animals, then pregnancies become unexpected and unwanted. Every unwanted thing is disposed of or recycled in our modern world.

One of the cruelest actions against the culture of life is abortion: stronger human beings killing weaker human beings who are not responsible for their conception. We live in a fake world, an insincere world. We are hypocrites! We speak about protecting nature; we speak about cruelties against animals. Our culture is more interested in animals like dogs and their welfare than the welfare of human beings. If little lives received the same love and care that we have for our pets at home, the rate of abortion would be much lower in the world. We vehemently speak about freedom of life and expression. People who demonstrate in the street for freedom of life and expression also demonstrate in the street for freedom for abortion, which is against freedom of life and expression for the fetus. What an irony! That is why I said we live in a hypocritical world. The Lord said, "You are like whitewashed tombs, which appear beautiful on the outside, but inside are full of dead men's bones and every kind of filth. Even so, on the outside you appear righteous, but inside you are filled with hypocrisy and evildoing" (Matthew 23:27–28).

Most pregnancies are the result of some sexual pleasure too. Can we deny that fact? If we enjoyed the pleasure of the moment, we must also be responsible for the result of that action. We are cowards to retreat from the phase of so-called trouble, which was the result of our passion and action. Abortion is escapism, not wanting to own up to the responsibility for our inordinate passion for the pleasures of life. Pleasures last only moments. One of the striking features of our time is that many people do not want to make any sacrifice, which can lead to the lasting joys of life. Cravings for the pleasures of life make our youth of today betray morals and values of life; cravings make them throw away life into the trash. St. Paul tells us that each of us is a temple of God and that the Spirit dwells in us, and so if anyone tries to destroy that temple, God will destroy that person. "Do you not know that you are the temple of God, and that the Spirit of God dwells in you? If anyone destroys God's temple, God will destroy that person; for the temple of God, which you are, is holy" (1 Corinthians 3:16–17).

But when I see many births that "just happen" today, and the abortion rate that shoots high each day, I feel that they were born by chance! No, certainly not. Every birth is by God's choice; every child is his masterpiece! But humanity, with its selfish motives, likes to think it was accident—or by chance. That leads to the murder of a fetus. The earth has been defiled and bloodied by innocent blood. Remember what God told Cain, "Your brother's blood cries out to me from the ground" (Genesis 4:10). I am sure humanity will have to answer before the throne of God's judgment for shedding innocent blood and for brutally destroying God's masterpiece.

Why abortion? Because the birth is not premeditated, not preconceived in the mind of man, not by choice, but by mere accident—the result of an act for pleasure. The Lord of the universe wills that every life should be preconceived in prayer, longing, and dreaming by the makers in their minds, thoughts, dreams, and, finally, in the act itself before the child is conceived in the womb. Since humans share the creative act of God in bringing forth life, God wills that every birth should be considered a gift from Him. Before a life comes into being in the womb of the mother by the sexual act of a couple, that life is known to the eternal mind of God. Every abortion kills the dream of God. It is a willful denial of the mind of God, the will of God, the dream of God.

Gay Marriage

Another major challenge that marriage and family life faces today is the issue of gay marriage. Though it has not become as big and rampant an issue as divorce or abortion, this strikes right at the root of marriage and family, and thus jeopardizes the stability of our society as it attempts to redefine these noble and traditional concepts. This "modern" problem, which again is found more in the West than in other parts of the world, is a disease that destabilizes the basic structure of society. I am not informed enough to speak at length on this issue, as I haven't really come to know many people who have entered into civil marriage, although I have personally interacted with many who have a gay orientation.

Here I would like to make a distinction between people who have a gay orientation and gay people who enter into civil marriage. Having a same-sex attraction, though it is not mainstream or "majority behavior," is not, in my opinion, anything dangerous. But one with this orientation getting married to another of the same pattern is a problem. I say *problem* because it causes moral issues in society. In other words, those who seek civil marriage are not positively contributing to build up society, but are negatively influencing society. In the long run, that would make society weak in terms of morals.

When we say gay marriage, we also mean gay family because they live together; they lead a family life, of course, by their own definition. In that family, if they try to bring up a normal child, what kind of identity will that child grow up in? Looking at same-sex parents, will the child be able to call one of them mom and the other dad? That would be very strange indeed! How will that child receive the love of a father and mother if both the parents are of the same sex? Loving *like* a father or mother is not the same as the love of a father or a mother. When the child is old enough to understand the normal law of the universe, what will that child learn, or how? When the child goes to school, how will that child explain things to its peer group? At the end of it all, will that child grow up to be heterosexual or homosexual? Are they not perpetuating confusion? Whatever theory we propose to accommodate this new trend, or however we try to redefine the existing traditional concepts of marriage and family, that would not be parallel. This would always remain strange to the child, because the experience of the child at home is not what the child sees around it.

We find an order in the universe. We find a principle that sustains the universe: the male-female principle. According to the Bible, God created us male and female. "God created mankind in his image; in the image of God he created them; male and female he created them" (Genesis 1:27). I think that the very basic order of the universe lies in this male-female principle. If we look closely around us, we can observe this male-female combination in almost everything; it is not only in living beings, but even in inanimate things. Just to give you a few examples that I observe around me: a pen goes into its top; a key goes into a keyhole; feet go into shoes; a plug goes into its holder. You might think I am nonsensical, crazy, but can't you see a male-female principle everywhere? To me, that is something wonderful. God sustains the universe by this male-female principle. And if humanity tries to change this order, that would be against God's design, God's plan for humanity. What would happen if the majority chose to embrace civil marriage? That would be a terrible disaster. That would be reversing the basic order of life and society, which God has ordained for the well-being of humanity.

I used to visit a ninety-three-year-old man with Holy Communion. One of his concerns was that one of his great-grandchildren was entering a civil marriage. He said he would not go to the "wedding" as it was against his convictions. He said, "I don't see it in nature. I don't see birds that way. I don't see dogs that way. I only see human beings getting married to persons of the same sex. It is against the laws of nature."

As far as Catholics are concerned, the Bible is our law of life and our guiding principle. We cannot compromise the Word of God and accommodate all the trends that develop in the world. Homosexual tendencies are found in the Bible, both in the Old Testament and in the New Testament. In the book of Genesis, we find men surrounding the house of Lot, looking for the angels who visited Lot. "They called out to Lot and said to him, 'Where are the men who came to your house tonight? Bring them out to us that we may have sexual relations with them'" (Genesis 19:5). This is what Lot told them in reply: "I beg you, my brothers, do not do this wicked thing! I have two daughters who have never had sexual relations with men. Let me bring them to you, and you may do to them as you please. But do not do anything to these men, for they have come under the shelter of my roof" (19:7–8). The reply of Lot gives us a clue that the homosexual act was considered to be a wicked act, and one that was not normal or approved of in the community.

St. Paul, in his letter to the Romans, says thus: "Their females exchanged natural relations for unnatural, and the males likewise gave up natural relations with females and burned with lust for one another. Males did shameful things with males and thus received in their own persons the due penalty for their perversity" (Romans 1:26–27). One thing is certain here: what Paul calls *natural* is the relation between male and female, not male and male or female and female. According to Paul, their act was "shameful." Please read once again the first part of verse 27: "And the males likewise gave up natural relations with females."

We do not know for sure the "sin of Sodom and Gomorrah," because of which, God destroyed these cities. God had decided to destroy these two cities before what happened at the house of Lot, because God said to Abraham, "The outcry against Sodom and Gomorrah is so great, and their sin so grave, that I must go down to see whether or not their actions are as bad as the cry against them that comes to me" (Genesis 18:20–21). The so-called sin of Sodom is the demand of the men for Lot's visitors, the angels (for homosexual rape happens later, in chapter 19). But the word *sodomy*, which means "sexual intercourse involving anal or oral copulation," a kind of sexual perversion, has come from Sodom.

You might ask, "Then why did God create them that way?" First of all, I don't think anyone is born that way, but as they grow up, they *become* that way. I told you I have no scientific evidence to prove this theory. But many scholars have told me that this orientation is largely environmental and includes factors such as domineering mothers, molestation as a youth, and ridicule by other boys or girls. This belief of mine came from my own interactions with a few youngsters with same-sex orientation. When I was in the United Kingdom, I met a young man who was gay. Let's call him Ben. As I befriended him, I asked him when was the very first time he knew he was gay. Ben was a normal boy; I mean, he was heterosexual in his youth. He had all kinds of dreams about his future life and future wife. He told me that he never "felt" that he was gay, but he *became* gay later in life because of his experiences with girls.

That brings us to look into what makes people gay, if they are not born that way. Ben told me that he tried to date many girls, many times. Many girls he came across intimidated him. At home, his mom was the controlling figure. He was used to seeing his dad being controlled by his mom. This experience of Ben from home, coupled with his experiences with the girls he tried to date, made him turn away from girls. That did not happen just over a day or two, but over many months and years. He felt more comfortable and confident in the presence of boys than girls. Well, he eventually "became" gay.

Another young man, we'll call him Jack, from the United States told me that he did not feel sexually attracted to women; rather, he felt an aversion for them, no matter how beautiful they may be. I probed into the why of it. He used to see his mom and his older sister in a bra and bikini when they were on vacation; he used to see them around their pool in summer. He said that was his very first experience with female bodies. He was exposed to the female nakedness of his own mom and sister. That made him repulsed by women later on. Men became more attractive to him than women.

This may be the case of just one Ben and one Jack. You might say these are poor examples. But, so far, no one has told me any more convincing reasons either. I am not saying that these are the sole reasons, but looking into our cultural side, I think there is some truth in what these young men had to say.

I wish that gay-oriented people refrained from getting married for the sake of stability of marriage and family life in our society. I am sure that is a huge sacrifice. But as I usually tell people, it is the sacrifices that make our life great and give a human face to the world. The world continues to be habitable because there are people who sacrifice many things that they could have easily enjoyed. If each of us starts to indulge in our own passions and desires on account of our given freedom and equality, we would be negatively influencing the world.

If anyone thinks that he/she is gay or lesbian, don't get discouraged; seek timely help. I am sure that timely help and support can certainly correct this problem. There are many who have successfully reversed the course of their lives. I personally know a few of them, and they now lead a happy life.

Divorce

One other major problem that threatens family life and marriage in the Western world is the rising rate of divorce. Most people don't like to talk about it, though many among us choose to do it. I once was talking to an eighty-year-old man whose eighty-one-year-old wife decided to divorce him! Why does the Western world have an increasing number of divorces? Is it because the people who enter into marriage seek to lead a more carefree life? A life of more freedom? Or are they trying to correct a mistake that they happened to commit at some point in time? They must not be making a mistake because they dated before they made the decision to marry, for many years perhaps, testing the "suitability" of the other. If the spouse is unsuitable or unfit now, what did they learn during all those years of dating? I've heard of a couple who dated for seven years before they got married, but their marriage did not last even seven months. They divorced. This means people are using the wrong parameters to test the compatibility of their future spouses.

People find all sorts of reasons for divorce, even Christians and Catholics. Catholics should remember that the promise they made before God and his people on the day of their wedding was not for a period of time; it was for the rest of their life. What are some of the common reasons for divorce that we hear today?

- "He was an alcoholic."
- "She/he was abusive."
- "She/he was bipolar."

- "She/he cheated on me."
- "She/he had an affair."
- "He/she was not the man/woman I wanted to grow old with."
- "Things were not going well between us."
- "When I became sick, he/she left me."
- "We didn't get along anymore. We were not on the same page anymore."

These are the phrases we continue to hear.

Actually, are these reasons for divorce? Maybe cheating is a big issue and one which might justify divorce. There is a beautiful passage in the Gospel according to Matthew, where the Lord reveals his mind on the indissolubility of marriage:

> Some Pharisees approached him, and tested him, saying, "Is it lawful for a man to divorce his wife for any cause whatever?" He said in reply, "Have you not read in that from the beginning the Creator 'made them male and female' and said 'for this reason a man shall leave his father and mother and be joined to his wife, and the two shall become one flesh'? Therefore, what God has joined together, no human being must separate." They said to him, "Then why did Moses command that the man give the woman a bill of divorce and dismiss [her]?" He said to them, "Because of the hardness of your

hearts Moses allowed you to divorce your wives, but from the beginning it was not so. I say to you, whoever divorces his wife (unless the marriage is unlawful) and marries another commits adultery." (Matthew 19:3–9)

Actually, what we listed above are not real reasons at all for divorce. The single major reason, according to many people with whom I've had discussions to get some enlightenment on this sad reality of our time, is that people no longer work at their marriage to make it successful. Most men and women I spoke to on this issue said that their marriage is not an ideal one either; they don't have a perfect marriage. If they wanted to divorce, they had a million reasons to do so. But they remain happy in their call because they constantly work at it, and they make it work. So it is against the argument that it doesn't work. Nothing "simply works"; people make it work. If you simply keep parroting that your marriage doesn't work anymore, your marriage is not going to be better. You need to take some pains to make it work.

If people are willing to work at their marriage, that is, if they are willing to talk, even if one of them cheats on the other (which of course is unmistakably stupid and which should never happen in marriage), there can be solutions. I have personal examples to give you. Not everyone whose spouse cheats on the other asks for a divorce. If he/she is willing to forgive, their marriage and family life would go on smoothly, without any hindrance. They are able to get on in life as if nothing terrible took place between them. I have seen and dealt with many families that went through some crises because one of the spouses cheated on the other, and the one who cheated acknowledged his/her sin, and the other was willing to forgive. It simply means that for them, divorce was not the first option. And it should not be the first option in marriage and family life. It should be the last option to be considered. Unfortunately, for most couples, divorce seems to be the first resort when things go wrong in their married life, because they do not want to take any pains, any sacrifice to make it work.

A year ago, on the Sunday before Christmas, I was walking to church to help with Communion, as was the custom of the parish. As I walked toward the church, a lady in her midthirties came to me, sobbing. She said she was going through a terrible agony because just that morning she found out that her husband had an affair with a woman, and he admitted that he cheated on her. She said hysterically, "Father, I really do not know what to do or where to go. It's just a few days away from Christmas. What will my Christmas be like this year? I am totally lost." I was at a loss for words. I tried to console her. I was sure no words of mine would console her at that time; she was terribly wounded just before Christmas. I felt sorry for her; but that wouldn't help her either. I told her to take some time to quiet down, to look at the situation more realistically. "The Lord will show you the way."

The following day, a young man came to see me around two in the afternoon. He said he wanted to talk to me. He said he made a huge mistake in life; he had cheated on his wife. Could he be the husband of the lady who came to me yesterday? I wondered. "I own my mistake. I am ashamed to look at the face of my lovely wife and children. I betrayed the trust of my wife. I offended my children. There is no excuse. I have left home with a few clothes. I am on my way to my parents' house, because I am not worthy to stay with my wife and children. I am not sure what else I can do at this time, except to hide myself from those whose trust I betrayed. No penance would ever be sufficient. I spoiled my beautiful family life. I spoiled every-thing my wife and children were doing to make this Christmas. I spoiled the joys of Christmas."

I interrupted to tell him that there was a lady who stopped by yesterday to tell me that her husband cheated on her. I said I didn't know if he was her husband. He pulled out his iPhone and showed me a picture of his wife. She was the same lady who had come to me the day before. That was quite by chance that both of them had come to me. "The affair developed around my job. It happened only once. I told her that I was married, and I could not be doing that. We discontinued the relation-ship. But my wife read a few e-mails that passed between us. She asked me about the affair, and I admitted it."

I listened patiently without saying a word. I was pretty sure that he was deeply contrite about his action. He said again that he was on his way to his parents' house, but he wanted to talk to me. I waited for a moment, and then I asked him if he wanted me to talk to his wife. I called her and said that her husband was with me, that I thought it was God's plan that both of them came to me. I repeated to her everything that he told me. I told her that he was deeply sorry about his crime, that he couldn't justify his action. I could hear her sobs on the other line. Finally,

I asked her if she was willing to come down to have a talk with me. She said she was willing. She agreed to meet me at around eight o'clock.

I asked the man to wait until his wife came. She arrived on time. We had a talk. "It is all in your power to accept the fact, to forgive and to get on with life, or to decide to separate forever," I said. "But I am begging you to consider your two lovely little children, and the trauma they will have to go through thereafter. If you are willing to forgive him, that would be the end of it all, and there will begin a new life. What I could read from what he said to me is that his act of cheating on you is not the result of a long, premeditated, or planned action. It was just a one-time stupidity that resulted from a bad situation. Forgiveness will bring healing, and healing will bring a new family life. But it requires real courage, a courage that will prove your mettle as a woman. Your husband is waiting to hear from you and me, whether you will leave or stay." She sat silent for quite a while, staring out through the window, tears rolling down her cheeks.

She acknowledged the fact that he was a loving husband and a great dad. But she said, "I thought he was different. But now I know all men are the same." I begged her again to consider giving him another chance, at least to do a penance for his sin against their family life. "You can punish him by deciding to separate, by driving him out of the house. But the biggest punishment you can mete out to him would be to forgive him. That would prove you are an extraordinary woman," I said.

She was an extraordinary woman. She said she was willing to forgive. Praise the Lord! I called the man to come in. He never justified his action, instead asked her pardon for his act of adultery. She forgave him. She was not comfortable to have him in her house that same evening; the wound was still fresh and bleeding. Therefore, he went to stay in a hotel for the night. But they had the Christmas together. A new life sprouted from there.

She is *the woman*. I told this story to prove that family life is still possible even when this kind of thing jeopardizes family life. It is an example that proves even the worst sins, like adultery, cannot shatter the dreams of a family, provided one or the other is able to forgive the offender. But it needs effort and sacrifice, the ability and strength to look at the broader spectrum of life. I told this to prove that there are families that are able to stay together when divorced couples say "Oh, he/she cheated on me" as their reason for divorce.

I had a chance to meet with a man who was in his midforties. He was a divorcee. I asked him the reason that led to the divorce. He said she was bipolar. Later on I reflected on what he said. Did she ask for that illness? No. Did she deserve it? No. She became ill; and bipolar is an illness. Maybe that was the time she needed him most. But he left her for that reason. Was that a reason for divorce, after all? Our society tells us that it is a reason. But I think it was an excuse, not a reason. Try to recall the wedding promise that couples make on their wedding day: "I promise to be true to you in good times and in bad, in sickness and in health. I will love you and honor you all the days of my life." The promise they make is for a lifetime. It is for good or bad, for poverty or riches, for sickness or health. What is happening to our times? Couples seem to be reversing the promise, "I promise to be true to you in good times, in health, in wealth. I will love you and honor you as long as I think you are useful to me." Most of the divorce cases show that the spouses did not want to stay with the downsides of the other. They did not want to stay together in poverty of life; they did not want to stick together in bad times, whatever that might be. The reasons that most couples find for divorce are not reasons, but excuses. That is a shame!

The rate of divorce is much less in India, and not because there are no similar situations there as we have here. In my understanding, many women do not even know what it is to be "happily married." But divorce is not an option for them. For them, marriage is a permanent commitment. They choose to live that life regardless of how tough the demands of that commitment may be. Every woman (there are exceptions, of course) considers her husband not only as her husband, but also as the father of their children. That is a big title. A woman may be personally dissatisfied with her husband and with her marriage, but she would choose to stay with her husband because he is also the father of her children, for their good future. When she thinks about the future of her children, she would gladly compromise her personal satisfaction or happiness for theirs.

I was talking to a girl whom I taught in college ten years ago. She is married and has three children now. She was a sad-looking girl when she was a student. Over our conversation, on New Year's Day, she sounded very philosophical, quite unusual for a girl of her age. I was sure she had some problems in life. Later on, she told me that she had a very difficult marriage. Her husband was a chronic alcoholic; he was even paranoid. It became impossible to stay with the man. She went to her parents' house for a while. Many people, including her mother, advised her to divorce him. But she told me, "I married him, he is my husband. Should I not love him, Father? We love with our hearts, don't we? I decided to stay with him. You know, I won him over after two years of my perseverance and persistence. I wouldn't say he is one hundred percent all right, but he is a good husband now. Actually, everyone had deserted us. He was considered to be a hopeless case. If I had divorced him, that would have been against the mind of God."

See the sacrifice of that young woman! Look at the philosophy of the person or the spiritual maturity of the woman! To be honest, I have never seen a divorce thus far in my family, either on my father's side or my mother's side. It is *not* because the marriages in my family are all perfect. Could anyone in the United States say that he/she has not seen a divorce in his/her father's or mother's side? Divorces are not common in my place, not because every marriage is perfect, as we saw, or every couple is happy and content in life; but rather, they consider their lives as a commitment, a sacrifice. The mentality that leads most people in our current times, I think, is one of consumerism: people try to consume, eat up the best, the juicy part of life; then when they get to the bones, they throw it away! It is a use-and-throw-away mentality. People consider life a glass of wine to be enjoyed. No, we should learn to consider life as a sacrifice, a libation. Life becomes meaningful only when it is poured out or spent at the service of others and for a nobler cause.

If every couple looks to serve their spouse in this unconditional surrender, which comes from unconditional love, there would be no divorce; no one would think of divorce when the other becomes ill—be it bipolar, alcoholism, or anything else. If we consider life as a sacrifice, no one will leave the other even when one makes the mistake of being unfaithful to the other, when the other feels betrayed, which of course, is a serious reason for divorce. Married life demands many sacrifices, especially when the couple encounters serious problems in their married life. When everything is super good, life may not demand any sacrifice. Consider every trial as a test of your true love for each other. Don't fail the test. If you fail, your love for the other was fake; you should be labeled an opportunist!

Once again I request you to call to mind the vow that you pronounced on your wedding day. I'd like to repeat one more time that the vow couples take on their wedding day is not only for the good days, but also for the bad days; not only for the days with good health, but also for the days of ill health; not only for riches and wealth, but also for poverty and the perils of life. Marriage today, especially in the Western world, is in many cases no more a permanent commitment; it is rather a temporary convenience. Society and the culture encourage people to follow their own passions. People take it to heart and are deceived. The society and the culture are deceiving us; we need more wisdom to understand its poisonous sting upon our life.

Any good family life is the result of commitment and many sacrifices. The most important and single failure of today's family life is that couples are no longer committed and faithful to their vocation to married life. They never even think that theirs is a vocation, a call.

I would like to compare the call to married life to the call to priesthood. If we go by the standards of present-day marriage and family life, there would be many priests who should leave the priesthood on many grounds and excuses. I agree that that there are priests who leave, but not many. I don't know if there is any priest who does not encounter some sort of challenges in their priestly life. Many of them are, as you know, unfairly criticized; some of them are misunderstood by their authorities, who sometimes can be unfair to their priests; the people they serve can be ungrateful; sometimes they are falsely accused. Certain pastors can be tough and even mean to their associate pastors; some of them treat their associates like teenagers. The list can go on endlessly. How many men leave the priesthood? Very few ordained priests leave the priesthood. They remain faithful to their call even when things don't seem very promising. Commitment to life matters very much. And that is what is missing in married life today.

In my opinion, the ill effects of divorce are far more serious than when a priest leaves priesthood. When a priest decides to leave, his decision does not directly affect as does a divorce. If one leaves, another comes to take his place. That is not the case when married people decide to divorce. There is usually a third party, their children, whose lives and futures will be affected, sometimes beyond repair. Their decision can shatter the dreams and futures of their children.

I am aware of human weakness. Not every marriage lasts because it is between two persons. If the marriage has to stay strong, it is not enough that only one of them works at it; both of them should. A marriage can easily fall apart if one of the spouses wants it to fail. The other might become helpless. Marriages might also fail if both are not compatible. In spite of all the good intentions and efforts of one of them to keep their marriage strong, the other can work against it, if that person wants a divorce and thus defeats efforts to make it work. What can the other person do then? Well, if divorce was forced upon you, that is, if you had all the intentions of staying together, but the other person said he/she did not want you, then face it. Be bold and get on with life. Remember, life should go on. Life is much bigger than a divorce, or any other failure in life. The Church, like a loving mother, stands by such people.

Horror of Pornography

Early exposure to sex and a sex-prone environment lead the youth of today to be slaves of pornography, which is dangerously cancerous to our society. Being a priest for just thirteen years in various parts of the world, listening to both young and old, married and unmarried, I can say with certainty that pornography is a monster under the clutches of which our men—more than women—are crushed beyond any easy escape. A very large number of people have been addicted to this infectious malady. Pornography is a major villain in any family today. I pray that your son/daughter, husband/wife, or friend is not a victim to this sin that sullies one's soul and body alike, and which destroys the marital life of a couple. But I am not sure how many of you realize this as a real problem!

It may be appropriate to recall the accusation that prophet Isaiah levels against the chosen ones of the Lord:

Hear, O heavens, and listen O earth, for the Lord speaks: Sons I have raised and reared, but they have rebelled against me! An ox knows its owner, and an ass, its master's manger; But Israel does not know, my people has not understood. Ah, sinful nation, people laden with wickedness, evil offspring, corrupt children! They have forsaken the Lord, spurned the Holy One of Israel, apostatized... From the sole of the foot to the head there is no sound spot in it; just bruise and welt and oozing wound, not drained, or bandaged, or eased with salve. Your country is waste, your cities burnt with fire; your land—before your eyes strangers devour it, a waste, like the devastation of Sodom. (Isaiah 1:2–7)

Responsible and Mature Dating Can Solve Many Problems

Since we have dating by means of which one finds a life partner—not like in India where there is arranged marriage—I wish people who date become a bit more responsible. They should keep in mind that marriage is not just taking a wife or a husband; it has much deeper and wider implications. Marriage means both man and woman becoming part and parcel of the family traditions of each other. Remember, man and woman come with baggage of their family, religious, and cultural traditions. They will never be able to completely rid of their respective tradition and culture; they will never be able, at the same time, to embrace entirely the culture and the tradition of the other.

They should remember that they are going to marry someone with whom they are expected to spend the rest of their life; they are to build up a family in which they should raise their children for the glory of the Lord. It is a very huge responsibility and commitment. It is good to recall here what the psalmist says: "Your wife will be like a fruitful vine within your home, your children like young olive plants around your table" (Psalm 128:3). This is the ideal family; this is the blessed home. An individual who enters into marriage is invited to build such a family.

If this should become a reality, then how careful should one be when he/she tries to find a husband or a wife? If you date a person who has nothing to do with your faith and values and has nothing in common with your family traditions, totally against what you and your family have been professing and practicing, your family life is very likely to be difficult on many grounds, like practicing your faith and values and sharing your faith with your children. You may not be able to work like an artist to create masterpieces.

In the Old Testament, we find people getting married to their own kindred, from their own family and lineage, precisely to keep their faith, values, morals, and customs of life and society intact. Marrying a foreign man or a woman was strongly discouraged. Here is the instruction of Tobit to his son Tobiah:

"Be on your guard, son, against every kind of fornication, and above all, marry a woman of your own ancestral family. Do not marry a foreign woman, one who is not of your father's tribe, because we are descendants of the prophets, who were the first to speak the truth. Noah prophesied first, then Abraham, Isaac, and Jacob, our ancestors from the beginning of time. Son, remember that all of them took wives from among their own kindred and were blessed in their children, and that their posterity would inherit the land" (Tobit 4:12). Marrying one from one's own kindred means marrying a person with the same faith, values, and morality.

You are the makers of the world!

What is the problem of a Catholic girl dating a non-Catholic boy? Or, more precisely, a person from an entirely different religion? Now, people who are deeply in love with their boy/girlfriends may say love will solve every problem. But in practical life situations, it doesn't. Consider this: I have seen, met, and had been in contact with many families here and in Europe, in which the husband is nonreligious and the wife, say, is Catholic. While they were dating, the mutual understanding was that the children will be brought up in the Catholic faith. Well, when they had children, as was agreed upon, they baptized their kids, which was a great thing to do. Now the kids are teenagers, none of them likes to go to church or to practice the faith. It is an irony that the woman who herself was a very strong Catholic until she got married is a nominal Catholic now!

What went wrong? Who is or what is responsible for this shift? Why did the woman who was a strong Catholic begin to drift away from her practicing of faith? It is all because of the incompatible alliance she chose. She took a man who is nonreligious, non-Catholic. Now his presence and influence have a negative effect on her and their children. The man has nothing against his wife practicing her faith; but as things are, she has lost her original love for the Lord and the Church. The kids are no longer interested, because they don't see their parents, especially their dad, practicing any faith. The children learned a negative lesson from their parents, who were supposed to be the first teachers of faith and values. They learned from their parents that religion and practicing of faith are not so important.

The faith-based life of people may become shallow and nil because of their marriage to a person who is much different on faith and religion. The moral fabric of a society loosens as time goes by because of lack of religious practice due to incompatible alliances. The couple that starts a family life without any common faith or value system is in danger of leading to a loose morality; they contribute to the moral decline of the society. The Catholics have a very strong ethical code that the Church tries to enforce and encourage followers to adhere to for the betterment of humanity and the strengthening of society. Other religions and non-Catholics may not necessarily have the same viewpoints as the Catholics. When people get married without taking into consideration the religious beliefs, they are jeopardizing the moral future of a generation. And we are responsible for that!

Those who get married to their sweethearts are of course happy, but they fail to foresee the religious future of their children. If you seriously reflect, you will see that the morality and the value system that make any nation have been evolved from religions. So when you compromise religion and faith and get married to anyone you seem to like and love, you might be compromising moral values that have come down to us from religions that helped a society to be strong on morality. When you cause your children, by your thoughtless actions, to become inactive in their faith life, you are actually endangering the future of an entire nation. The best examples are the United States, United Kingdom, France, Italy… you name it.

Try to recall the story of Solomon, the son of King David, who loved the Lord and walked in his statutes. The Lord was very much pleased with Solomon that the Lord said, "Whatever you ask I shall give you" (1 King 3:5). Well, Solomon asked for "a listening heart to judge the people and to distinguish between good and evil" (9). "Moreover, God gave Solomon wisdom, exceptional understanding, and knowledge, as vast as the sand on the seashore. Solomon's wisdom surpassed that of all the peoples of the East and the all the wisdom of Egypt… and his fame spread throughout neighboring peoples" (5:9–11). His fame was so widespread that the queen of Sheba came to test him with subtle questions (cf. 10:1–13).

But this same Solomon fell out of God's favor! In chapter 11:9, we read that "the Lord became angry with Solomon, because his heart turned away from the Lord, the God of Israel." Why? To know the reason, we should read the same chapter, verses from 1 to 8: "King Solomon loved many foreign women besides the daughter of Pharaoh," his wife, "from nations of which the Lord had said to the Israelites: You shall not join with them and they shall not join with you, lest they turn your hearts to their gods. But Solomon held them close in love… and they turned his heart. When Solomon was old his wives turned his heart to follow other gods, and his heart was not entirely with the Lord, his God, as the heart of David his father had been. Solomon followed Astarte, the goddess of the Sidonians, and Milcom, the abomination of the Ammonites. Solomon did what was evil in the sight of the Lord, and he did not follow the Lord unreservedly as David his father had done. Solomon then built a high place to Chemosh, the abomination of Moab, and the Molech, the abomination of the Ammonites, on the mountain opposite Jerusalem. He did the same for all his foreign wives who burnt incense and sacrificed to their gods."

People ask me, "But is there not a possibility that the non-Catholic will be converted to Catholicism?" Of course, there is. If the person can be converted, it is great. But our experience tells that it is not always the way. In many cases, the non-Catholic remains a non-Catholic for the entire life. It is possible, in some case, the non-Catholic convert to Catholicism after many years of marriage. By then the grown-up children may be away from practicing faith and religion or may not have any faith at all! If you marry a person who is not of your faith and religion with the hope of converting him/her to your faith at the cost of three or four of your children's faith-based life, it is not justifiable. Well, when you give me an example of one spouse converting to the Catholic faith, and thereby forming a great Catholic family, or "winning souls for the Lord," I can show you hundreds of spouses who stand far from practicing their Catholic faith, or practicing their faith once in a while, and the entire family ending up in having no faith and religion due to the influence of the other spouse. The religious confusion due to "mixed marriage" or incompatible marriage today in our society is much bigger than the expected religious conversion. The risk is not worth taking. What would happen if Catholics start marrying Muslims with the hope of converting them to Christianity? In all probability, Catholics would end up becoming Muslims, as their religious conviction is much more radical than that of the Catholics. But I am aware that there are also spouses who, through their tireless prayers and examples, lead their spouses to Catholic faith. That indeed is great!

A person dating another person from another religion, say, a Catholic girl dating a Muslim boy; do you think that there will be no effect on the later life of the girl? There will surely be. Another religion means an entirely different culture of life. When kids are born, what religion will they profess? Even if they are baptized, they may choose differently later on in their life. What will the family look like? Catholic mother, Muslim father, nonpracticing children. When the children are old enough to date, they might repeat the same thing that their parents did. Some practice, some don't; some go to church once a year, and some go to church on special occasions; some receive sacraments, and some receive some of the sacraments once in a while; some parents sometimes take their kids to religion classes and some compromise. Is that a very stable situation? Is there anything in common? Will there be any unbroken family tradition or any noble cultural element of the family? Just because of an incompatible alliance, are you not bringing into the society tons of chaos? Don't you see how the fabrics of the moral life slowly unravel?

I have hundreds of examples to show that incompatible alliance contributes to moral and religious anarchy. Here is another example: The woman of the house is a very religious person, because that is how her parents brought her up. Her husband has no religion; I doubt if he believes in God! They have three children. The oldest one is a daughter of twenty-four now. She is very much like her mother and her grandparents. But the two younger ones are like their father; they have nothing to do with God or religion. They never baptized their children. The oldest became a Catholic on her own, when she was seventeen. Well, she made a good choice. The other two chose to be "free." Well, that, again, is their choice. But all three would likely have been Catholics if both the parents were practicing Catholics. The woman is very sad over the fact that her husband and the two younger children don't practice any faith or religion. Why this frustration now? Of what use? This is an invited situation. When she dated the man, she knew he was going to be this way. Maybe she did not care at that time. Can you see how irresponsible and incompatible alliances aggravate religious dilemmas in our society?

Since people know that I am from India, some people ask me, "Father, are all your family members Catholics?" They are so innocent to ask that question. I would tell them that that question does not arise in my culture. If the family is Catholic, the entire family is Catholic; if the family is Hindu, the entire family is Hindu; if Muslim, the entire family is Muslim. There is no "ecumenical family" in my country, because marriages are arranged. Even if someone would like to date a boy or a girl, he or she will certainly consider the entire socioeconomic, religious-cultural background of the person he/she is intending to date before the affair becomes serious. People date from the same religion and culture. In other words, there is no "blind" dating over there. One considers many other things like religion, faith, values, family background, education, etc. It does not mean that no one ever marries a person from outside of one's religion or strikes an incompatible alliance. There are exceptions.

That is what I mean by responsible and mature dating. Since everyone marries from the same religion, there is no religious confusion. There is nothing like some practicing and some don't in the same family. There is no Catholics/ Hindus/ Muslims mix in the same family. Even within Christian families, there is no marriage between Catholics and non-Catholics. There is a very fine line. Therefore, there isn't much religious confusion. Because there is a strong sense of religion, there is also a strong morality. The society and families do not approve of irresponsible or immature dating. The people are not willing to take chances for no reason. So there is a much better and stronger Church over there. Though the percentage of Catholics is very small, the Catholic community is very strong and powerful. There is also a deeper awareness among the people of their religion and religious practices. Just imagine for a moment how it would be if people had married others of their choice. There would have been many moral and religious confusions; the strong social fabric that exists today would have been lost. India, though a land of diversities as you may not find in any other country, remains a very strong nation because of social stability, a stability that has been the result of stable families, which again is the result of "wise, mature, and responsible" marriage.

As people who are expected to be the makers of the world, young people are to be responsible, disciplined, and mature in finding a suitable date—and then a suitable wife. They need to be responsible because they are to establish a family, which is the basis of a society, which should be a place of turning their children into masterpieces for the Lord. If the society is bad, it is because many families are loose; many families are loose because many people who enter into family life are not responsible and disciplined enough. This seems to be a cyclical problem. To reverse the present situation, we need young people who are mature enough to embrace family life.

Right in our midst we also see great families. I would credit the greatness of those families to the parents. The parents are deeply devoted Catholics who practice their faith and teach their children the same. They are able to do so because the father and the mother have a common faith and value system. It is so much easier for them to practice their faith and to instill the same faith into their children than if one of them is Catholic. I have met many parents who have told me that they are praying that their children would get practicing Catholics to be their future spouses. Many parents have told me that their prayers were answered when their children brought home their Catholic dates for the very first time. These are the parents who contribute to the making of the world!

Know the Greatness of Your Vocation

When the Lord commissioned the prophet Jeremiah, the Lord said, "See I place my words in your mouth! Today I appoint you over nations and over kingdoms, to uproot and to tear down, to destroy and to demolish, to build and to plant" (Jeremiah 1:10). I think this should be the core mission of the youth today as they prepare to enter into the sacrament of Matrimony. Their call is to be the *makers of the world.* Their mission is to be the watchdogs of the values of life, to be the guardians of the future, to be the cultivators of virtue for a better tomorrow. To be able to create a better tomorrow and to plant "whatever is true, whatever is honorable, whatever is just, whatever is pure, whatever is lovely, whatever is gracious" (Philippians 4:8) when they get married and build a family, the youth of today need to "uproot and tear down, destroy and demolish" whatever is false, whatever is dishonorable, whatever is unjust, whatever is impure, whatever is ugly, and whatever is contrary to the mind of God. They need to (before they get married) make sure that there is nothing in them that might jeopardize marriage. I am sure they are able to do that, because as St. John says, they are strong, and the Word of God remains in them (cf. 1 John 2:14).

It is a tough, very tough, mission today, because our society is very much estranged from the ideal situation, very far from the right track. It will take hard work and commitment to straighten this crooked situation. But it would be very easy if the youth of today could realize the importance of this sacrament: their call to be guardians of the future and cultivators of discipline and virtue. I say the *youth* because things are in their control now. They should realize the nobility of their call to create a more suitable and stable society and a world for the glory of God and the welfare of humanity, when they enter into this sacrament. If young people realize that the future of our society and the world is in their hands, and conduct themselves accordingly, with discipline and responsibility, knowing that the Lord is calling them to a mission, which is one of supreme importance, they can certainly save our society and the world, because they are strong. They are able to conquer the present situation. For them, a fresh start is easier than for people who are already married and have finished more than half their journey. Our young men and women, our future parents, can rewrite the destiny of our nation and the world.

One of the ways we desecrate the sanctity of marriage is when people with no moral values and convictions enter into this holy sacrament. A person who had been through premarital sex, who perhaps cohabited, who was used to contraceptive methods, who thinks abortion is not an issue, what can that person contribute to create a stable family? What is the value system he/she can give to his/her children? What will the children of that person later become? I think the greatest and the best gift parents can give to their children is, first of all, a good education, and secondly, moral values, or a strong value system. I am pretty sure that even if they do not have a billion-dollar bank balance for their children, the children will do well because the parents gave them the best they could.

But the real challenge of our times is that we do not have many men and women with convictions and who are able to distinguish right from wrong. I also think that many of the youths today do not have a vision for their future family. This happens maybe because they are born of parents who perhaps had no values of life like God, religion, or family. They perhaps never introduced their children to religion, never encouraged them to practice any faith, never became an example for their kids. You see how it all becomes a vicious circle. That is a major reason our families are no longer stable; thus, we have an unstable society. Let us not repeat the mistake; let us not contribute to the existing moral confusion; but let us, by being morally grounded, create a better society and a better nation.

As I conclude these scattered thoughts, I wish to thank the Lord with all my heart; may I praise Him for His never-ending love. I thank God in a very special way because He gave me great parents. My parents are the visible "gods" in the world, who brought me forth with boundless love; my mother, who carried me in her womb with great love and brought me up with many sacrifices; my dad, who worked day and night to provide for me. All that I am and all that I have today are all because of them; it is because they gave me life. I am able to see the beauty of the world, and I am able to enjoy all the good things of this world, because they made me.

I thank God the Father, whose love became tangible through the love of my parents. I learned to love the Lord and fear Him through them. It is they who taught me to love God and honor Him; not only this, but all the lessons about God came from them. They were my first teachers, and home was my first school. Not only school, but also my university, I must say, because as I grew up, I learned all the great lessons of my life and its values from my parents, from my home. How can I thank God enough for the gift of my parents?

They watched me grow, inch by inch, every day. The amount of sacrifice they underwent, even now they undergo, is immeasurable; the prayers they have prayed for me are countless; the sweat of their brow for me is unforgettable. How many days have they been without sleep when I was sick! How many times had they been on their knees with hands outstretched for my well-being! How many days have they gone without good food, because they wanted to make sure I had enough to eat! I still remember the rough and tough days in their life. The financial discussions between my parents (because our financial situation was not so good) every night after the family prayer and dinner still echo in my ears. What struggles they had to undergo to give my two siblings and me a good education!

It was from my parents that I learned to make the sign of the cross on my forehead; it was they who taught me to pray; they taught me to love God and to cling to Him. It was they who instructed me to grow up in "favor before God and man" (Luke 2:52). In short, I haven't learned anything that did not first come through my parents. I thank God for the gift of the sacrament of Matrimony, which gifted to me my parents. If He hadn't given us this sacrament, I wouldn't have had my parents.

Matrimony is an amazing sacrament. Humanity continues to exist in and through this sacrament. The Lord brings a man and a woman together as one flesh through the sacrament of Matrimony for the preservation of humanity. The Lord enables them to be coworkers in His creative and generative work through this sacrament. They are given the key to the procreative role here in this world; to them alone it is given!

The Lord established a sacred union between a man and a woman as the canvas on which they would help Him portray His masterpiece. A masterpiece means the best of one's creation! As coworkers of God, people who enter into marriage are expected to bring forth the best out of their union! I consider this world to be a garden that can be beautified with lovely flowers, children. The parents are gardeners who tend the garden. If all those who enter into marriage had realized the importance of their mission of turning this world into a garden for the Lord with beautiful people, they could turn this world upside down with virtues and goodness, instead of people who crush the world with hatred and vices. In that sense, don't you think that married people are responsible for cultivating and nurturing goodness in their children, who will be "like young olive plants around your table" (Psalm 128:3)? Don't you think that they should be responsible builders and makers of this world?

The Lord is not going to have the best creations from His coartists and sculptors, people who get married, if they are not trained and qualified. If marriage is so important a sacrament, those who plan to enter into this sacred covenant should prepare themselves to work with the Lord and to meet His expectations. If marriage is the canvas for the masterpiece of God, and people who enter into this covenant are His coworkers, the youth of today, who would be parents tomorrow, should be more prepared and qualified for the mission they are going to undertake.

I wish our young people enter into this vocation with a greater awareness that they are called to reshape the society and the world, and thus the future and destiny of humanity, by creating great and value-based families. One must have a vision, a dream for his/her future family life with a man/woman as his/her husband/wife. He/she should pray that he/she meets the best suitable partner for life so that they will build a family together; a family that will become a field where all virtues of life may be cultivated, where, perhaps, many children will grow up as their masterpieces.

When I see all the many moral issues related with marriage and family, I feel that many of the people who enter into this way of life are not informed and qualified enough for the job; they are not well prepared for it. I went through eleven years of formation before I was ordained. What kind of formation do people have before they enter into marriage, one of the seven sacraments? A few hours of marriage guidance course and natural family planning and a few sessions with the priest who witnesses their wedding! That is all the preparation we have now for such an important sacrament, which should become the cornerstone of society. I think we have more preparation and formation for the sacraments of First Holy Communion, Reconciliation, and Confirmation! This shows how careless we are about the sacrament of Matrimony. Of course, we speak highly of this sacrament as the basis of everything, but in actual context, we place very little importance on it. This sacrament is simply taken for granted. The only qualification seems to be is age!

No one can be a great artist, sculptor, or musician—even if he/she has inborn talent—if he/she is not trained well in his/her area of interest. He/she may be able to produce something without proper training, but that won't be the best of their capacity. This is exactly what happens today in marriage and family life; the people, because they are not qualified or trained well to be great parents, have a "*kind of* marriage and family," not the best of their capacity, not what the Lord expects of them. That is the reason we have not the best families, society, the Church, and the world. If you think that we have great actors, musicians, or sportsmen, it is because they are trained well; they are prepared well to do their part, whatever that may be.

No one can be a great parent just by procreating children. The real test is in bringing up their children in values of life. If they should do that, they have to be rooted in values of life themselves. No one can give what one does not have. People complain that the youth of today are not well disciplined. They are not disciplined because, perhaps, they did not receive it from their parents. So when they get married and procreate children, what can they pass on to their children? Lack of discipline. It is a vicious cycle! So if you want to give to your children values of life, you need to acquire them now. So that you can pass it on to your children. That is how you contribute positively to creating a better world.

Actually, the couples who come together in this sacrament are responsible for the continuation of humanity. They are also responsible, as noted earlier, for handing over values of life to the young ones. They are the first teachers; home is the first school. They are responsible for creating the cycle of good or bad. If the parents are good, from them come forth good children, and from these children come, again, good children. Jesus once said, "Do people pick grapes from thorn bushes, or figs from thistles? Just so, every good tree bears good fruit, and a rotten tree bears bad fruit. A good tree cannot bear bad fruit, nor a rotten tree bear good fruit" (Matthew 7:16–18). In this context, good children come from good parents. Generally speaking, it is hard to see bad children coming out of a great family. Children can go wrong way even if their parents are great people because human beings possess free will. But my general experience, maybe yours too, is that great parents have great children. And when these children get married to great men and women, again, they bring forth great children. So it becomes a cyclical process: good children from good couples; and from these good children, again good children. Therefore, I think, the sacrament of Matrimony should be given a bit more importance. All the great popes, bishops, priests, religious, and laymen and laywomen in the Church are the result of this great sacrament. This sacrament can make a difference in the world!

CHAPTER 2

The First Divine Touch of God

I have called you by name: You are mine.
—Isaiah 43:1

When parents procreate a life, the care of the soul is given over to the Church, which begins to perfect the soul by the sacraments of the Church. We should keep in mind that the image of a person was conceived first in the mind of God. But the Original Sin corrupted us both spiritually and physically. I am of the opinion that the Lord perfects a person born of Catholic parents over the years with the sacraments. Baptism is the first divine touch of God upon the soul of an individual conceived first in the mind of God and brought forth by God's coworkers, the parents.

One of the greatest gifts of God, the sign of His everlasting love that I received as a child, is the sacrament of Baptism. My parents say that I was baptized at my parish church when I was three months old. The same may be the case with you. That made all the difference in my later life. The Prophet David says in Psalm 51, verse 7: "Behold, I was born in guilt; in sin my mother conceived me." Yes, I was born with Original Sin, the result of the first fall of the First Parents. They were driven out of the Garden of Eden due to their disobedience. They were condemned to toil, and pain was their punishment. But by the sacred sacrament of Baptism, the Lord cleansed me with hyssop; I was made pure. He washed me in the waters of grace and truth, and I became whiter than snow. I, through this great gift of cleansing, was claimed to be God's with an imprint of grace on me. The gates of the kingdom of God were wide open to me! The door that was shut to our First Parents, due to their disobedience, was thrown open to me once again through this sacrament.

This is clear from the Baptism of the Lord. "It happened in those days that Jesus came from Nazareth of Galilee, and was baptized in the Jordan by John. On coming up out of the water he saw the heavens being torn open and the Spirit, like a dove, descending upon him" (Mark 1:9–10). When Jesus was baptized, the heavens were opened; when I was baptized, the heavens were opened for me too. The Spirit descended upon Jesus; the Spirit came upon me too. The voice said, at the baptism of the Lord, "You are my beloved Son; with you I am well pleased" (Mark 1:11). God's choice of me shows his predilection for me. I became his beloved son in Jesus. I was given the grace to move toward spiritual perfection. God breathed not only air to sustain my body but also His divine spirit of life into my soul.

I was born again through water and the Spirit. I was given entry into the kingdom of God. The Lord said, "No one can enter the kingdom of God without being born of water and Spirit. What is born of flesh is flesh and what is born of spirit is spirit" (John 3:5–6). My parents brought me forth biologically; the Church regenerated me spiritually. This is even more wonderful; this is of more importance, because the Lord said, "It is the spirit that gives life while the flesh is of no avail" (John 6:63). I was reborn, spiritually, into a spiritual edifice: the Church. I was set like a city on a mountain; like a lamp, I was set on a lampstand, the Church. I was regenerated by water and the Spirit so that I could live by the Spirit as a child of God. God made me a member of a much bigger family, the Church, which I know is the depository of grace. On that wonderful day, you also gave me a name, by which I am now called. Baptism was the occasion by which you called me by my name.

Over the years, I have been blessed to witness hundreds of baptisms. I know exactly how the Lord performs that divine touch through an ordained minister. Though I do not remember the day of my baptism, now I am in a position to recall how God claims an individual for Himself through this sacrament. I am sure that is the way the Lord claimed me too.

On that beautiful day, with great rejoicing, my Christian community welcomed me into the Church. That was the first time a crowd of people looked at God's handiwork and admired and glorified the author. In the name of the Church, the priest traced the sign of the cross on my tender forehead, then on the foreheads of my parents and godparents, and claimed me for Christ my Savior. For the very first time, I was led into my parish church; symbolically, I was led into the Church. My godmother, standing in front of that most beautiful altar on which the sacrifice of the Mass is offered daily, held me in her arms. My older brother said I was like a cute doll. The priest proclaimed the Word of God to my tender ears. I think that was the very first time I received God's Word through a priest, who represents Christ in my life, though my mother might have read some scripture passages into my ear as my family prayed their evening prayers. But that day, as I was led into the Church, the seed of the Word of God was sown in my life to grow and to bear fruit thirty-, sixty-, and a hundredfold. Ever since that first time, the Word became my rule of life, my guiding light; the Word became my prayer and praise; the Word became my light and my salvation.

Then the priest said the prayer of exorcism to free me from the clutches of Satan. Jesus came to defeat the power of evil and to free humanity from the grip of evil and to lead humankind into the light of God's kingdom. The priest prayed for me, asking that I be set free from original sin and made a temple of God's glory. Later, he anointed me with the oil of salvation in the name of Christ our Savior to strengthen me with the power of Christ, who strengthens the weak.

Later, my community of relatives and friends prayed for me. They prayed not only for me, but also for my parents, godparents, relatives, and friends. They prayed that I would grow up in the favor of God and men, as the Child Jesus grew up. They prayed that I would enjoy God's predilection. They interceded for me; they sought the prayers of Our Lady and those of all the saints and all holy men and women. Their prayers, I believe, have been answered. I have always enjoyed God's love and mercy, his choicest blessings. Later, I was carried toward the baptismal font; my parents and godparents professed the faith of the Church for me on my behalf. But now I am proud to profess that faith that they professed for me with my own conviction.

When I was probably asleep in the arms of my godmother, the priest called me by my Christian name; he pronounced the formula of the sacrament of Baptism and poured water on my tender head. I was thereby immersed into Christ's life and grace. Thus, You called me by my name (cf. Isaiah 43:1) into Your sheepfold. I remember what Jesus said in the Gospels: that He calls each sheep by its name and leads them out (cf. John 10:3). By this great sacrament, He was calling me by my name to follow Him, the Good Shepherd. He was calling me out to the mountaintop to become a light to the nations.

My new name gave me a new identity. In the Bible, we see God giving new names to people. The conferring of new names implies a new mission too. In the book of Genesis, we see God changing the name of Abram, Sarai, and Jacob into Abraham, Sarah, and Israel. The Lord said to Abraham, "No longer will you be called Abram; your name will be Abraham" (Genesis 17:5). His new identity, we read in the same verse, was associated with his new mission: the mission to become the father of a multitude of nations. God also changed the name of Abraham's wife, Sarai, into Sarah. God said to Abraham, "As for Sarai your wife, do not call her Sarai; her name will be Sarah" (Genesis 17:15). This too was for a new assignment, a new mission. Her mission was to give rise to many nations and rulers of people. "The Lord said to Abraham, 'I will bless her, and I will give you a son by her. Her also will I bless; she will give rise to nations, and rulers of peoples will issue from her'" (17:16). We also see God changing the name of *Jacob* into *Israel* (Genesis 32:29). That, again, was a sign of God's love for Jacob, a call to become the father of a new nation for God. He called me by my name to bear the light of Christ, to bear the light of the Gospel, to become a tiny light itself in the world.

The priest, in the name of the Lord, anointed me with the sacred chrism, by which he marked me out as one sharing in the divine life of Christ and in his kingship and priesthood, and I was anointed a prophet for the Lord. As St. Peter (whose name had been also changed by the Lord) said, I became one of "a chosen race, a royal priesthood, a holy nation, a people of his own" (1 Peter 2:9) so that I could start my new mission of announcing the Gospel. He touched my ears and opened them to hear the Word and every tiny sound, the music of the world. My life would have been very different indeed if the Lord hadn't opened my ears and given me the gift of hearing! How could I ever hear His Word? How could I hear the music of nature and enjoy the sounds: the sweet murmur of the breeze, humming of birds, trickling of streams, roaring of seas, and everything else? How could I enjoy the music created by gifted people? If the Lord hadn't opened my mouth that day, how could I sing His praises, how could I proclaim His Word to the world?

By this gift of baptism, I was set apart to be a light in the world, to bring His salvation to the people. By this sacrament, I was led from darkness to light. The Lord showed me a path to eternal life; He gave me a key to the knowledge of divine life; He touched my ears to receive His word and my mouth to proclaim His praises; He whispered in my tiny ears that there is a heaven awaiting me; the Lord marked me so that I would live in the world, but would never belong to it. He said to me that I was destined for a higher life and purpose. What else do I need? When there are millions in the world who haven't known Him or who do not know the secret of His love and salvation, He revealed it to me as a child. "I give praise to you, Father, Lord of heaven and earth, for although you have hidden these things from the wise and learned you have revealed it to the child-like. Yes, Father, such has been your gracious will" (Matthew 11:25–26).

On that marvelous day, the Lord gave me a white cloth, which signified that my life was pure, holy, and innocent; that He had divested me of the person of sin and had clothed me in the person of Christ. As St. Paul said, I became a child of God through adoption in Christ (cf. Romans 8:14–27). "In Him we were also chosen, destined in accord with the purpose of the One who accomplishes all things according to the intentions of His will, so that we might exist for the praise of His glory, we who first hoped in Christ. In Him you also, who have heard the word of truth, the gospel of your salvation, and have believed in Him, were sealed with the promised Holy Spirit, which is the first installment of our inheritance toward redemption as God's possession, to the praise of his glory" (Ephesians 1:11–14).

That day, the priest placed a burning candle in my small hands and asked me to receive Christ, the Light. Yes, Jesus is the Light of the world, for He said, "I am the light of the world. Whoever follows me will not walk in darkness, but will have the light of life" (John 8:12). From that day onward, Lord, you became "my light and my salvation" (Psalm 27:1), and "in your light we see light" (Psalm 36:10). That day was a day of promise that I will have security under God's protective light, that I will never have to "fear the terror of the night, nor the arrow that flies by day, nor the pestilence that roams in darkness, nor the plague that ravages at noon" (Psalm 91:5–6).

I received Christ, the light who would lead me through darkness into the abode of eternal life. By this sacred act, the Lord was telling me to keep Christ the light always in my life, to be a tiny light in this darkened world, to light it up in my own way. I received Christ, the Light, and now I have to become the light of the world; for the Lord said, "You are the light of the world. A city set on a mountain cannot be hidden. Nor do they light a lamp and then put it under a bushel basket; it is set on a lampstand, where it gives light to all in the house. Just so, your light must shine before others that they may see your good deeds and glorify your heavenly Father" (Matthew 5:14–16).

When God called me by name through the sacrament of Baptism, He made me a member of the Church, the bride of Christ, the mystical body of Christ. And I thank the Lord for calling individuals to be part of the Church. If there is one thing of which I am very proud, it is the Church. And I have a great many reasons to say this. Sometimes I wonder how the world would have been if there were no Church! You set the Church as a light to the nations. And She, down through the centuries, has shone her light upon the world. She became a beacon in this dark world. She illuminated the minds of millions of people; She illuminated the dark regions of the world. That is why I said I am proud of being a member of the Catholic Church. As Catholics, we have every right to be proud, because there is no other organization or institution in this world that does what the Catholic Church does for the well-being of humanity, spiritually and materially! Allow me to explain along this a little bit more.

The Church Made the World Humane

The sacrament of Baptism brings us into the community of God, the Church. The Church, from the time of the apostles until now, has been carrying out the same mission of the Lord. She has been a beacon of hope in this world—by all that She does; by all that She teaches; by the sacraments, devotions, prayers; by all her great popes, bishops, priests, deacons, religious men and women, and laypeople, who down through the centuries, have died for their convictions, declaring to the world that the powers of darkness cannot overcome the light, that virtues will always prevail over vices. The Church was telling the world that it may nip away all the flowers from a garden, but cannot prevent the spring from coming. By her struggles for justice and peace, by her advocacy for the poor of the world, by her uncompromising positions on the culture of life, marriage and family, by denouncing everything that stands in the way of life, by negotiating with world leaders to pursue peaceful solutions to world problems, by asking her followers to lay down their lives for noble causes instead of taking life for vested interests, by becoming the voice of conscience for the world, by her countless humanitarian activities, and by many other means, which no other religions or religious organizations have tried to do, or could do to this day, the Church continues to be the light. She brings salvation to the world.

The Church's role in saving mankind is something that the world conveniently forgets. Can there be an honest history rich with goodness without the Church? The ignorant may say there can be. But there will never be an *honest* history rich with goodness without the Church. There may not be another religious or nonreligious organization that touched the world as positively as the Church did. What would the situation of the world be if the Church did not concern herself with issues of peace and justice? What would the world look like if She stopped speaking against the exploitation of the poor, the marginalized, the downtrodden, and the underprivileged? The earth we live in would be much bloodier, stained with the blood of the innocents, if the Church did not raise her voice against crimes like abortion. The world, in my opinion, will become a crazy hub of people with loose morality if She stops her endeavors to stabilize marriage and family in the world. The world learns to look through the lenses of morality and a value system because the Church wears them! The world is not completely clouded or in darkness because the Church, as the watchdog of morals and values, is always on guard.

Education

The world would have remained largely illiterate if the Church did not open schools, colleges, and universities for the poorer sector of the world. I can say this with 100 percent conviction, because it is the Catholic Church that opened schools for underprivileged children back in my state in India, at a time when education was the prerogative only of the upper classes. St. Chavara Kuriakose Alias, the vicar general of the vicariate in 1861, who was canonized in October 2014, asked every pastor under his jurisdiction to open a school attached to his parish. In my language, a church is called *palli*. Even now in my mother tongue, which is *Malayalam*, a school is called *pallikoodam* because it was attached to a *palli*, a church. Even the word for *school* was coined for the very first time by the efforts of the Church. St. Chavara opened schools, not only for Catholics, but for everyone—for Hindus and Muslims alike. Now, of course, Hindus and Muslims have huge educational institutions of their own, but they all followed the blueprints of the Catholic Church. This may be the case in most countries in the world, including communist countries. You should be able to track all the numerous famous educational institutions in this country. Wherever Catholic missionaries went in the world, they also brought the light of education along with the Gospel of the Lord.

Medicine

Think about the medical centers that we have today. I honestly believe that the medical care that we have today is the result of the endeavors of the Christians. Organized medical care and hospitals might have originated first in the mind of the Church, or at least in Christianity. I don't mean to say that there was no health care before the time of Christ. But we know from the Bible that certain diseases, like leprosy, was dreadfully feared by people. Lepers were not even allowed to live in the same village. They were driven out from mainstream society; they were condemned to lead a kind of hidden and isolated life. But when Jesus came, He touched them and cured them and restored them to health. Jesus cured the blind and the lame first. The Church, following the command of the Lord to cure the sick (cf. Matthew 10:8), took upon herself the healing ministry of Christ.

Think about all the popular medical centers that we have today in our country. This element is much more explicit in various other parts of the world, especially in mission countries. India is no exception. The contribution of the Church to the field of organized medical care is unquestionable. It is the Church that opened what we call dispensaries, especially in the rural parts of India, for the service of the poor. This continues even today. As in the case of education, today there are many other religions that build huge medical centers. They got the idea of establishing hospitals from the missionary spirit of the Church; they follow the footprints of the Church. Is not the Church becoming a light, a ray of hope for the sick?

Social Welfare

Think also about various charity institutions that the Catholic Church runs. Here in this country, old-age homes are called nursing homes. But back in my country, this has not yet become a business. There, leaving parents in nursing homes or old-age homes is a shame on the children, for they consider it their duty to look after their aging or dying parents. We do not have so-called nursing homes as we have them here, because the children usually take care of their parents at home. In other words, the parents, when they are old, continue to live with their children. But there are old-age homes for the homeless. Old-age homes also are available for poor households that are not able to take care of parents at home. The Church started caring for the homeless, the poor, and the aged. Even now, if we take a count, the Church will be far ahead of all other religions in this regard. This is also true in the case of private mental asylums, orphanages, halfway homes, rehabilitation centers, and the like. If all the inmates of old-age homes, orphanages, mental asylums, halfway homes, and addiction centers that are run by the Church were let out just for a day, Kerala would become the most chaotic place. This shows how substantial the effort of the Church is, in taking care of the sick and the less fortunate. Don't you think that the Church is the light of Christ in the world? Can you find any other religion or religious organization in the world that does as many charitable works as the Church does? This is something the media of today hides from people. The media tries to minimize the efforts and contributions of the Church in making the world more humane.

The Church Is the Conscience of the World

Consider for a moment all the efforts of the Church in maintaining the moral or value system in the world. Who else but the Church would so vehemently speak out for life, against abortions, against gay marriage and cohabitation? Who else speaks up as loud as the Church for the sanctity of family life? How many times do you see, in the media, other world leaders speaking against abortions, or for marriage or family life, as does the Pope? Who else in the world can influence world leaders to pursue peace and justice, as does the Pope? Can you show me a single world religious leader today (there may be one or two who appear on the media once in a while) who can negotiate with other nations for peace, or ask for an end to hostilities among nations, like the Pope? Remember, when I say "the Pope," it is *the Church*! Is there any other religion that takes public initiative in the world as does the Church?

If the Church had kept silence about the violation of human rights around the world, the rights of millions more would have been violated more intensely than it is today. If the Church did not take an uncompromising stand on the sanctity of human life, the world would have certainly become lax on the value of life; thus, abortions, contraception, euthanasia, suicide, war, and the like would have been uncontrollably on the rise. Even if the Church may not be able to eradicate these evils completely, certainly the Church puts a check on them. Catholics and Christians are not the only beneficiaries of the interventions of the Church on these matters: the entire world is. And no one should forget that.

We don't often hear or read in the newspaper about any other religion or religious leader voicing against human rights violations across the world as the Pope and the bishops do. People might say Gandhi did; Desmond Tutu and Nelson Mandela did! But that is not equal to what the Pope as the head of the Church continues to do. Gandhi is no more; so is Nelson Mandela. We don't hear much about Desmond Tutu anymore. But there will always be a Pope who continues to intervene in the big issues of the world.

I don't often see any other religions standing up for life as Christianity does. I am not sure how many religions and religious organizations call upon their youth to march for life in front of the White House in Washington DC every year, as the Church does. I don't know how many religious leaders speak for peace as the Pope does, or of any other religion that raises large sums of funds to alleviate poverty, or for helping a disaster-stricken country, as the Catholic Church does. I am not saying other churches or religions are not doing anything, but the Church as a powerful institution is able to do much more than perhaps other religious institutions. I don't often see any other religion working as much as the Church does for racial equality; I don't know how many other religions pray constantly for flourishing peace, harmony, and justice in the world as does the Church; every Catholic church, I believe, does pray for this almost every Sunday! The Church daily prays for wisdom, grace, and the light of God to be sent to leaders of the nations and world leaders, that they will govern the people with a sense of justice. The Church prays for the military personnel, law enforcement officers, fire fighters, and the like. Are they all Catholics? I hope the beneficiaries are not only Catholics!

God Plants Us by the Waters of Grace

The sacrament of Baptism plants us by the waters of grace, or the fountain of grace: the Church. Those who are planted in the Church are "like a tree planted beside the waters, that stretches out its roots to the stream: It does not fear heat when it comes, its leaves stay green; in the year of drought it shows no distress, but still produces fruit" (Jeremiah 17:8). The Lord expects His people to stay evergreen by receiving the nourishment that flows from the Church so that we will have the strength to do the mission that God enjoined on us on the day of our Baptism.

When the Lord calls us by our name through the sacrament of Baptism, He calls us to be part of a much bigger light, the beacon, which, in spite of the hostilities of the world, continues to be the single ray of hope. It is the time the Lord calls us and chooses us out of the world to go forth and to bear fruit. This is what the Lord told his disciples, "It was not you who chose me, but I who chose you and appointed you to go and bear fruit that will remain" (John 15:16). The Lord, through the sacrament of Baptism, chooses us in His rich mercy to be part of His wonderful mission of bringing the light of the Gospel to the world. By belonging to the mystical body of Christ, we bear much fruit.

The Lord planted us like the cedars of Lebanon by running water. The Church is the overflowing river of God's graces. The prophet said, "That you may drink with delight from her abundant breasts! For thus says the Lord: I will spread prosperity over her like a river, like an overflowing torrent, the wealth of nations. You shall nurse, carried in her arms, cradled upon her knees; as a mother comforts her child, so will I comfort you; in Jerusalem you shall find your comfort" (Isaiah 66:11–13).

Why Is the World Hostile to the Church?

I wonder why the world becomes so antagonistic toward the Church, even when She tries to do good for its people. I know it is out of sheer jealousy, because She is very productive in this unproductive and ruthless world. We as kids, on the way to school, used to throw stones at mango trees that stood elegantly laden with golden fruits. None of us ever threw any stone at a tree that didn't have any fruit. Many people out there in the world, and the media, attack the Church constantly because She is productive; She bears golden fruit day in and day out. The world has nothing to say about other religions, because they don't do anything as much as the Catholic Church does. They don't seem to intervene in the life of the world; they don't seem to advocate for the poor, the needy, the oppressed, as publicly as the Church does. As the Middle East is constantly at war, where innocent people are caught up in the middle of violence, there was only the Pope to appeal to that part of the world and to its leaders to stop the devastating conflict. I did not see any other world religious leaders pleading for nonviolence.

But I am not surprised about what her enemies are doing to the Church. Neither am I discouraged or frustrated. On the contrary, I thank the Lord for calling me to be a Catholic, for making me a member of the Church that follows a Catholic from birth to death, and even after death; that caters to the needs of millions of people, both Catholics and non-Catholics; that constantly strives to safeguard the morality of the world; that fosters and protects the culture and the sanctity of life; that is the moral conscience of the world; that asks its members to sacrifice their lives for the well-being of one another, while some religious groups teach their followers to fight and kill in the name of God. I can say with conviction that there is but one organization, the Catholic Church, that has influenced the world so positively in the past; there is nothing like the Church in the present; and I don't think there will be another like the Church in the future.

A few months back, I noticed that a man, who was in his mideighties and a regular church attendant, was absent from church for a time. I was curious to know what had happened to him. I gave him a call. He argued that he had lost faith in the Church, because it was not the kind of Church he was looking for. He said to me that priests were pedophiles. He recounted to me how he felt when he read in the newspapers the story of a man who was abused by a priest many years ago. I said to him that I had read in the newspaper that a Boy Scout was molested by his troop leader. Does that mean that we should not have Boys Scouts anymore? I read in the newspaper that a patient was abused by a doctor in a hospital. Does this mean that we shouldn't go to hospitals anymore or that all the doctors are molesters?

I know that the anti-Catholics and anti-Catholic media have only one thing to say these days about the Church: priests are pedophiles. While it is a big failure, not of the Church itself but of a few individual priests, they should also remember that the Church is not just that. They always keep repeating that the priests of the Church are pedophiles. They willfully and intentionally forget that there are also so many great men and women: religious, deacons, priests, bishops, and popes in the history of the Church who have shed blood for various noble causes and died for the rest of humanity, at different times in the Church, and who do the same even today in different corners of the world. Why does the media not speak of them? That is why I said these people try to ignore the contributions of the Church to humanity and to the world. These people intentionally downplay the achievements of the Church. They are ravenous wolves; they are enemies of the Church, enemies of Christ.

If the world hates the Church, there is only one reason: the Church achieves what nobody else can achieve in the world. I know that the world is jealous of the Church; it fears the light, because the world's works are evil. It was the same with Christ too. He went around doing good to the people of His time, but they rejected and crucified Him. His life was a threat to the vested interest of the people of His time. The situation is the same today. What the Church does is a threat to the world and even to some other religions. Therefore, the world tries to downplay the value of the missionary activities of the Church and sees fault in everything She tries to do.

Another reason some people unfairly criticize the Church is that they know we are tolerant. The command of the Lord to us is to offer no resistance. For He said, "Offer no resistance to one who is evil. When someone strikes you on your right cheek, turn the other one to him as well. If anyone wants to go to law with you over your tunic, hand him your cloak as well. Should anyone press you into service for one mile, go with him for two miles" (Matthew 5:39–41).

These same people are afraid to talk about some other religions; they never utter a single word against them. Why? They know that other religions don't have the same philosophy as the Christians do. If they are struck, they will strike back. So they don't dare to speak about them or against them as they do with the Catholics. But that is all right, because the Church is not the work of man, but of God. Therefore, human efforts to put down the Church will never be successful, because we have security under God's protection. "He will rescue you from the fowler's snare, from the destroying plague, He will shelter you with his pinions, and under His wings you may take refuge; His faithfulness is a protecting shield. You shall not fear the terror of the night nor the arrow that flies by day, nor the pestilence that roams in darkness, nor the plague that ravages at noon. Though a thousand fall at your side, ten thousand at your right hand, near you it shall not come... because you have the Lord for your refuge, and have made the Most High your stronghold, no evil shall befall you, no affliction come near your tent" (Psalm 91:3–10). Down through the past centuries, kings and emperors, philosophies and arguments tried to eliminate the Church, but could not. The Church withstood them all for the past two-thousand-plus years! I firmly believe in what Jesus said when he established the Church: "And I say to you, you are Peter, and upon this rock I will build my Church, and the gates of the netherworld shall not prevail against it" (Matthew 16:18).

The foolish think that they can destroy the Church by physical damage. They will never be able because the Church has been built not on sand but on rock. The Church sprouted and flourished in a soil that was soaked in the blood of martyrs, those great men and women who were unflinching in front of the anti-Christians. As the second-century Church father Tertullian wrote, "The blood of martyrs is the seed of the Church." If people gave their lives in the past, as people continue to give their lives in the present, God will protect her for us and for Him. As St. Paul asks, "If God is for us, who can be against us?" (Romans 8:31).

Actually, the Lord did not promise any good times to His followers in this world. He, on the other hand, warned His followers of persecutions and agony. He said, "Nation will rise against nation, and kingdom against kingdom; there will be famines and earthquakes from place to place. All these are the beginning of the labor pains. Then they will hand you over to persecution, and they will kill you. You will be hated by all nations because of my name. And then many will be led into sin; they will betray and hate one another. Many false prophets will arise and deceive many; and because of the increase of evildoing, the love of many will grow cold. But the one who perseveres to the end will be saved" (Matthew 24:7–12). This is the actual situation a Christian will have to encounter. But by our perseverance, we will bear witness to the Lord and to His

Gospel. Therefore, when the Lord calls someone by his name into the Church, He is calling him/her to be a light. But he/she has to give light to the world like a candle: by melting out, by suffering with the Lord, and for the Lord.

Baptism Is the Right of the Child

It is the duty of Catholic parents to bring their children to this sacrament at the earliest stages of life. When I am assigned to give a preparation class to the parents of a child soon to be baptized, I usually tell the parents not to baptize their child purely for a social reason alone or to ensure a seat in a Catholic school. These reasons are not only imperfect but also underevaluating the worth of God's gift. A good number of parents decide to baptize their children for these kinds of petty reasons. Most of them are not aware of the seriousness of what they undertake. They never are aware of their obligation to bring up their child in Catholic practices and faith. Some of them don't even return to Church later on; some of them only come back when their children receive the other sacraments. That is very sad indeed.

Baptism is an invitation to grow in the grace of God through the medium of the Church, to draw nourishment for spiritual life. Chapter 55 of Isaiah has been entitled "An Invitation to Grace." The first verse states: "All you who are thirsty, come to the water! You who have no money, come, buy grain without money, wine and milk without cost!" (Isaiah 55:1). At the time of Baptism, the candidate is taken to the "waters," the baptismal font. Once the person is baptized, he/she becomes eligible to "eat and drink" from the spiritual wealth of the Church. Once the person grows old enough to understand the deeper nuances of Catholic life, he/she furthers in spiritual maturity by other sacraments. One sacrament that nourishes life with "milk and honey" is the Sacrament of the Eucharist. But to enjoy the sweetness of the Eucharist, a person must come to the waters of Baptism first.

When the child was in the womb of its mother, the child drew its nourishment through the umbilical cord of the mother. The umbilical cord was the feeding tube for the child, which connected the child to its mother and gave it all nourishment. The umbilical cord played a very significant role in the physical growth of the child in pregnancy. So, too, to remain spiritually nourished, one needs to remain connected to God. This happens in the life of a Catholic by means of the Church. If an umbilical cord was that which made nourishment possible, without which, the child would have died in utero, then the Church is the umbilical cord of a person, through which one receives all spiritual nourishment. There is no spiritual life for a Catholic without the Church.

In the early life of a child, it is the parents who should make sure that their child receives all the spiritual nourishment at the proper time. They should make sure to keep the child connected to God through the umbilical cord of the Church. Any laxity on the part of the parents will result in the spiritual anemia of the child. The Lord will hold them accountable. If the new generation is not God-oriented or religion-oriented, it is because the parents failed to inculcate into them the basic virtues of life. Their priorities were wrong. They took their children to sports, movies, and amusement parks. They did not have time to take them to church or to religion classes. Do not forget what we said in the section on the sacrament of Matrimony: the parents are the makers of the world.

It may be noted that when the child grows older, when he/she is able to make decisions for himself/herself, he/she might reject his/her faith and religion. But that is his/her choice. They will be held responsible for their actions; you will be free before God. But if you failed to instill and inculcate into a young mind the basics of faith and religion, and because of which your children drifted away from their baptized faith and religion, then you will be answerable before the judgment throne of God, because you failed in your responsibility to shape and reshape the lives of your children.

When I go around our parish school and ask the students, "How many of you have seen me before?", some of them would say no, which would certainly surprise me. I also ask them if they go to church on Sunday, to which some of them reply no. I ask them why they don't go to church on Sundays. They would say, "My parents don't take me to church." So it is the failure of the parents, not of the children. Therefore, when you lament that the younger generation is not morally upright or value-oriented, you must examine yourselves to see if you gave them a value system when they were young. Maybe it is time for the parents to say, "Mea culpa, mea culpa, mea maxima culpa."

Some of the parents—born, raised, and married in the Catholic Church—do not even care to baptize their children. Thus, they cause their children to become barren fig trees. They turn them into a heap of dry bones, spiritually speaking. The present spiritual amnesia is the result of their slothfulness, their spiritual amnesia. They passed their spiritual dryness onto their children; these children will, in turn, pass it on to their children. Are they not contributing to spiritual decline? Are they not perpetuating their lack of faith and moral standards? The Lord will hold them accountable for the present spiritual crises.

If the world remains unchristian, it is the failure of these so-called insipid Catholics, who are neither hot nor cold, who have lost the original love for the Lord. And see what the Lord will do to us who are insipid! The book of Revelation is a reminder to us all, and an invitation: "So, because you are lukewarm, neither hot nor cold, I will spit you out of my mouth. For you say, 'I am rich and affluent and have no need of anything,' and yet do not realize that you are wretched, pitiable, poor, blind, and naked. I advise you to buy from me gold refined by fire so that you may be rich, and white garments to put on so that your shameful nakedness may not be exposed, and buy ointment to smear on your eyes so that you may see... Be earnest, therefore, and repent" (Revelation 3:16–19).

If all the Catholic parents had worked hard to instill into young minds the basic principles of Catholic life, by their life and examples, if they had been a bit more serious in practicing the faith, their children would have surely been more religious; the culture would have been far better, the Church would have been stronger in this country, and the nation would have been more stable!

Why the Shadows?

There are, of course, shadows in the Church; not everything is holy or perfect; not everything is clean. But that doesn't bother me. I know that the Church is also subject to human frailties. We are the Church, we are the people of God; and we are not perfect. Therefore, the Church is not perfect. But it would be unfair to ignore or minimize the works of the Church just because there are some shadows of imperfection. The imperfections and weaknesses of the Church are not certainly bigger than the amount of good works that She does, the strength that She has. I like to look at the brighter side of life. It is better to light a candle than to blame the darkness.

This is what I received on Facebook as a message:

> When I say that "I am a Christian," I am not shouting that "I am clean living." I am whispering "I was lost, but now I'm found and forgiven."

> When I say "I am a Christian," I don't speak of this with pride. I'm confessing that I stumble and need Christ to be my guide.

> When I say "I am a Christian," I'm not trying to be strong. I'm professing that I'm weak and need His strength to carry on.

When I say "I am a Christian," I'm not bragging of success. I'm admitting I have failed and need God to clean up my mess.

When I say, "I am a Christian," I'm not claiming to be perfect. My flaws are far too visible, but God believes I am worth it.

When I say "I am a Christian," I still feel the sting of pain. I have my share of heartaches, so I call upon His name.

When I say "I am a Christian," I'm not holier than thou. I'm just a simple sinner who received God's good grace, somehow!

CHAPTER 3

A Time God Smiles Upon Us

I give you thanks, O Lord; though you have been angry with
me, your anger has abated, and you have consoled me.
—Isaiah 12:1

I have been told that the sacrament of Reconciliation is the time when God the Father waits at the threshold of heaven with open arms, to embrace me and welcome me back into the joys of heaven. Well, I like to think it is the time when God the Father is smiling down upon his prodigal sons and daughters.

When God sees all that happens around the world today, like wars, terrorism, racism, human trafficking, idolizing sex, pornography, corruption, oppression, poverty amid wealth, and so forth, He might regret that He created human beings. When God learns that ISIS (Islamic States of Iraq and Syria) has killed more than 200,000 Christians alone, that there are never-ending wars where Jesus was born as King of Peace, that terrorism has laid waste certain countries of the world, that many people are victims of pornography, especially in the West, and that the United States alone has killed more than 60 million babies, I can imagine God shedding tears on account of humanity's wickedness. God might certainly be regretting that He created human beings. "When the Lord saw how great the wickedness of human beings was on earth, and how every desire that their heart conceived was always nothing but evil, the Lord regretted making human beings on earth, and his heart was grieved" (Genesis 6:5–6).

The Lord shaped us on the canvas of marriage with the help of our parents as coartists. The Lord gave us His first divine touch when He called us by name in the sacrament of Baptism. Though we may look perfect physically, we are not perfect spiritually. As we know, human beings are made of both body and soul. We are not perfect human beings; our lives are not perfect, because our souls are sullied. Therefore, the Lord has to continue shaping us until we get near to His image and likeness.

One other way the Lord continues to touch us is in the sacrament of Reconciliation. This sacrament is a continuous renewal of our baptismal promises, an ongoing process in which God shapes our most vital parts: our souls. As we are beings with the gift of freedom, we often make wrong choices that are against the will of God. Human beings, as God's masterpieces, exist to glorify the Maker; we are expected to make Him smile upon us. God smiles when we do the will of Him who made us.

One of the most beloved books in the Bible, for me, is the book of Psalms, which embodies the genuine human feelings and emotions of helplessness, sorrow, frustrations, defeat, anger, vengeance, hope, joy, gratitude, self-surrender, victory, and so on. I love this book so much that I read it daily. As I read and pray over the Psalms, each of them seems to reflect my life and my feelings; this makes the Psalms very personal to me. Lord, I believe that there is no one who does not feel helpless or is not sorrowful in life, no one who is not frustrated, no one who is never angry or never feels defeated. There are also moments of happiness, joy, gratitude, self-surrender, and victory in life, at some point in everyone's life.

Among the Psalms, Psalm 51, which is the prayer of the repentance of David, is special to me. David, who was a "man after the heart of God" (cf. Acts 13:22) fell into sin. The man God chose and anointed to be king over the people of Israel was not strong enough to resist temptation. He fell from the shouts of victory to the agony of the defeat of his own spiritual life. He fell like an animal of prey into his own spider's web. But then came God's voice through the prophet Nathan, who pointed out to David the sin he had committed. David was humble enough to say, "I have sinned against the Lord" (2 Samuel 11:13). This psalm should be our daily prayer too, because we are sinners. We are very much like David. One day we soar high like an eagle; the next day we are so low. From the zenith of our spiritual life, when everything seems great and wonderful, all of a sudden we swoop down to nothingness, sins, and follies. We need God's mercy and forgiveness.

As we grow older, enjoying all the privileges of being children of God, we begin to stray. Maybe that is part of being human. I don't know what makes us go away from God's path; how on earth can we forget His blessings so soon? Why are our hearts so calloused? Why do we lose all the innocence and purity of life that He bestowed upon us on the day of Baptism, when He called us by name and possessed totally for His own? How we lose His grace; how the beautiful smile fades on our faces when we lose the sparkle of our eyes, or when His voice becomes silent within us. We violate almost all the commandments in certain ways. The Lord said in the Gospels, "But what comes out of a person, that is what defiles. From within people, from their hearts come evil thoughts, unchastity, theft, murder, adultery, greed, malice, deceit, folly. All these evils come from within and they defile" (Mark 7:21–23). Many of us are indeed defiled by most of these evils.

> Blessed is the one whose fault is removed, whose sin is forgiven. Blessed is the man to whom the Lord imputes no guilt, in whose spirit is no deceit. (Psalm 32:1–2)

I thank the Lord because, in His abundance of love and mercy, He gifted us with another wonderful sacrament, the sacrament of Reconciliation, by which He continues to wash us and cleanse us. If the sacrament of Baptism washed away our Original Sin, the sacrament of Reconciliation for us is a continual baptism, because it continues to remove our guilt and shame. If the sacrament of Baptism washed us clean at the waters of the baptismal font, the confessional washes us in His mercy and compassion.

The sacrament of Reconciliation, as I said, is an ongoing second baptism, as it is a continual cleansing from our sins. In the sacrament of Baptism, we promised before the Lord to reject Satan and all his glamorous ways; we promised to accept the Lord Jesus as our king and savior. But as we grow older, we seem to forget the many promises we made before the Lord. At least sometimes we walk with Satan; we take sides with him, and/or we appreciate the glamour of the devil. Thus we sin against our own promise. Therefore, we need the sacrament of Reconciliation, which makes us clean.

If there is one place on earth that I love the most, it is the confessional. There, He makes us new persons in Christ. How can I thank the Lord for bringing us back into His fold of love and grace as He carries the lost sheep on his shoulders (cf. Luke 15:4–6)? There is the deep mercy which encompasses the confessional: "I declare my sin to you; my guilt I do not hide. I said, 'I confess my transgression to the Lord', and you took away the guilt of my sin" (Psalm 32:5).

When we commit sin, we stray from His path. We become prodigal sons and daughters who waste God's graces and the riches He gave us as our share from His own riches for petty and momentary pleasures and selfish gains. We sully that white and pure garment which He gave us on the day of our Baptism. We sully our souls, which He sealed with His eternal love. We end up in faraway places, very far from our true home and our Father; we end up in unbecoming, unedifying, and undesirable places. But Jesus, as the Good Shepherd, comes after us. Each time we sin, we cry out like David, "Cleanse me with hyssop that I may be pure; wash me, and I will be whiter than snow" (Psalm 51:9); and each time, He waits for us with open arms as the Father in the parable of the Prodigal Son (Luke 15:11–32). When we squander His grace and blessings imprudently along the way of our worldly life, and when we come back to Him through this marvelous sacrament, God showers His love on us; He celebrates our return with great festivity. I thank the Lord and praise Him for having "more joy in heaven over one sinner who repents than over ninety-nine righteous people who have no need of repentance" (Luke 15:17). I am *that one person* who needs repentance, who needs to be forgiven, not once but many times—not even seven times, but seventy-seven times (cf. Matthew 18:22).

As the book of Psalms says, "Sin directs the heart of the wicked man; his eyes are closed to the fear of God. For he lives with the delusion: his guilt will not be known and hated" (36:1–3). As a priest, I come across people who say, "I haven't been to confession for the past forty years"! For quite a few years, especially these days, at least a few people stay away from the confessional; they try to hide themselves from God's presence; they try to avoid God. They try to justify their deeds. I would say that they are blind. They are quite foolish to think that the Lord God does not see. But now, at this most compassionate place, they pray: "Lord, do not punish me in your anger; in your wrath do not chastise me! Your arrows have sunk deep in me; your hand has come down upon me; there is no wholesomeness in my flesh because of your anger; there is no health in my bones because of my sin. My iniquities overwhelm me, a burden too heavy for me" (Psalm 38:1–5). That is the time when God makes a sigh of relief, the relief of a parent seeing his son/daughter coming home after many years.

I can never thank God enough for the gift of forgiveness. That is one thing that makes my life hope-filled. When I am exhausted from carrying the burden of sins and follies, the Lord, through the sacrament of Reconciliation, relieves me; He renews my life once again, giving me a chance to put away the old self of my former way of life, corrupt through deceitful desires, and to put on the new self, created in God's way, in righteousness and holiness of truth (cf. Ephesians 4:22–24). There in the confessional, He puts in a new wick and pours new oil into my lamp; He lights once again that which was put out by sin. There, in the confessional, the Lord dispels the darkness of the soul and asks me to walk by the light of the Lord. "For you, Lord, give light to my lamp; my God brightens my darkness" (Psalm 18:29). "Lord, your mercy reaches to heaven; your fidelity to the clouds. Your justice is like the highest mountains; your judgments, like the mighty deep; human beings and beasts you sustain, Lord. How precious is your mercy, O God! The children of Adam take refuge in the shadow of your wings. They feast on the rich food of your house; from your delightful stream you give them drink. For with you is the fountain of life, and in your light we see light" (Psalm 36:6–10).

"If you, O, Lord, keep account of sins, Lord, who can stand?" (Psalm 130:3). Nobody can, because, "There is not one who does what is good, not even one" (Psalm 53:4). And I am no exception. Jesus, Lord, my loving savior, may I repeat the brokenness which St. Paul, your most zealous apostle, expressed: "I do not do what I want, but I do what I hate" (Romans 7:15). It seems to me that he was voicing my brokenness too. I, therefore, need this sacrament most urgently.

If Jesus hadn't given us the gift of the sacrament of Reconciliation, we would have been lost in our sins; we would have been crushed under the weight of sins and the follies of life. Our souls, which God created and marked out to be His own, would have been lost. And I dread that loss! "What profit is there for one to gain the whole world but forfeit his life? What could one give in exchange for his life?" (Mark 8:36–37). Loss of one's life, that is, his/her soul, should be the biggest of spiritual tragedies. The forgiveness that the Lord extends to humanity, out of love for it, and the acceptance or refusal of that forgiveness is what decides the destiny of humanity.

I know that my sins make Him dismayed, even angry. He may be disappointed at times with me. I, as one who has received much more than I deserve, should be eternally grateful to Him. Each sin is an act of rejection of His goodness, a turning of my back to His light and grace, a craving to be at the side of Satan, a willful denial or disowning of His gifts. Staying close to Him, or walking in His path and in His light, is the way to show my gratefulness to Him for all His marvels in my life. Humbling myself before the sacrament of Reconciliation is the time when His anger passes and His mercy consoles me. It is the time He smiles upon me!

The Lord Jesus spoke to us of His love for sinners in the Scriptures. He told us that the Son of Man came to seek out the lost sheep, the prodigal son, and the sinful woman; he told us that it is the sick that need a doctor, not the healthy. Yet we are afraid to come to this sacrament. Maybe we need greater trust in His words. Sometimes we hide our sins from him and make dishonest confessions, as though God is not aware of our sins! I know our sins are open before Him. How can we flee from His presence? How can we hide our face from Him? The Lord is all-knowing and ever-present. As the psalmist says, "Lord, you have probed me, you know me: you know when I sit and stand; you understand my thoughts from afar. You sift through my travels and my rest; with all my ways you are familiar. Even before a word is on my tongue, Lord, you know it all. Behind and before you encircle me. Such knowledge is too wonderful for me, far too lofty for me to reach. Where can I go from your spirit? From your presence, where can I flee? If I ascend to the heavens, you are there; if I lie down in Sheol, there you are. If I take the wings of dawn and dwell beyond the sea, even there your hands guide me, your right hand holds me fast" (Psalm 139:1–10).

Therefore, I pray, "Remember no more the sins of my youth; remember me according to your mercy, because of your goodness, Lord" (Psalm 25:7). We most humbly confess our sins to you. In your kindness, make us clean. Lord, let us never postpone turning back to you. Let us never be presumptuous, for the Scripture says, "Do not say, 'I have sinned, yet what has happened to me?' For the Lord is slow to anger! Do not be so confident of forgiveness that you add sin upon sin. Do not say, 'His mercy is great; my many sins he will forgive.' For mercy and anger alike are with Him; His wrath comes to rest on the wicked. Do not delay turning back to the Lord, do not put it off day after day. For suddenly His wrath will come forth; at the time of vengeance, you will perish" (Ecclesiasticus 5:4–7). Let us never try Your patience and flare up Your anger. May we love You wholeheartedly and belong to You entirely.

I know that the sacrament of Reconciliation is an invitation to walk with God again. I know that it is an opportunity to restart my life, a chance to begin all over again. It is a challenge for me to divest myself of the old self of sin. In the words of St. Paul, "That you should put away the old self of your former way of life, corrupted through deceitful desires, and be renewed in the spirit of your minds, and put on the new self, created in the God's way in righteousness and holiness of truth" (Ephesians 4:22–24). The sacrament of Reconciliation invites us to become aware of our weaknesses and brokenness and to be strengthened by the power of God's forgiveness. I know that it is the time the Lord "pours oil and wine over our wounds and bandages them" (cf. Luke 10:34). When we sin, we fall victim to the attacks of Satan, and we are beaten by the sins we commit. We lie helpless, abandoned by all, like that man on his way from Jerusalem to Jericho. When the Lord passes by us, He doesn't hurry away like that priest and the Levite, but takes time with us, takes pity on us; He carries us on His shoulders to the inn, which is the Church. There He entrusts us to a priest, as the innkeeper, who will pour wine and oil on our wounds in the confessional, in His name and person. He will bandage us up for the Lord. Actually, the Lord Himself becomes our Good Samaritan. If He had not come at that moment when we lay helpless in the filth of our sins, we would have died on the roadside.

At the sacrament of Reconciliation, the Lord invites us: "Come now, let us set things right… Though your sins be like scarlet, they may become white as snow; though they be red like crimson, they may become white as wool" (Isaiah 1:18). He asks us, "Wash yourselves clean! Put away your misdeeds from before my eyes; cease doing evil; learn to do good" (Isaiah 1:16).

When we open the bundle of our misdeeds before His divine but merciful presence, He tells us that He will pay the price for our life, with His own lifeblood; thus, He will settle the account for us. We know He will come back to pay the penalty of our arrogant and deceitful life. The prophet Isaiah said, "Yet it was our pain that he bore, our sufferings he endured. We thought of him as stricken, struck down by God and afflicted. But he was pierced for our sins, crushed for our iniquity. He bore the punishment that makes us whole, by his wounds we are healed. We had all gone astray like sheep, all following our own way. But the Lord laid upon him the guilt of us all" (Isaiah 53:4–6). Saint Peter, in his first letter, said, "He himself bore our sins in his body upon the cross, so that, free from sin, we might live for righteousness" (1 Peter 2:24). Thus, the Lord Jesus kept His promise. He came back to pay the penalty for us by dying for us on the cross. He snatched us away from the clutches of sin.

We were like a ram caught up in a thornbush; we were bleeding all over our body. Our wounds were deep. As the psalmist cries out, "Foul and festering are my sores because of my folly" (Psalm 38:5). But every time we walk over to that marvelous box that we call the confessional, we seem to pray with the psalmist the following psalm, one that is our prayer too: "Lord, do not punish me in your anger; in your wrath do not chastise me! Your arrows have sunk deep in me; your hand has come down upon me. There is no wholesomeness in my flesh because of your anger; there is no health in my bones because of my sin. My iniquities overwhelm me. Foul and festering are my sores because of my folly. I am stooped and deeply bowed; every day I go about mourning. My loins burn with fever; there is no wholesomeness in my flesh. I am numb and utterly crushed; I wait with anguish of heart. My Lord, my deepest yearning is before you; my groaning is not hidden from you; my heart shudders, my strength forsakes me; the very light of my eyes has failed. Friends and companions shun my disease; my neighbors stand far off" (Psalm 38:1–12).

How rightly does the psalmist describe our situation, Lord! Everything he says applies to us. Actually, that is the prayer that we make every time we inch toward the confessional. There were many days and nights that we have spent between the time we sinned and our decision to go to the sacrament. Those days and nights were a nightmare for us; we were restless. We were desperate beyond words to unload the burden of our sins, to tell You that we want to be new again, want to restart our life as clean as possible. The thoughts about our shameful sins had been like burning coals within us. How correct is the psalmist to say that the light of his eyes was lost. We ourselves have felt many a time that we have lost the light from our eyes; that is, we are blinded and clouded. We were "very near to falling" (Psalm 38:18). But in the confessional, "you changed my mourning into dancing; you took off my sackcloth and clothed me with gladness. So that my glory may praise you and not be silent. O Lord, my God, forever will I give you thanks" (Psalm 30:12–13).

Lord, You know our pitiful situation; You know that we want to stay with You and avoid sins and sinful occasions. As we make an act of contrition, every time after confession, we seem to place extra emphasis on our words: "I firmly intend, with your help, to do penance, to sin no more and to avoid all occasions of sin." But we fail miserably. With all our good and strong resolutions, with all our mighty promises, we fall again and again. Maybe the temptations are much stronger than all our resolutions. We need your support and strength to fight against them. We consider all temptations our enemies, who war against us to win us over to their side, to the side of the evil one. But we want to be always at Your side, the side of eternal beauty. Therefore, "in you, Lord, I take refuge; let me never be put to shame. In your righteousness deliver me; incline your ear to me; make haste to rescue me! Be my rock of refuge, a stronghold to save me. For you are my rock and my fortress; for your name's sake lead me and guide me. Free me from the net they have set for me, for you are my refuge. Into your hands I commend my spirit; you will redeem me, Lord, God of truth… Be gracious to me, Lord, I am in distress; affliction is wearing down my eyes, my throat and my insides. My life is worn out by sorrow, and my years by sighing. My strength fails in my affliction; my bones are wearing down" (Psalms 31:1–6; 10–11).

Don't You, O Lord, know the anguish of our hearts each time we fail? Each confession reminds us that we are weak, weaker than we think. We come to You. No, we run to You for help, because we know that You are there in the confessional, waiting for us, writing on the ground with Your finger (cf. John 8:6). We are beyond recognition! We are now not the persons You created. We are far from our original state. Now, one who looks at us may not glorify You; he/she may not appreciate the hands that made us; their thoughts may not rise to You, our Maker, because we are no more a masterpiece. Somewhere along the line, we lost that wonderful form; our innocence and purity disappeared. We are not the kind of persons You made us to be. We are very far from Your plan, Your design.

Lord, we are humbly kneeling before You for Your forgiveness for the sins that we committed; forgive the wrongs our heart meditated on; cleanse the sins of our loose and defiled thoughts; forgive the sins our hands committed; kindly wash us clean from all the sins our eyes committed and our tongues spoke; cleanse the sins of our lips; let the fire of Your love touch our lips, so that hereafter, our lips will proclaim Your praise and sing Your glory. Remove the filth in our ears so that Your Word will fall in them. Forget the wrong paths our feet took; we are yearning for Your mercy. We wish to wash Your feet with the tears of our eyes, as Mary Magdalene did. We are sorry for our sins; so sorry, not just because we are afraid of the punishment, but because we offended You, who are all good, all loving, and all holy.

Lord, we are broken down to the depths of our soul, to our very being. Our body is covered with the filth of sins; our souls are infected with the effects of all that we did. The seal of Your ownership on our souls is hardly visible now. Sins cover the seal of Your grace in us. We are ashamed of our deeds. We are ashamed to look at Your divine countenance, which reflects holiness. But still, we trust your mercy, which surpasses Your justice. "Who is there like you, the God who removes guilt and pardons sin for the remnant of his inheritance; who does not persist in anger forever, but delights rather in clemency, and will again have compassion on us, treading underfoot our guilt? You will cast into the depths of the sea all our sins; You will show faithfulness to Jacob, and grace to Abraham, as you have sworn to our fathers from days of old" (Micah 7:18–20). Pull us out from the pit of heinous sins, especially our sin of forgetting our worth in Your sight. Write off our many sins of omission too, the good we did not do intentionally and unintentionally. We postponed our obligations indefinitely, and thus we missed many chances to do good. We ignored the needs of many whom we could have easily helped; and we had nothing to lose. What can we say to You now about love we wasted, about the times our hearts did not leap to help someone else. We are too weak to walk with all the burden of our sins.

Lord, only You, who has compassion on the straying and the lost can make us whole. You who came as the physician for the sick can heal our broken hearts and bind up our shattered lives. We are waiting for Your soothing hand to anoint our crushed souls and bodies; embrace us once more, just once more.

Lord our God, when we think about the sacrament of Reconciliation, what comes to our mind is the parable Your Son, our Lord Jesus Christ, spoke to us of in the Bible. The picture of You waiting for our return warms our hearts. There in the confessional, as we humbly kneel and fumble over our long list of filthy sins, You tap on our shoulders reassuringly and wipe our tears with Your most divine hands. Looking into our eyes, You lovingly smile and gently ask us to restart our life all over again, to learn once more, to walk as a child learns to walk for the first time. You seem to tell us the same words You said to the woman caught in the very act of adultery: "Neither do I condemn you. Go, and from now on do not sin any more" (John 8:11). The joy of being forgiven unconditionally is beyond all telling. "Blessed is the one whose fault is removed, whose sin is forgiven. Blessed is the man to whom the Lord imputes no guilt, in whose spirit is no deceit" (Psalm 32:1–2). The bigger our sin, the greater is the joy that we experience.

I think that the gift of being forgiven is priceless. Every night I sleep peacefully because I know that I am forgiven.

As this sacrament makes us happy, I know it makes God happy too, for He said, "There will be more joy in heaven over one sinner who repents than over ninety-nine righteous people who have no need of repentance" (Luke 15:7). It is so good to know that the Lord rejoices when a sinner repents; it is so good to know that the entirety of heaven rejoices. When a sinner steps into a confessional, the celebrations in heaven begin. The absolution of the priest is the time when we are reunited with God our Heavenly Father and the joys of heaven.

It is the time the Lord runs to meet us at the gates, to embrace us, and to cover us with His fatherly kisses. It is the time He tells His servants to bring the finest robe and to put it on us; to put a ring on our finger and sandals on our feet; to take the fattened calf and slaughter it; to celebrate with a feast because His son/daughter who was dead has come back to life, who was lost but is found (cf. Luke 15:11–32).

The Other Side of the Coin

As a priest having worked in many places, even in other countries, I see fewer people going to receive this sacrament. The lines of people to get to this sacrament shorten, perhaps, every year. I now work in a parish with around three thousand families. The percentage of people going to the sacrament of Reconciliation on a regular basis is maybe less than 10 percent! Another 10 percent may go once a year, say around Easter. The other 80 percent don't go at all!

Why don't people go to this sacrament anymore? Why do people fear this sacrament, even when they know that it is a channel of God's unending and forgiving love? Is it because people don't sin anymore? Certainly not. St. John says, "If we say, 'we are without sin', we deceive ourselves, and the truth is not in us.... If we say, 'we have not sinned', we make him a liar, and his word is not in us" (1 John 1:8, 10). Listen to what the prophet Micah says: "The faithful have vanished from the earth, no mortal is just! They all lie in wait to shed blood, each one ensnares the other. Their hands succeed at evil; the prince makes demands, the judge is bought for a price, the powerful speak as they please. The best of them is like a briar, the most honest is like a thorn hedge" (Micah 7:2–4). The psalmist says, "There is no one who does what is good, not even one" (Psalm 53:4). This is what St. Paul cites in his letter to the Romans: "There is no one just, not one, there is no one who understands, there is no one who seeks God. All have gone astray; all alike are worthless; there is not one who does good, [there is not] even one. Their throats are open graves; the venom of asp is on their lips; their mouths are full of bitter cursing. Their feet are quick to shed blood; ruin and misery are in their ways, and the way of peace they know not. There is no fear of God before their eyes" (Romans 3:11–18). This is a clear statement of the general nature of human beings; we all carry the burden of sin. The text above mentions many organs of the body: the throat, tongue, lips, mouth, feet, and eyes. It simply indicates that we commit sin, maybe many times a day, at least with some of them. I do not believe there are Mr. Perfects among us. But fewer people going to the sacrament of Reconciliation points to the fact that the "Mr. Perfect mentality" is on the rise.

The main reason for this situation is that people have lost the very sense of sin, the ability to distinguish between right and wrong. People have no guilty feelings; they are not sorry about anything. For most people, what used to be a sin once upon a time is not sin anymore. People take everything as all right. Kindly keep in mind that we live in a world in which people demonstrate in the street to have abortion legalized! Pornography is not "uncommon," divorce is "common," cohabiting is "okay," premarital sex is "all right," extramarital affairs are "no problem" affairs, contraception is what "everyone does," abortion is "normal," color difference is "still in our minds"! This is a very loose mentality. When these "big issues," which create big moral problems, are taken lightly, we slowly end up in darkness. Sense of sin slowly disappears from our lives.

One other reason I hear from high school and college teachers, counselors, and ministers for not having guilty feeling is that young people today are afraid of failures and unable to admit failures because they think they have no value if they fail. They are raised on a diet of relentless praise; they are not taught to admit and evaluate any failure and to learn from their mistakes.

When I was in Europe, I could see many youngsters shamelessly getting physical with their boy/girlfriends in public parks, in cars, under bridges and trees, behind bushes and deserted buildings. No one has any moral stamina to say aloud to such an infected culture that this is shameful and wrong; nothing but abominations. It is because of all these abominations that our world is so cancerous.

If you ever visit India, you will notice animals straying in towns. They meet and mate in public, without any inhibitions. Aren't we belittling and reducing ourselves to being mere animals? Haven't we lost all sense of shame? If all that we said is normal, okay, all right, and so on, then what is *not* normal? What is not wrong? What is not all right? What is not okay? For many people, these are not upsetting elements anymore. Sadly, we should admit that we live in an "all right" society and culture; we turned our culture into an "all right culture." Anything and everything goes with us. The so-called big issues we mentioned above, which used to be uncommon or even unheard-of until a few decades ago, are all right to most people—I mean, to the 80 percent who do not go to this sacrament anymore. This is reflected in our religious practices. Though the Church does not compromise on her positions, She becomes helpless at times. What else can She do except to remind people to make use of this sacrament of God's unconditional love and mercy? When people willfully turn their backs to God, even God becomes helpless before human choices. He created us without our consent, but He cannot redeem us without our consent and cooperation.

Everyone who commits sin commits lawlessness, for sin is lawlessness. (1 John 3:4)

Advantages of the Sacrament of Reconciliation

1. Keeps alive the voice of God

When the sense of God disappears from the lives of people, when the voice of God, which is the voice of conscience, is feeble and low, that is the time people begin to lose the sense of right and wrong. When the spiritual life is too clouded, our vision is blinded. Therefore, even wrong things become *right* to people who have lost that important voice, their conscience, speaking to them. It is here that the sacrament of Reconciliation becomes important in our lives. Frequenting this sacrament on a regular basis helps us keep the voice of conscience, which is the voice of God, loud and clear. This is a very important advantage of the sacrament of Reconciliation. Our moral lives remain intact when we are able to distinguish between right and wrong, an ability that is helped by this sacrament. When all in our parishes try to keep their consciences clean by washing them with the divine hyssop (cf. Psalm 51:9), the moral life of our parishes becomes high. They will, in turn, contribute toward a very high moral life in society. That is how Catholics, the followers of Christ, become light and salt in the world (cf. Matthew 5:13–16).

When one walks away from this sacrament due to any reason, the conscience slowly becomes deadened over the years. That is the first sign of spiritual death in a person. Spiritual death is disastrous. When the voice of conscience is no longer evident and clear, then the person will have no worries about committing any sin. Repetitions of serious and mortal sins, in turn, deaden the conscience. This is a vicious circle: not frequenting the sacrament of Reconciliation for a few years or for many years weakens our ability to hear God's voice within a person; not being tuned to God's voice makes a person prone to commit any kind of sin.

After all, this wonderful sacrament allows one to reflect upon one's life. The more frequently one celebrates this sacrament, the more chances there are to reflect on his/her life. Reflecting on one's life, that is, on what a person did (act of commission) or what he/she failed to do (act of omission) gives him/her a chance to evaluate and assess himself/herself. That is the first step toward spiritual progress. In ordinary terms, we call this the examination of conscience. Before we go to this sacrament, we should take some time to think about what we are going to confess in the confessional. Going over the activities of the past, that is, examining our consciences, helps us realize the things that were bad, that we shouldn't have done; we might even be alarmed at what we see. How could we ever do such a thing? We become ashamed. Or we might wonder why we didn't do something (sin of omission). All this is possible only if we sit back and take some time to evaluate ourselves, to examine our consciences. Examining ourselves lets us know where we stand. We would check ourselves regularly only if we had something like this sacrament. Otherwise, how many of us would regularly make an examination of conscience without fail? That is why the Church encourages us to celebrate this sacrament more often than only once a year. The Church reminds us to make a good confession at least once a year, but this doesn't mean we should be satisfied with the bare minimum. Confession allows us a better chance to keep our ability to hear the voice of God loud and clear within us, which will prevent us from disastrous failures in life.

What will happen if we look in a dusty mirror? Certainly our reflections will not be clear. Or what happens if we don't polish a bronze vessel or vase for a long time? It will tarnish and lose its shine. So too our souls, if we don't celebrate the sacrament of Reconciliation for a long time, it becomes dusty; it loses its shining grace! That is why David, the prophet, prayed, "Cleanse me with hyssop, that I may be pure; wash me, and I will be whiter than snow" (Psalm 51:9).

This reminds me of Miss Martha, who was in charge of all the bronze items in my former parish in the United Kingdom. She was an older lady, close to eighty. She would come in to polish all the bronze things in the church—like vases, candlesticks, and utensils—every two weeks. She would take almost two hours to finish her work. But once she finished polishing, they would shine like new! I used to tell my folks that the sacrament of Reconciliation does the same job: it makes our souls shine like new. Of course, Jesus takes the place of Miss Martha in the confessional.

2. The gift of God's forgiveness

The best gift we receive through this sacrament, of course, is God's forgiveness and pardon. The Lord does not question you; He does not ask you to explain the situation that led you to that sin. He does not even care to weigh the weight of your sin. The priest might ask you a few questions to clarify certain things to determine the gravity of the sin. All that the Lord asks you is to "go, [and] from now on do not sin any more" (John

8:11). This is what the Lord tells anyone who celebrates this wonderful sacrament. Jesus did not condemn sinners; rather, He offered pardon to all, even the thief who was put to death with Him on the cross. When the man said, "Jesus, remember me when you come into your kingdom," the Lord replied, "Amen, I say to you, today you will be with me in Paradise" (Luke 23:42–43). St. John tells us, "God did not send his Son into the world to condemn the world, but that the world might be saved through Him" (John 3:17).

The priest in the confessional (who is the ambassador of Christ, because the Lord said to his disciples, "Whose sins you forgive are forgiven them, and whose sins you retain are retained" (John 220:23) is the one whom the Lord appointed to forgive and to retain sins here on earth. Saint Paul, in his second letter to the Corinthians, says the same thing about priests being the ambassadors of Christ in the ministry of reconciliation. This is what he says: "And all this is from God, who has reconciled us to himself thorough Christ and given us the ministry of Reconciliation; namely, God was reconciling the world to Himself in Christ, not counting their trespasses against them and entrusting to us the message of reconciliation. So we are ambassadors of Christ, as if God were appealing through us. We implore you on behalf of Christ, be reconciled to God" (2 Corinthians 5:18–20). It is clear from what St. Paul says that priests, as the coworkers of bishops, who are the successors of the apostles, are entrusted with the ministry of reconciliation.

They are the people through whose healing touch in the confessionals, the Lord reshapes his artwork and makes it more shining. Every sin is an estrangement from God's way, moving far from God's original design. Sin is a rebellion, a refusal to be God's masterpiece, a movement away from the way God wants us to be. But the sacrament of Reconciliation is the potter's wheel, and the priest is the visible potter. There the Lord is trying to reshape us through His forgiveness. That is the attempt of God: to reinstate our original shape. When we cry out to God in the confessional as the prophet Isaiah did: "Yet, Lord, you are our father; we are the clay and you our potter: we are all the works of your hand. Do not be so very angry, Lord, do not remember our crimes forever" (Isaiah 64:7–8), the Lord gladly reshapes us by His divine mercy.

Try to recall that beautiful story of the potter and the clay, which the prophet Jeremiah tells: he went down to the potter's house; rather, he was asked by the Lord to go over. The Lord wanted him to see how the potter was making pots. When the pot the potter was making turned out badly in his hands, he made another one. The text says, "Whenever the vessel of clay he was making turned out badly in his hand, he tried again, making another vessel of whatever sort he pleased" (Jeremiah 18:4). This is a beautiful reminder to us that the sacrament of Reconciliation is a process of reshaping us until we become whatever would please the Lord.

How will that reshaping take place, if we do not go to the potter's house and wheel? How can the Lord forgive our misdeeds and give us back the best of our shape without this sacrament? Try not to resist the Lord; try not to wrestle with God as Jacob did (cf. Genesis 32:23–31). You may have to limp physically and spiritually all your life because your hip socket may be dislocated by your wrestling with God and choosing to be at the devil's side.

3. Gift of peace

It is beyond doubt, from my own personal experience and also by spending some time almost every day in the confessional, that the foremost result of forgiveness, which is received from the sacrament of Reconciliation, is *peace*! That is something beyond my ability to explain. When I come out after making a good confession, I feel as if I am floating in the air; I am lightweight! The heavy burden has been lifted from me. The weight of big and small sins I carried around has vanished. My heart becomes light. Joy fills my soul. It is so, so great to know that I am forgiven. That brings me peace.

When I confess my sins to another priest, I sometimes cry because I am deeply sorry for offending the immense love of God and also ashamed of my follies. But when the priest raises his hands to forgive my sins through his prayer of absolution, I feel a smile passing across my face. When I hear confessions myself, as I said, I often hear sobs on the other side of the confessional screen. If the person is right in front of me, I see him/her wiping eyes or blowing his/her nose. I think that the weight of their sin is disappearing in their tears. Then I see them smiling with joy. Many have told me that it was great to know that they are forgiven. Some of them must have been carrying around that burden for many months, or even years. But now they are free. The psalmist said, "Blessed is the one whose fault is removed, whose sin is forgiven. Blessed is the man to whom the Lord imputes no guilt, in whose spirit is no deceit" (Psalm 32:1–2).

Reconciliation allows us to share our burdens with someone else. Remember, sorrow shared is sorrow halved, and joy shared is joy doubled. In a very mundane sense too, the sacrament of Reconciliation gives us a great relief. Why do some people become sad and depressed in life and are sometimes even led to commit suicide? Because they think that there is no way out of that particular situation. But for Catholics, we have a way out: in the sacrament of Reconciliation. But if we choose to shut up ourselves in a world of our own, most probably the result will be that we end up on the negative edge of life. "Because I kept silent, my bones wasted away; I groaned all day long. For day and night your hand was heavy upon me; my strength withered as in dry summer heat. Then I declared my sin to you; my guilt I did not hide. I said, 'I confess my transgressions to the Lord, and you took away the guilt of my sin'" (Psalm 32:2–5). See the difference between the impact of confessing our sins to the Lord and holding them inside ourselves; I mean, carrying that weight around with us. When we keep silent about our sins, that is, when we hide from God by walking away from the sacrament of Reconciliation, we feel the heaviness of our sins within us; we call it a *heavy heart*. The psalmist calls it "bones wasting away" and "groaning all day long." He felt the hand of God very heavy on him. But when he decided to confess to the Lord, the whole picture became different: the Lord took away the guilt and burden of his offenses.

I personally feel that that the rate of suicide and suicide attempts are very low among practicing Catholics. It is very unlikely that a person who goes to church and receives all the sacraments on a regular basis would consider suicide as an escape from his/her problems. It should be noted that many suicide cases are persons who do not practice their religion or do not practice any faith at all. Let us "not be like a horse or mule, without understanding" (Psalm 32:9). I wish every one of us had the wisdom to know the difference this sacrament makes in our lives. If only we had the strength to walk over to the confessional to unload the sorrows of our sins, and be freed!

This sacrament promises the mercy and the forgiveness of God. It should be remembered that the sacrament of Reconciliation does not "solve" all the problems that we face. Celebrating the sacrament does not promise that everything is going to be perfect overnight. The sacrament of Reconciliation does not even promise that you will be immune to temptations and weaknesses thereafter; it doesn't promise that we will not sin anymore. So we must not approach this sacrament with wrong notions; that is, the thought that celebrating this sacrament will solve all the problems we face, or that we will not sin again. Though we firmly resolve, in the confessional, to sin no more, we might fail and fall again because we are human beings. After we step out of the confessional, we will have to face all the challenges that were in front of us before we celebrated the sacrament; situations will not change. But we receive supernatural strength to face the challenges of life; we obtain a new and divine strength to encounter baffling situations in a far better way. The Lord helps us to walk away from certain situations that will pull us into sinfulness.

The real change in life happens when God's grace and mercy, received from the sacrament, meet our efforts to fight a good fight. Our sinful lives will not change, even if we frequent this sacrament often, unless we make a real effort to change ourselves. Therefore, we must remember that this sacrament, apart from granting us God's forgiveness, which of course is the purpose of the sacrament, will be "useful" to a person in the practical context of life only if the penitent is willing to work at his/her weaknesses with a genuine desire to overcome those weaknesses. That is the personal responsibility of the penitent. If the penitent does not make an effort to overcome his/her weaknesses, he/she will always find himself/herself in the same situation. That is when people become frustrated with this sacrament; that is when people say, "I am not making any progress. Why should I celebrate the sacrament?" That is why I said earlier that the sacrament does not guarantee a better situation. Situations will get better only if a penitent is keen on making improvements.

Maybe the following example will help you to understand better. If you know that meeting with your boyfriend/girlfriend at your house with nobody else present will lead you to engage in sex, you should avoid meeting him/her at your house. That is your responsibility. That is what we mean by "I resolve to avoid near occasion of sin." If you don't avoid that occasion, and if you fall into sin, that is not the problem of the sacrament; that is your problem. So if the sacrament should bring about some explicit changes in your life, you should have the courage to tell your boyfriend/girlfriend that you cannot meet him/her there, but should choose a place where you have less chance for a fall into sin. That is the time the sacrament of Reconciliation begins to create some ripples in your life apart from granting you forgiveness for your sins; that is the time the sacrament molds you and perfects you by helping you to align yourself with the design God had in His mind before you were born.

4. Rejoining God's community / coming home

Every sin is an alienation from God and one another. The Church is the family of God. When one commits sin, he is sinning not only against God, but also against his family, that is, against all other members of God's family. "If [one] part suffers, all the parts suffer with it; if one part is honored, all the parts share its joy" (1 Corinthians 12:26). Most of the sins that we commit are done against someone. For example, of the Ten Commandments, seven of them are against others. Only the first, second, and third directly deal with God. From fourth to tenth, it's all related to others. When the prodigal son went away with his share of the estate, he was sinning against God and his family. That is why when he returned, he said, "Father, I have sinned against heaven and against you; I no longer deserve to be called your son" (Luke 15:21).

The sacrament of Reconciliation is the time when we are brought back into the joys of God's family. That is why the Lord said, "There will be more joy in heaven over one sinner who repents than over ninety-nine righteous people who have no need of repentance" (Luke 15:7). This joy of God's family over the lost one coming back is well said, again, in the parable of the Prodigal Son. The father tells his servants to bring the finest robes to clothe him and the best sandals for his feet because he was in his rags. Certainly he was not at his best, as he was with pigs; the father commands his servants to put a ring on his son's finger because the ring is the symbol of authority, of belonging to his kingdom. He was out of God's circle, as he decided to cut himself off from the family, when he asked for his share of the property and left on his own accord. The father instructs his servants to kill the fattened calf and to prepare a feast in honor of his son who has rejoined his family.

This reunion literally happens also in this world. For example, if you sin against your wife/husband, you are breaking the joy of your family. Making a good and sincere confession means you are also willing to reconcile with the one whom you happened to offend. If someone tells me that he or she sinned against his or her wife or husband, I would say that the confession does not rectify the family problem without being willing to forgive and forget. That needs personal effort. The joy of your family life can be reinstated only when you are able to reconcile with your husband or wife, either before or after the sacrament of Reconciliation. Celebrating the sacrament does not automatically rebuild your strained relationship; that is your duty. My personal suggestion would be that you first be reconciled with the one against whom you sinned, *then* celebrate the sacrament of Reconciliation. That way you are reconciling with God and the person you offended. I think that is the mind of the Lord too, for He said, "If you bring your gift to the altar, and there recall that your brother has anything against you, leave your gift there at the altar, go first and be reconciled with your brother, and then come and offer your sacrifice" (Matthew 5:23–24). I am prone to think that when you rebuild your broken relationship with your near and dear ones, you are automatically reconciling with God too. But reconciling with God does not automatically rebuild relationship with others. You need to personally work at it.

5. A restart is possible

Most of us are upset about our wrongs in life; some of us get depressed and frustrated with the fact that we continue to fall in the same areas of life, that we are not making progress. Most of us are ashamed of some of our actions. Some of us wonder why on earth we did this or that. Or how we could possibly do such a terrible thing. I have seen penitents weeping and expressing frustrations that they are "way below what they should be." Some of them try to explain to me the situation and what made them do that. They seem to relive the past when they are in the confessional.

I tell them that there is nothing unusual about having done something wrong in life. That shows we are weak human beings, that we are not perfect. Weaknesses are part of being human; both good and bad, weakness and strength, all come in the same package of being human. Though God designed man "little less than a god, crowned him with honor and glory" (Psalm 8:5), we are fallen beings. Remember what we said earlier on that: though God had the perfect design in His mind, we were not made perfect because we were also created by our parents: that is, we are human. If we were perfect, then we wouldn't need any sacraments; even Jesus wouldn't have had to come to save us. Our call is to become perfect over the years through the graces of the sacraments of the Church. But that will take time. We may have to receive a million times the sacraments of the Church before we get there. So there is no need to be upset.

One of the most important benefits of the sacrament of Reconciliation, I tell penitents, is that it allows a restart in life. The past is past, we cannot undo it; that is not in our control anymore. All that is left to do is to try to forget the past, and to start over. That is what the sacrament is calling us to do. While it is true that the past cannot be undone, the sacrament of Reconciliation gives you and me an opportunity to start afresh in life. The sacrament tells us that a new life is possible from that moment forward. The invitation is to be a new man, a new woman, a better husband or wife, mom or dad, brother or sister, colleague or neighbor. The Lord simply tells us to go and start over. St. Paul tells us to divest ourselves of the old self and to put on the person of Christ, to be renewed in life. This is what he tells us in Ephesians: "That you should put away the old self of your former way of life, corrupted through deceitful desires, and be renewed in the spirit of your minds, and put on the new self, created in God's way in righteousness and holiness of truth" (Ephesians 4:22–24). What a wonderful opportunity to get on with life as a new person. Is there any reason for us to be disappointed or frustrated?

The parable of the Barren Fig Tree is an example here (cf. Luke 13:6–9). Jesus told this parable just after calling people to repentance at the beginning of the same chapter. Chapter 13, verses 1 to 5, speak about the need for repentance. This parable was told when someone told the Lord about the Galileans, whose blood Pilate had mingled with the blood of their sacrifices. Jesus then asked them, "Do you think that because these Galileans suffered in this way that they were greater sinners than all other Galileans? By no means! But I tell you, if you don't repent, you will all perish as they did! Or those eighteen people who were killed when the tower at Siloam fell on them—do you think they were more guilty that everyone else who lived in Jerusalem? By no means! But I tell you, if you do not repent, you will all perish as they did!" (Luke 13:2–5).

Then the Lord told the parable of the Barren Fig Tree. We must note what the landowner—I take him as God the Father—tells his gardener: "For three years now I have come in search of fruit on this fig tree but have found none. [So] cut it down. Why should it exhaust the soil?" (13:7). But the gardener—I think he is Jesus—tells him, "Sir, leave it for this year also, and I shall cultivate the ground around it and fertilize it; it may bear fruit in the future. If not you can cut it down" (13:8–9). God the Father was looking for fruit from us; we failed. The Lord expected sweet fruits; we produced sour or rotten fruits. Here I am reminded of the Song of the Vineyard from the book of the prophet Isaiah: "Now let me sing of my vineyard, my beloved's song about his vineyard. My friend had a vineyard on a fertile hillside; he spaded it, cleared it of stones, and planted the choicest vines; within it he built a watchtower, and hewed out a winepress. Then he waited for the crop of grapes, but it yielded rotten grapes" (Isaiah 5:1–2). We are the vineyard the Lord planted; He does everything for us; He waits for the finest fruits from us.

Actually, the gardener was asking for another chance for the fig tree to bear fruit. This is exactly what happens in the sacrament of Reconciliation. The Lord gives us another chance, and again another chance, and again another chance in the expectation that next day, next week, next month, or even next year, He will have a season of good fruit from us. He spares us. The priest in the confessional does not condemn penitents; rather, he says, "Go in peace." Jesus, the gardener, begs on our behalf to

God the Father, the landowner, to allow Him to dig around us, to cultivate the soil, to fertilize. The Church gives us water and manure, light and grace through the sacraments—here, in this case, through the sacrament of Reconciliation. The Lord gives us chances. He tells us to "go and bear fruit that will remain" (John 15:16) for the next season. Will the Lord find fruit in us when He visits us the next time?

Renewal should be an ongoing process until we get to the actual image designed by God, the master artist. The Lord continues to give us polishing touches through the sacraments of the Church. The sacrament of Reconciliation and the Eucharist are the two most frequent ones through which the Lord continues to reshape our image.

6. Taking a U-turn

Consider life a spiritual journey. For most of us, it is a long journey for sixty, seventy, eighty, or more years. It is a long trip indeed! Every long trip takes planning ahead. But despite all the planning, the trip can be delayed on the road. Tires can go flat, certain lanes may be closed, weather conditions can slow us down, we may go off the road, miss the right exit. But do we give up on the trip? *No.* When we miss the exit we should have taken the GPS renavigates us, it tells us to make a U-turn when possible. When the road we are on gets unexpectedly congested, and thus indefinitely delays us, we reroute. But we don't give up the trip entirely. When the car breaks down, we call for roadside assistance and wait until it arrives. Waiting can be frustrating, but we hope to get back on the road soon.

Every sin is a spiritual breakdown; every sin is going off the road. We get delayed on our spiritual trip. But the Lord, through the sacrament of Reconciliation, tells us to make a U-turn, to renavigate, to reroute. There are people who come to me and say, "My last confession was my first confession"! But I am not disappointed, though a bit surprised, because they decided to make a U-turn, although a bit late. They knew they would not get to their "destination" if they continued on that road. They decided to reroute their spiritual trip; they decided to get out of the loop.

The Lord whispers within us, as does a GPS, to get back to our spiritual highways so that we will not be unduly delayed on our trip. The sacrament of Reconciliation, for me, is a GPS, or a road map, that shows us a better way to reroute our lives; a better way to renavigate our trip. All that we need is the courage to make that U-turn. Ask the Lord for His help.

7. An occasion to be carried on the shoulders of the Good Shepherd

I consider the sacrament of Reconciliation an opportunity to be carried on the shoulders of the Lord back to the sheepfold, the Church. A sinner is a little lamb that goes away, that is lost from the group of a hundred. Reconciliation is the time the lost sheep returns to the group, the community of God's people. Jesus the Good Shepherd looks for the lost ones, as the book of the prophet Ezekiel says, "The lost I will search out, the strays I will bring back, the injured I will bind up, and the sick I will heal" (34:16). After all, the entire content of the books of various prophets in the Old Testament is nothing but a constant invitation of the Lord to return to Him. In the sacrament of Reconciliation, Jesus the Good Shepherd searches for the lost and brings us back on His shoulders; He binds up the wounds that our sins have caused; He heals our spiritual sickness through this miraculous sacrament. What a wonderful privilege for the lamb to be carried by Jesus the Good Shepherd. As I write this, I actually visualize the picture of the Lord with a lamb on his shoulders.

How to Make a Good Confession

Try it this way: When you decide to celebrate the sacrament, you need to take some time to prepare to receive the sacrament. This should be a deliberate action, not a situation when you get to church for Sunday Mass, and you happen to find the priest in the confessional. You might think, *Well, he is waiting for some "customers." Let me go in and see.* No, that is not the way you should receive this sacrament. (Well, not only this sacrament, but any sacrament.) Kindly take some time to prepare. You can consider the following steps for making a good confession.

Try to recollect your sins in order. Some people come in and fumble. Even if they were in line for an hour, they seem to think right at that moment about what they want to say. Some say, "Well, let me think"; others would say, "Okay, all right, let me see." They go on repeating these words for some time. No, you shouldn't do that. First of all, you are wasting time. There may be others waiting to celebrate the sacrament. You can't afford to take all the time for yourself. So to make it easier, try to recall your sins in order before you step into the confessional. If needed, write them down.

Some people say they don't remember anything in particular. Well, if you don't remember anything in particular, it is possible that you haven't done anything really bad. Thank God for sparing you from serious sins. If you have done something really bad, then certainly, you will not forget that. So when I say you have to remember your sins in order, begin with the big ones first and then move to the venial sins.

Most people think of going to the sacrament of Reconciliation because they think they have done something bad that bothers them; they are "heavy in their hearts." They need to clear it from their minds as early as possible. Definitely they will not miss those kinds of sins. If you miss even the bigger ones, there is some problem.

Be repentant. The second, and the most important element, is to repent of your sins. This is one essential element of this sacrament. Without repentance, you will not have forgiveness. Repentance is compunction of heart. It is a true feeling of sorrow for your misdeeds that offended God and others. This should lead you to the next step.

Be resolved to sin no more. The sacrament of Reconciliation becomes personally effective in your life when you resolve to sin no more. Your resolution shows how determined you are to stay away from sin. This is a promise you make before the Lord: that you will do everything possible to avoid sin and occasions that might lead you to sin. This is the core of the Act of Contrition that we make after confession.

True repentance is not just feeling sorry for our sins. It is also a promise, a resolution to do good in the future. This is what St. John the Baptist says when he preaches the baptism of repentance and forgiveness of sins: "Produce good fruits as evidence of your repentance" (Luke 3:8). So by avoiding evil and doing good, we prove that we are sorry about our past misdeeds. Psalm 34:15 exhorts us to "turn from evil and do good." Listen to what the prophet Isaiah tells us: "Cease doing evil; learn to do good" (1:16). What does this mean? It is not enough to turn away from evil; we need to learn to do good also. That is true repentance; that is called a change for the better.

The prophet Joel shows us what true repentance is or how we must return to the Lord: "Return to me with all your heart, with fasting, weeping, and mourning. Rend your hearts, not your garments, and return to the Lord your God, for he is gracious and merciful, slow to anger, abounding in steadfast love, and relenting in punishment. Perhaps he will again relent and leave behind a blessing" (Joel 2:12–14). The people are asked to show their repentance by fasting, weeping, and mourning. The sacrament of Reconciliation is an invitation to walk away from the darkness of sin and into the wonderful light of the Lord!

Inform the priest. This is the time you actually step into the confessional to receive the sacrament. There, you kneel or sit before the priest and humbly tell him what you have done (sins of commission) or what you haven't done but that you should have done (sins of omission). This is the hardest part for all of us—at least, most of us. I know that it is not easy for people, myself included, to tell anyone the most personal things of our lives. The natural tendency is to hide them from others.

Informing the priest is the humbling part of the sacrament. It is good to remember that you are talking to Jesus, not to the priest, though he is physically there. If you don't want to reveal your identity, that is fine. You can kneel where the priest cannot see you, and most probably you cannot see the priest.

The Church is aware of this limitation of people. That is why we have a space for anonymous confessions. From my experience as a priest, having listened to many confessions, I can tell you it is no fun to hear what people have to say. It is rather painful. Therefore, you don't have to worry about priests carrying around what you say. I don't remember what people tell me, especially in the confessional.

Be open before the Lord. He sees us and knows us; everything before Him is like the day. I hope you know that the priests are not allowed to reveal the confessional secrets under any circumstance. That is called the *seal of confession*, which no priest will ever break even if he has to die. If he does, he will be in trouble. He will be automatically suspended from his office of being a priest. It is that serious. Priests don't break the seal of confession, not because he is afraid of the consequences, but because of the very nature of his office. So you can be 100 percent confident of this secrecy.

When you finish your confession, he will give you some thoughts for your consideration, based on what you told him. If the priest needs some clarifications, he might ask you. Don't get upset over this. Maybe you were not clear enough, or he did not hear you well. Therefore, he may ask you for some clarifications. A doctor cannot treat his patient without first knowing what the problem is. He might run many tests and ask many questions before he finalizes his conclusions. The priest is a spiritual doctor the Lord has appointed to help you overcome your spiritual ailments. He asks for clarifications to help you with his insights, which might be of great help to you to overcome your habitual sins and weaknesses.

Some priests talk a lot, and some priests talk less, in the confessional. Priests who talk a long time honestly think that they need to tell the penitent at least a few basic things, especially if the person is returning to this sacrament after thirty or forty years. That is very fair. Some priests finish with the penitent in a few minutes; they may think that the sacrament of Reconciliation is nothing but God's forgiveness and that their duty is to absolve sins. They might say that this sacrament is not the time for spiritual direction. They are also correct. They may not care to talk long, especially if there are many waiting in line for the sacrament. If you want to have a long conversation, a kind of spiritual guidance, approach him at a different time.

Some people come into the confessional after many years. There are people who go to confession after forty or more years! I am glad they thought of going, at least at that point. It is better to be late than never. But they don't seem to be ashamed; instead, they seem to tell of some feat; the way they explain things might look as if they are coming after having done something great; they are not sorry about having missed all those forty years. This might make the priest think that they are not repentant. Some priests might even tell it to their faces. If any priest tells you that he thought you were not repentant, don't get upset with him. It is your problem; you failed to *express* your sorrow. If you are truly repentant, you will certainly sound like you are truly sorry about your negligence. Usually we don't tell someone sorry about any serious issue with a big smile. If you do, that will mean that you are not *really* sorry, but you are saying it for the sake of saying it. When you come into the confessional after so long, you should first of all tell the priest that you are sorry that you missed this sacrament for that long. Actually, that should be your first sin to start with.

This could also be a defense mechanism, expressed in a particular cultural form, just as some cultures teach to laugh when receiving correction to show that they are not offended. I personally believe that the person knows the seriousness; he/she does not know how to hold that seriousness. Or they may be trying to make light of it. It helps them face the truth. Not all priests may be aware of this situation.

Once you inform the priest of everything that you wanted to say, and the priest gives you the absolution, praise the Lord: you are free forever. You never have to even think about it again. You don't have to bring up the sins that you already confessed today in the next confession. There are many people who carry around the burden of their past, even after a good confession. That shows your inability to trust in the forgiveness of God. When you confess your sins, the Lord tells us: "It is I, I, who wipe out, for my own sake, your offenses; your sins I remember no more" (Isaiah 43:25). In the book of Jeremiah, the Lord says, "For I will forgive their iniquity and no longer remember their sins" (Jeremiah 31:34). Micah 7:7–20 expresses confidence in God's future. Verse 19 says, "You will cast into the depths of the sea all our sins." When God says that He does not remember our sins anymore, He means that He does not hold our sins against us, that He is willing to begin the relationship again. When God does not remember our sins, why should we remember it? We should learn to forgive ourselves; forget it too. We must let go of the past and move forward.

Reconciling with the past does not mean that you will never ever remember a particular sin that you happened to commit at some point, which caused you a lot of pain and suffering. That is not the meaning of forgetting the past. Even after making a sincere confession, even when you know that you are forgiven, you may still remember that sin that you did long ago. That is quite normal. That does not mean that you are not forgiven. For example, a parent who had an abortion will most likely always remember that, even if he/she confessed it before God and received forgiveness. That is most probable. Allow me to explain it this way: If you get a deep wound on your body, a doctor may stitch it up; the wound will heal in due time, but the scar may remain for many more years, sometimes for life. When I was in my early twenties, learning to ride a motorcycle left a big scar on the left side of my right calf. The motorcycle leaned over to the left side; my right calf was right on the hot exhaust pipe. It took only a few seconds to burn my flesh. The burn healed in about two weeks' time. Even after many years, the scar left by the burn is still visible. Whenever I see it, I remember the accident. I don't think it will ever disappear. I have to live with the scar. But the accident does not hurt me anymore, nor am I disappointed. That accident made me stronger in life. I still enjoy motorcycles. So too with wounds left by the sins of the past. Let the scar be there; you get on with life, learning a lesson from that "accident."

The Lord transforms wounds of sins in the sacrament of Reconciliation.

Do the penance that the priest suggests. This is the last step of a good confession. Usually the priest asks you to do some small act of penance for your sins. Remember, it is not your penance that makes you forgiven of your sins. It is a visible act of repentance; neither is it a punishment for your sins. The forgiveness is granted through the act of reparation by Jesus by way of his Passion, Death and Resurrection; and He also bore on the cross the punishment our sins deserved. Your act of penance is a very small gesture of your love for the Lord, whom you offended by your sins.

As a priest who hears confessions almost every day, it is a time for me personally to become humble before the Lord, when I see how humble and open people are in making their confessions, how sincere they are. They open the book of their life before the Lord, page by page. They have nothing to hide from the Lord. Sometimes I ask myself, "Am I that open and sincere before the Lord?"

The Lord continues to refashion us into His own image day by day through the sacrament of Reconciliation; He fashions us into a dwelling place so that He can come to us to dwell within us in the Sacrament of the Eucharist. The immediate purpose of the sacrament of Reconciliation is to make us worthy to receive the Lord Himself in the Sacrament of the Eucharist, which is the symbol of God's everlasting love, through which the Lord abides in the world after the promise, "I am with you always, until the end of the age" (Matthew 28:20). I cannot explain how much I trust in the sacrament of Reconciliation.

CHAPTER 4

Human Becomes Divine

Do not fear, for I have redeemed you.
—Isaiah 43:1

The Lord conceived us in His mind before our birth, painted us on the canvas of the sacrament of Matrimony, called us by our name in the sacrament of Baptism, reshaped us through the sacrament of Reconciliation, and now he saves us with His everlasting love. The death of the Lord is the sign of his unfathomable love, which is made present through the Sacrament of the Eucharist.

Another more radical way in which the Lord perfects us is with the Sacrament of the Eucharist. This is yet another sacrament that the Lord established to perfect us. Certainly, the sacrament of Baptism is the first divine touch of the Lord toward our perfection; the sacrament of Reconciliation is the ongoing process of God's touch that makes us worthy recipients of the Sacrament of the Eucharist and enables us to taste the divine life of God.

The best and the biggest gift that I ever received from heaven is not wealth or riches—my small bank balance, or the ability to read and write; neither is it my parents who became instruments in my birth and who vied with each other in loving me; nor my good home, nor the good food that I eat more than three times a day; nor good health. It is nothing that I enjoy as a creature living in this world. But it is God's beloved son, Jesus Christ, God's ultimate gift to humanity. How on earth can I express my joy over this most wonderful gift to me and to the rest of the world? This beloved Son of God, who was born in history as the "Wonder-Counselor, God-Hero, Father-Forever, Prince of Peace" (Isaiah 9:5) is the one I received as the most touching and influential gift from the Father, the gift that totally changed my destiny forever! If God hadn't given me this gift, the salvation He promised would have been impossible for me. I would have wandered in this world hungry and thirsty. I would have perished eternally.

There are hundreds of thousands of reasons for me to say that Jesus was the best gift I ever received. Jesus taught me to call God Father. In him, as St. Paul said, I became God's adopted son and He became my Father. Up until then, I never knew God was love. Nobody had ever told me that He was an ocean of boundless love. It is Jesus who unveiled for me God's love, the secret of His nature. Though the people of the Old Testament had sung of God as "merciful and gracious" and "slow to anger, abounding in mercy" (Psalm 103:8), Jesus became the embodiment of that merciful love. I saw in him what I failed to understand clearly prior to His coming. I was able to get closer to

God and behold His face. For me and for my generation, God became a Father who anxiously awaits the return of his children.

It is Jesus who taught me and the rest of the world to hope for a life after death. He taught us to think of heaven as a mansion with many rooms: "In my Father's house there are many dwelling places" (John 14:2). Until the Savior came, was there any real hope of a resurrection as we have it now? I don't know. There must have been some vague hope of life after death. But Jesus gave a clear picture of it. He also proved that salvation is possible through his life, death, and resurrection. And most importantly, He showed us the way to the Father because He Himself was the way. I know from His own statement that Jesus is the sure way to the Father: "I am the way, the truth and the life. No one comes to the Father except through me" (John 14:6). Now I know that He is the door, though it is narrow; and I can certainly come to the Father because Jesus my Savior has gone ahead of me. He will come back again to take me to Himself so that where He is, I also may be (cf. John 14:3).

The world has seen many saviors and many leaders. But Jesus is the only one who promised everlasting life, for He said, "I am the resurrection and the life; whoever believes in me, even if he dies, will live, and everyone who lives and believes in me will never die" (John 11:25–26). The world has seen many prophets who taught the people to look for light; but Jesus, the precious gift of God to me, was Himself the light. He is the only one who said, "I am the light of the world; whoever follows me will not walk in darkness, but will have the light of life" (John 8:12). Light is that which expels darkness and reveals what is hidden. Your absence was darkness itself. But the birth of Christ brought light; You led humanity from darkness to light. That is why the prophet Isaiah said, "The people who walked in darkness have seen a great light; upon those who lived in a land of gloom a light has shone. You have brought them abundant joy and great rejoicing. They rejoice before you as people rejoice at harvest, as they exult when dividing the spoils" (Isaiah 9:1–2).

Jesus, who was born into the lowliest of situations, became the greatest influential factor in the world. He is the dividing point of history. The Son of Man, who walked along the streets of Palestine, who touched and reawakened even the lilies of the field, became the greatest inspiration to the world. Millions and millions today carry on His mission in numerous ways—teaching, preaching, healing, and many other good deeds. Every single thing that the world enjoys today has come about as a result of His influence. In a world where only the rich and the powerful had a place, He made space for the poor and the marginalized; He opened the door of the kingdom to the poor by being born poor, by living with the poor, by being with the poor, and finally by dying a poor criminal's death. In a world where the sick and the suffering were condemned to die by the wayside, Jesus brought healing to them and made them whole. And as mentioned earlier, hospitals, education, the social welfare concept, morality, and discipline are all embedded in the person of Christ, whose works today the Church carries on in various ways. All because of the *person* of Jesus.

Jesus, the ultimate gift of God to humanity, gave us many memorable gifts. He promised us and breathed on us the Holy Spirit to lead us and guide us in the world; He gave to us His own mother, the Virgin Mary, to be our mother at the foot of the cross when He said, "Behold your mother" (John 19:27); He established the Church for us and made us a member of the Church, which is the repository of graces for the salvation of all souls; He gave us the sacraments, for which we should be constantly thankful; and finally, He gave Himself on the cross, which we daily celebrate in the Eucharist and which is the visible sign of His everlasting presence "until the end of the age" (Matthew 28:20): the Eucharist, which continues to nourish the faithful, that gives everlasting life to the faithful, that gives us a foretaste of the promised life in heaven and the eternal banquet therein.

We make this wonderful gift our own for the very first time through our First Holy Communion.

As a child, I watched with curiosity as older people lined up for Communion. I didn't know what they were receiving on their tongues. I wished I could receive one too. I stood by my parents as they moved up to the priest to receive the divine bread, and how many times have I screamed for that "bread from the priest"! Once I even pulled at the edge of his long robe and begged, "Can I have one, please?" The priest smiled at me and gave me a blessing instead. As my dad dragged me back to the pew, I kept turning and looking at the priest. This continued for almost four more years.

At last the day came: the day of my First Holy Communion. If the most memorable day in the history of humanity, especially for the Christians, is the day on which the Son of God died on the cross for the salvation of many, one of the most memorable days of my life is the day I received my First Holy Communion, the self-gift of Jesus in the Eucharist. It is a day that is still vivid in my memory, even after many years. I can still recall how devoutly I received the Body of the Lord and then the Blood; how slowly, with folded hands, I walked back to my seat; how carefully I knelt down and immersed myself in prayer. I do not remember now all the prayers I made to the Lord. Was I saying many prayers, or simply praising the Lord present in my inmost being? I am sure those were moments of intense joy. That day was the day of real communion with the Lord, for I became one with Him, and He became my all.

I don't think I can thank God enough for the marvel of the Eucharist, because through this, I taste the divine life on earth. When I received Jesus, I was receiving Him entirely: the life of God, the Word of God, all that He stood for, and all that He came to realize in this world. The day I received the Lord was the day I was invited to grow into His likeness, to become like Him. Ever since my First Holy Communion, I have received the Lord into my heart nearly every day. And each day, I wish to grow a step closer to the image and likeness of Jesus. I hope to receive Him many more times, until I become one with Him in heaven, when I see him face-to-face as He really is; that is the ultimate union of the masterpiece with God, the master artist.

> Take it; this is my body... This is my blood
> of the covenant, which will be shed for
> many. (Mark 14:22–24)

Through the frequent celebration of the Eucharist, I was able to know the depth of this sacrament of Your Son's love for me and the rest of humanity. As I grew older, I learned to see the face of Christ, who places Himself on the altar of sacrifice. Now as I stand at the celebration of the Eucharist, I see the gentlest face I have ever seen in my life. That is the face of the Nazarene who was born among cattle, grew up around Nazareth, walked the roads of Palestine, challenging the thoughts and traditions of His time, who became a question to which His times could not find an answer. Therefore, the people of his time tried to eliminate the question, thinking that eliminating the question was the solution to the question. Neither before nor after did the world see one who posed such strong challenges, ones that shook the very foundations of the world. He was not only a question for the generations to find an answer to, but He Himself was also the answer to the questions He raised. He challenged the world, and He showed the people how to face challenges. He was one who hadn't had any place to lay His head in a world where even the birds of the air had a nest and foxes had holes. He was the poorest man, the most detached man the world ever saw. But the challenge He raised was the toughest in the world. Even after His death, the challenge He raised continues. As long as humanity celebrates the Eucharist, the challenge will continue.

Who could forget that evening that touched the conscience of the world? That was the beginning of an evening that witnessed the fading of the sun before the actual sunset: everything was unusual. The carpenter's son, the son of Mary and Joseph, that young man who chose fishermen and tax collectors as his companions, who performed great and small miracles, who with His gentle presence awakened even the lilies of the field and the birds of the air, who walked along the streets of His hometown, preaching a new form of worship, preaching a new image of God, which was alien to the people of His time until then, and writing a new commandment of love on the tablets of human hearts. The Messiah, the Christ, was going to sign the completion of His mission with His own blood, whispering in the ears of the world the formula for reversing the course of the world. That formula became the remedy for all the problems the world encounters. He became the key to every lock for all those who really wanted to open wide the door. For the most part, the world, at least secretly, considered Him the solution to every puzzle; He was thought to be the answer to every question that baffled humanity. He was the first and the last formula of its kind, which was to be taken on by millions across the world, the formula that explains the chemistry of the salvation of the world.

I see the Last Supper: the Master in the center and the twelve at his sides. That was a supper prepared for the life of the Master, for the life of the world. That was His last supper while the world would continue to eat many more suppers. That was the last sip of wine until He would drink it anew in the kingdom of heaven with his disciples (cf. Matthew 26:29), while the world would sip many more drinks. He was setting a table so that humanity could have life and have it abundantly (cf. John 10:10).

That was a supper at which many things were foretold; many things were said and many things done. The face of the Master was composed; the serious face of the Master reflected the gloom of the night, because He was going to miss His friends. The time was running short. He must have seen the shadow of the cross behind the table of love. The mission was coming to a decisive conclusion; the toughest part of the mission was in front of His eyes. He must have seen with His divine intuition His impending crucifixion. He must have already begun to feel the grip of death looming around Him. Even the air smelled of the death of the Lord. But His determination was also written on that comely and loving face.

That must have been the most heart-wrenching farewell supper the world ever witnessed. The Master setting a table for His chosen friends and serving the food and drink with His own hands, knowing that was the last chance for a meeting of all thirteen, for He said, "I tell you, from this time on I shall not drink of the fruit of the vine until the kingdom of God comes" (Luke 22:18). I see the Master looking into the eyes of the one going to betray Him as he served dinner to him. But His hands did not shake at all! There was no difference in His look. It had all the love and affection it used to have. As He kept looking into the eyes of each, the look seemed to burn away all the filth from the lives of all He served at the table and the world they would serve later. It was the most powerful gaze, and one that went right into the depths of hearts; a gaze that read the past and the present and that knew the future; a gaze that read the hearts of people yet unborn. It was a gaze that made Peter weep bitterly after his denial; it was a gaze that broke the heart of His mother Mary on His way to Calvary.

I see the disciple whom Jesus loved, leaning over the breast of the Master. That was a privilege he alone had, a privilege to be described as "the one Jesus loved." He was finding a special place in the life of the Lord. The Last Supper reminds you and me that we have a special place in the heart of God, a love beyond all telling, because of which He dies for us. The Eucharist is the assurance of that love. As the Lord served the meal to each of them, His death was but moments away; he was serving not just bread and wine, but He was serving *love*, the gist of His life. Khalil Gibran, the prophet and the poet of Lebanon, wept: "Love never knew its depth until it was time to part." The Lord was silently telling them the three most important words: "I LOVE YOU; before I walk into the hands of death, let me tell you how much I love you and allow me to show you how much I love you; before the world wipes me away from its unkind surface, let me carve your images upon the tablet of my heart; before some of you denounce me, let me embrace you with an eternal love; before you are shattered due to fear, allow me to hold you to my breast; before you begin to experience the bitterness of the night, let me express the warmth of this evening; before I sink into the depths of agony, let me conceal you in the depths of my heart, where everyone, even the one who betrays me, has a place, so that you will not be drowned in the turmoil of life."

I see the betrayer receiving the bread from the hands of the one who trusted him, as though he was not aware of anything that was going to happen. The cravings of the world had calloused his heart. His love for money had blinded him; or was it his blindness that made him love money more than the Master? The words of life that had drifted from the lips of the Nazarene had done him no good; being with the Lord for the past three years did not change his destiny. Though he was born to love and to be saved, he opted to be lost! Not waiting for the final thanksgiving hymn to be sung, he disappeared into the darkness to plot against the one who fed him like a mother. He, like a serpent, was going to bite the hand that fed him with milk and honey. He was going to betray the Master for thirty silver coins. His Master was worth thirty silver pieces? The secret signal he would use is one of the most beautiful gestures of love and acceptance: a kiss. It was like slicing the throat while smiling, a stab in the back.

I hear the prayer of the Lord for the disciples: "I pray for them… Holy Father, keep them in your name that you have given me, so that they may be one just as we are. When I was with them I protected them in your name that you gave me, and I guarded them, and none of them was lost except the son of destruction, in order that the Scripture might be fulfilled. But now I am coming to you… I do not ask that you take them out of the world but that you keep them from the evil one" (cf. John 17:9–19). As this prayer comes to my mind, I feel my heart melting within me, a sense of sadness enveloping me.

The Lord Jesus is about to fall like a grain of wheat. He had said much earlier that a grain of wheat must fall to the ground and die so that it could produce much fruit. If it does not fall, it will just remain as it is. The death of one grain becomes the source of many grains; and here, the death of the King renews the life of the world. This is an unusual situation, for most often the victory and power of the emperors of the world were the result of the sacrifices of the *subjects* they ruled. They established their dominion by sacrificing the lives of their people. Their names are written in gold letters on the pages of history books. But the name of Jesus, the Supreme King, has been written on the hearts of humanity. Here the Master surrenders His life so that the people who belong to him "might have life, and have it abundantly" (John 10:10). This is the difference between Christ and the other kings of the world. No, the kings of this world cannot even be compared to Christ. If we do so, that would be a crime!

As Jesus broke the bread for the twelve, He must have seen Himself in the bread as the grain ground under the weight of the cross; the wine poured into their cups was the blood that he would shed on the following day on the way to Calvary, as He would carry the cross and on it die the death of a criminal. The bread broken and wine poured that night at the table would be the body shattered and the blood spilled the next day. Jesus the Lord on Holy Thursday was anticipating Good Friday. He was not serving bread and wine; he was serving His *life*. As He served the food, He was saying, "Eat my life and live." He was serving it not only to his friends, but also to His foes. But had He foes? I believe not. He had no enemies; all were His friends. It was the others who considered Him an enemy to be destroyed. He called even the one who betrayed Him "friend"; He looked with sympathy and understanding on the one who denied Him not once, but three times.

I remember the carved picture on the front side of the altar in a church that was three miles away from my home parish. It was a picture of a pelican—a name that I did not know then—feeding its brood with its own lifeblood. The mother bird tore open her heart and fed her chicks with the blood that oozed from her heart. That was such a striking picture; I have not seen a similar one since. I used to visit that church just to see that picture. It was beyond my ability to understand the motive of the mother bird that tore open her heart for her brood. Neither could I comprehend the motive of the Lord, who died on the cross for the world. Whenever I looked at that altar, it reminded me of the sacrifice of the Son of Man. That must have been the most fitting picture that could remind the faithful of the sacrificial nature of the Eucharist. As the mother bird feeds her brood with her lifeblood flowing from her own heart, the Lord feeds us with His body and blood. As the mother bird falls dead, the brood flies away to freedom, fluttering their tiny wings. The death of the Lord is the life of the world.

I remember His words: "A man can have no greater love than this, that he lay down his life for his friends" (John 15:13). That was the greatest expression of love; the noblest form of love. Christ was showing humanity that no one can exceed Him in love; no one can express love in a better way. I have never truly loved anyone in my life. All my expressions of love were nothing but pretensions of love. My love was never seasoned with sacrifices; it was never unconditional, but had many "ifs and buts." I don't even smile at a person from my heart. The smile that I put on comes not from the depths of my heart but is merely a work of my lips just to bluff the passerby.

What a blessedness the Lord has filled us with by letting us receive the body and blood of the Lord—His very life! We are invited to eat and be nourished by His body and blood, to grow like Jesus. And one day, like Him, we will offer our entire life too for the salvation of souls.

Lord, how blessed we are to taste Your life on earth! How blessed we are to be promised everlasting life because we eat this divine bread! We completely trust in the words of Jesus: "Whoever eats my flesh and drinks my blood has eternal life, and I will raise him on the last day" (John 6:54). We know that the Eucharist is the pledge of salvation; it is the true food with which God feeds His children. Since we are not of the world, God knew that we also needed food that is not of the world. Therefore He prepared a divine banquet that "comes down from heaven [and] which gives life to the world" (John 6:33). And we know that Jesus is that food, for He said, "I am the living bread that came down from heaven; whoever eats of this bread will live forever; and the bread that I will give is my flesh for the life of the world" (John 6:51).

I am filled with joy every morning as I walk to church, for I know Jesus is going to be with me again in a very personal way through the Eucharist. After receiving Communion, I experience His nearness wherever I go and whatever I do. The presence of the Lord guides my steps day in and day out; that is the fuel that drives many miles without becoming weary. As I walk the road of life, which often is difficult and burdensome with the worries and cares of life, He becomes a cotraveler as He did on the road to Emmaus (cf. Luke 24:13–35). He becomes an "all-knowing and ever-present God."

Lord, "you know when I sit and stand; you understand my thoughts from afar. You sift through my travels and my rest; with all my ways you are familiar. Even before a word is on my tongue, Lord, you know it all. Behind and before you encircle me and rest your hand upon me" (Psalm 139:2–5). In Holy Communion, He becomes one with me and I with Him. This wonderful union of the Lord with me is called communion.

This communion of the Lord makes me feel great; it enables me to walk all the ways that I should take, whether I like them or not. As the sun goes down the horizons dispelling darkness, blurring my sight, He becomes my light; as the sun strikes me with its scorching rays, He becomes my shade and breeze to comfort me; when my burdens become too much for me to carry, He tells me to unload them on Him. He whispers in my ears, "Come to me, all you who labor and are burdened, and I will give you rest. Take my yoke upon you and learn from me, for I am meek and humble of heart; and you will find rest for yourselves. For my yoke is easy, and my burden light" (Matthew 11:28–30).

We are most thankful to You, our Father, for saving us by the body and blood of the Lord; for allowing us to receive Him who redeemed us by His Passion, Death and Resurrection, and thus fulfilled the prophecy of Isaiah, "Do not fear, for I have redeemed you" (Isaiah 43:1). We feel that redemption each time we receive the Lord in the Eucharist. What a privilege to behold the Lord, to touch Him, and to receive Him into our life. What more could we want? "None beside you delight me on earth" (Psalm 73:25). When we receive Him in the Eucharist, our joy doubles and our life becomes sanctified. Thank You again, my Lord, for the sacrament of the Holy Eucharist, the sign of God's everlasting presence in the world. We can walk many miles in this arid world because the Lord continues to live within us like the dewfall!

But this sacrament also challenges us: it is a challenge to become another sacrament on earth. That is the mission the Lord enjoins on us at the end of every Eucharistic celebration.

Our First Holy Communion was an initiation into the mission of the Lord. Though I did not understand the full significance of that initiation and the mission on the day of my First Holy Communion, I began to get a better picture of the challenge as I grew older. Everyone should be able to understand the numerous possibilities of the Eucharist. The reason, I realize now, the world remains unaffected and unchanged by the reception of this great sacrament is that the participants of the Eucharist do not understand the many nuances of the Eucharist; they don't personally take the challenges the Eucharist poses before them. The Lord, at the end of the celebration, is asking the congregation only one question, as He asked the prophet: "Whom shall I send? Who will go for us?" (Isaiah 6:8). That is a very poignant question for the participants to answer. If we want to change the world, or rather, if we wish to see a better world, go for the Lord. The Lord strengthened us to do the task. Now say, "Send me, Lord; I will go for you." Most people are not able to say yes to the invitation of the Lord because they don't correctly understand the many nuances of the Eucharist.

Know What We Celebrate

I am not sure how many of us really understand what we celebrate. Of course, all of us know that it is the sacrifice of the Lord. But how many of us are able to find the reflections of our lives in the Eucharist, though most of us might know that the Eucharist should be reflected in our lives? How many of us remember that it is our lives too that we celebrate in the

Eucharist? The Eucharist simply does not become meaningful to us if we don't try consciously to find the meaning of what we celebrate. Not understanding the many hidden riches of the Eucharist would be a terrible loss. Try to reflect on the Eucharist in a different way. The celebration of the Eucharist will make much more sense if we see our own lives reflected on the altar. What becomes the body and blood of the Lord is what is offered up: the bread and wine. But we must remember that the bread and wine are the symbolic representations of *our lives*. When the offertory procession moves forward, we must be able to place ourselves—that is, our struggles, pains, sufferings, achievements, failures, dreams, hopes, and everything we have and are—in that offering. In short, everything that makes us should be turned over to the Lord at the time of the offertory.

It should be remembered that the collection we take just before the offertory is a representation of our lives too, with all their ups and downs, joys and sufferings. The envelope that we drop in the offering box should sum up our lives. That is a more convenient way of showing our *self-gift* to the Lord, a small share of our labour. The general collection and the offertory will make sense to us only if we see them in the light of our *self-surrender* to the Lord. When the priest offers up the offerings, which are taken from the "fruit of our labour and the work of human hands," he is actually offering up *our lives* to the Lord, on the altar.

Well, if we are offered with the bread and wine, then we too are consecrated along with the bread and wine on the altar. This means we too are changed into the body and blood of the Lord. We become divine too! The challenge of this understand-

181

ing is that we too are *broken* with the Lord when the bread is broken. At the time of Communion, what we receive is not only the body and blood of the Lord, but also one another, because we were offered up, consecrated, transformed, and broken. The Communion we receive becomes truly meaningful when we receive each other into our hearts and into our lives, along with the Lord. This is the time of "communion of hearts": we are in communion with the Lord and with one another. I think that is why we call it communion.

> Whom shall I send? Who will go for us?
> (Isaiah 6:8)

The celebration of the Mass comes to an end with one of the following invitations: "Go forth, the Mass is ended" or "Go and announce the Gospel of the Lord" or "Go in peace, glorifying the Lord by your life" or "Go in peace." When the Mass ends, the mission of Christ does end, but our participation in that mission begins. The final invitations are the start of our part of the mission or, rather, continuing the mission of Christ. It is exactly the same mission that the Lord enjoined on His disciples: "All power in heaven and on earth has been given to me. Go, therefore, and make disciples of all the nations, baptizing them in the name of the Father, and of the Son, and of the Holy Spirit, teaching them to observe all that I have commanded you" (Matthew 28:18–20).

The mission of Christ ends at the end of the Mass, that is, with His Passion, Death and Resurrection. There is nothing more for Him personally to do to complete His mission in the world. He has done everything that He came to do. But our part of the mission begins at the end of each Mass we celebrate. The challenge is thrown open to the followers of Christ, to the people who celebrated the Mass. When the Mass ends and the worshippers disperse to their separate ways, they should begin their mission of being *broken* in their own walks of life. That is the meaning of the call "Go and announce the Gospel of the Lord" or "Go forth, glorifying the Lord by your lives."

The Eucharist is to become a living celebration; and a participant is to become a "Eucharist, after the Eucharist." A participant is to become a sacrament to others in the world: a sacrament of God's unfathomable love, through which Jesus was broken and died for us; a sacrament that nourishes the participants. Therefore, the participant should become a symbol of God's unending presence in the lives of all people—the "eighth sacrament." This is achieved when the participants take one of the formulae of dismissal seriously and try to personalize the Eucharist in their lives.

Whenever I preside at a Mass, I like to dismiss the congregation by saying, "Go in peace, glorifying the Lord by your life" or "Go and announce the Gospel of the Lord." I personally feel that these two formulae directly and more pointedly commission the participants to take the life of the Eucharist out into the world than the other two formulae of dismissal, namely, "Go, the Mass is ended" and "Go in peace," as these two formulae do not seem to commission directly as do the other two. The first two directly and clearly invite the participants to carry on the mission of the Lord by being agents of change in their own walks of life.

Our society does not change, or its participants don't become agents of social change, because most Mass participants hurry back from church without taking upon themselves any challenging invitation from the Lord; or they do not want to be commissioned by the Lord at all. They do not want to challenge the existing structures; they do not want to shake up the system; they do not wish to make straight what is crooked in their life; they do not want to fill up the valleys of life; they do not want to bring low the mountains of life; they do not want to make smooth the rugged parts of life (cf. Luke 3:4–6). In short, they do not wish to be sent out. They want to enjoy the merits of the Mass, but do not like to face the challenges the Mass offers.

Most Catholics today *like* Jesus. They don't actually *love* Him. They like to follow Him at a distance but not closely. Following at a distance makes one a nominal Catholic; following the Lord closely makes one a *radical* Catholic, a follower of the Lord. If everyone who professes himself/herself a Christian had followed Christ closely, the world would be a much better place. It is sometimes sad that even people who claim to have the ownership of the Lord and His teachings are unwilling to think and act "outside of the box" and find new ways of proclaiming the message of the Gospel in our quickly moving and changing times. As a result, the message of the Lord goes unheard by millions of people.

Actually, the Eucharistic celebration is the time when the Lord asks, "Whom shall I send? Who will go for us?" as He asked the prophet. The prophet said, "Here I am, send me!" (Isaiah 6:8). The Lord is challenging us to leave behind our own boats and nets of life and to follow Him closely, not at a distance, so that He will "make us fishers of men" (cf. Matthew 4:19). He is sending us out as He sent out the prophet Jeremiah "to uproot and to tear down, to destroy and to demolish, to build and to plant" (Jeremiah 1:10). Jesus places His words in our mouths during Mass as God placed His words in the mouth of the prophet (cf. Jeremiah 1:9); He touched our lips with His Body and Blood and purged our sins and removed our wickedness as God touched Isaiah's lips (cf. Isaiah 6:7). He made us ready for a job, a mission. It is unfair, even a breach of trust, to say no to His invitation at the end of the Mass, which we celebrated at the cost of the Lord's life. If we ever walk out of the Mass to follow Him merely at a distance, we are not trustworthy Christians.

Formulae, a Recipe to Make a Better World

The dismissal rite is very important because the Lord is commissioning those of us who participated in the Eucharist to share with the rest of humanity in the joy of the celebration. That is the challenge of the Lord. This is the *practical* or *action* part of the sacrament. The world will change, I am sure, if we find our own means of living the message of the Gospel. When the Lord tells us, for example, to "go in peace," He is asking us to extend the sign of peace that we exchanged inside the church to people outside the building, those people with whom you are not at peace. The symbolic expression should become a reality. We become peacemakers; we become children of God. "Blessed are the peacemakers, for they will be called children of God" (Matthew 5:9).

Perhaps one of the greatest gifts of the Lord to us is the gift of peace. The Lord said, "Peace I leave with you; my peace I give to you. Not as the world gives do I give it to you" (John 14:27). So when the Mass invites the participants to go in peace, the Lord is asking us to strive for peace in the world. If we can become an element of more peace in the world, what better way to fulfill the commission of the Lord? The question is, how to do that? How will the participants contribute to a more peaceful world? Let us start from our hearts, from our homes, from our workplaces, from our neighborhoods, and then spread it to the world. Let us remove elements of hatred and jealousy from our hearts that spark a fire of restlessness and war.

There are law enforcement agencies and personnel in our land who help us enjoy peace by enforcing law and order. Their lives are mostly at risk, especially at this time of global unrest. Think about our military personnel here in the United States and those serving overseas for national interests and for world peace and security. What would happen if they didn't protect us? Why do we sleep peacefully every night? It is because there are men and women who—twenty-four/seven, with a finger on the trigger, without even blinking an eye, at different borders, in cold and heat, far away from their loved ones—keep watch, looking for those elements that are threats to peace. When the Mass ends with the invitation to go in peace and we hurry back home, let's not forget the fact that we are able to go home in peace because someone else has taken upon themselves the challenge of the Lord to build a more peaceful world. Let's not forget to pray for them.

There are many nations around the world that are constantly undergoing trouble. Countries like Afghanistan, Israel, Libya, Palestine, Pakistan, Syria, and Nigeria haven't known peace for a very long time; there people don't sleep in peace as we do; they can't "go in peace" from place to place. For them, peace should be the most sought-after value, the rarest thing they have known and seen. Maybe what upsets the Church and the Pope today must be that this unrest is often in the very same areas where the Prince of Peace was born. It is an irony that the land the Lord chose to be His own has become a land of never-ending war, the opposite of peace. The Church constantly tries to mediate for peace. We can become ambassadors of peace in those countries by cooperating with the efforts of the Church. While we appreciate the peace we enjoy in our country, let's be resolved to do everything in our capacity to build a more peaceful world. When we stay away from all those elements that undermine peace in our own communities, we actually become ambassadors of peace.

Usually peaceful solutions among the nations are undertaken by the leaders of those nations. It is the duty of every Catholic, no, of every follower of Christ to elect people to high positions who are morally upright, who are morally properly formed. Being Catholic and electing a person who has no clear values of life is anti-Christian and is against the mind of Christ. A person who celebrates the Eucharist is expected to uphold certain values. Every Catholic needs to use careful consideration when using their voting power. When Catholics elect a person to a very important position who is clearly against the values of Christ, be it peace, justice, life, or any other sublime value of life, they work against the ideals of Christ, and they are working against the invitation to go in peace.

"Going in peace" after the Eucharistic celebration, with the resolve to create a more peaceful and just world, is glorifying the Lord. But "glorifying the Lord by our lives" and "announcing the Gospel of the Lord" can certainly have many more extensions. Catholic life is a witnessing to the values of the Gospel and to the person of Christ. When the world looks at us, it should be able to see God. Then God is glorified through our lives.

It resembles someone looking at a masterpiece of artwork. When people appreciate the work of an artist, they are actually appreciating the artist, the hands that made it; the credit goes to the artist, not to the artwork. So too are our lives. When others, especially non-Catholics, look at Catholics, who are the handiwork of God, for the Scripture says, "We are his handiwork, created in Christ Jesus for the good works that God has prepared in advance, that we should live in them" (Ephesians 2:10), they should be able to see the face of Christ. They should be able to see a difference between our lives with the Lord and our lives without the Lord. That is how we glorify the Lord with our lives. From time to time, we go to church and receive the sacraments; and yet, if there is no difference between our lives and the lives of persons who never receive these "growth factors," then there is something wrong. All that we receive, then, is useless. Why all the sacraments, sacramentals, prayers, devotions, this and that, if they do not help us to be better human beings in this world? Are we not just wasting time?

If we have to glorify the Lord by our lives, we should be doing something different than what the world does now. I think this is a huge challenge before Catholics and Christians, especially in the Western world. Catholics and Christians fail to withstand the currents of the time; they fail to swim against the cultural tides. Rather, they seem to float along with the negative forces. Practicing Catholics, Catholics who have walked away from the Church at some point, non-Catholics, anti-Catholics, religious, nonreligious, and antireligious, believers, and nonbelievers all do the same things. Our country, being a Christian country, could have been a real beacon in the world; it could have changed the destiny of the entire world. Yet today we find things sliding; the soil is eroding from under our feet. Judging by the very fact that Christians and Catholics equally contribute to the dark and gloomy clouds that envelop our nation, "glorifying the Lord by our lives" is still far away from being a reality.

Try to announce the Gospel of the Lord by good deeds. The world always stands in need of men and women who are wide awake to its needs. Here are we, Christians and Catholics, able to change the course of the world. There is no doubt: each parish offers unending possibilities of being at the service of humanity; thus, they have an opportunity to be at the service of the Lord. Usually, I tell people to look for the Lord in the events of the day and in the eyes of the people around us. Everything that we do for others is done for the Lord. "Amen I say to you, whatever you did for one of these little brothers of mine, you did for me" (Matthew 25:40); this is what should motivate us as we walk out of church after each Eucharistic celebration.

Try to look around us; we will see a number of ways to be of service to others. Be practical. There are many older people who want a ride to church; they might not go to church every week simply because they have no ride. If we can offer someone a ride to church, that would be great. There are many who are wheelchair-bound; when we push someone on a wheelchair, we are actually walking with the Lord. When we humbly smile at a person who may be much less fortunate than we are, we are making the face of the Lord come alive before that person. If we are not physically fit to physically help others, think of dedicating some time to praying for people in need. Pray for the sick, the dying, the homeless, the unemployed, and the childless; there are broken families, people who are forgotten by others, who have no one to think of them or pray for them. Pray for the success of the mission work of the Church. Pray for the priests who make the Lord present through the sacraments of the Church. St. Teresa of the Child Jesus is the patroness of all the mission works of the Church. She never left the cloister. She became the best known "missionary" by her prayers. I promise: we can turn the world upside down with our prayers for others. Even the smallest act of kindness will leave our signature in this world. We will be remembered, not for how long we lived, but how we lived.

At Ascension, where I served, there is a church that is called the "little church", which was built when the parish was much smaller. When the parish grew to over three thousand families, a much bigger church was built. The weekday Masses at 6:30

a.m. are always in the "little church", as well as a few other Masses on weekdays. It is open twenty-four hours, all days of the week, throughout the year. People can come in any time of the day or night and spend time in prayer. There is also adoration every Thursday from 8:00 a.m. to 7:00 p.m. Sometimes there are time slots that are open, but there may not be anyone to fill in these slots. I used to encourage people to consider spending some time on Thursdays in that "little church" before the Blessed Sacrament. That is a wonderful opportunity to pray, a wonderful means of preaching the Gospel.

Maybe when we were younger, we were busy with caring for our family and building up our career; we may not have had the time, though we wished to have it, to spend in prayer, to be at the service of the Church and the people. In other words, we could not become part of "preaching the Gospel" in that active way. However, leading an exemplary family life is itself preaching the Gospel. But now we are perhaps retired, maybe in good health; we may have plenty of free time. We can certainly think of compensating for the so-called lost time by engaging ourselves with works of charity and prayer. So let's not say we have nothing to contribute to the activities of the Church and to the needs of world.

The very purpose of the Eucharist is to transform us into a Eucharistic people for God, making us ready for fullness of life with Him in heaven. As noted earlier, the Eucharist is the foretaste of the heavenly banquet prepared for us in heaven. It foreshadows what is going to come. While we are in this world, we can turn this life into a much better one by celebrating the Eucharist here below. That is possible only if we apply the many nuances of the Eucharist we celebrate into the daily activities of our lives.

When Jesus came into the temple, He quoted the prophet, "The Spirit of the Lord is upon me, because he has anointed me to bring glad tidings to the poor. He has sent me to proclaim liberty to captives and recovery of sight to the blind, to let the oppressed go free, and to proclaim a year acceptable to the Lord" (Luke 4:18–19). Jesus proclaimed the Good News by curing the sick, raising the dead, setting people free from the slavery of sin, feeding the poor, forgiving sinners, and challenging oppressive systems and traditions of his time; He called men and appointed them to be His coworkers to continue this mission; He established a new system, the Church, to carry on His mission; and He gave us the sacrament of the Eucharist as the pledge of His love. Finally, He died on the cross to complete His mission for the salvation of the world. This salvation is the very mission of the Church.

Our mission today is to bring glad tidings to a world that is often gloomy and corrupt, clouded by the hypocrisy of the devil. Many people seem to fall victims to this trick of the devil. People lose hope. As Catholics and Christians, we should be champions of glad tidings. We need to proclaim to the world all that the Lord and the Church are doing, even now.

Go, therefore, and find your own ways and means of joining your hands and voices with the mission of the Church. Go from your church to your homes and, from there, to your offices, schools, farms, and your jobs. There you should live like true Christians, leading uncompromising lives. That is the way we should announce the Gospel of the Lord today. Those of us who have time think of expressing our love for the Lord in more concrete ways, by some humanitarian works; thus, we shall be a light to the world. Announce to the world that the Lord is good, that God has saved us, that we are a Eucharistic community. Then will we become a "Eucharist after the Eucharist"!

Find Your Own Way of Being a Eucharist after the Eucharist

Most people don't feel the changing effects of the sacrifice of the Lord, as noted earlier, because they don't see any connection between the Eucharist and the lives they lead. Actually, these are not two different things. The lives we lead must be an extension of what we celebrate in church. In other words, our daily activities must be conducted in the light of the celebration of the Eucharist. This means that the participants should become Eucharistic people.

We can create a Eucharistic community only when each participant takes the challenges of the Eucharist to heart. When I say "be a Eucharistic person," don't think it is something beyond our reach. It is very simple. Recall the challenge of the Lord: "If you bring your gift to the altar, and there recall that your brother has anything against you, leave your gift there at the altar, go first and be reconciled with your brother, and then come and offer your gift" (Matthew 5:23–24). Does this not simply tell us that we need to mend our relationships before we come to the sacrifice of the Lord, that is, to Sunday Mass? When we celebrate the Eucharist, which is for the reconciliation of the world with God, and we go home and are reconciled with our brothers or sisters, or anyone else for that matter, whom we might have cut off from the circle of our lives, *that* will be the time when the Eucharist touches us in our personal lives. Until we are able to do that, the Eucharist will remain far from our personal lives, without any real impact on our lives. Without this aspect, we might celebrate the Eucharist our entire lives, but we are not going to feel the effects of the Eucharist in our lives. We will be as a "resounding gong or a clashing cymbal" (1 Corinthians 13:1).

One of the major issues we face today is that people can be religious, but they may not be ready to listen to the invitations of the Lord on a very personal level. They can be very rebellious when it comes to certain core issues, like reconciling, forgiving, and compromising. I remember a certain incident: when I was in my old parish in the United Kingdom, I noticed that a lady (a very pious woman), when coming for the Stations of the Cross, would not kneel down at the seventh station. I noticed it and wondered why. On the last Friday before Good Friday, out of my curiosity, I asked her the reason. She told me it was because the image at the seventh station was donated by her neighbor who had done her a lot of harm! What are all her prayers and devotions for? Why be in church every morning for Mass, carrying all the burdens of enmity and unwillingness to forgive or let go of things? Do you think the Lord will listen to the many prayers we offer before Him? This is what the prophet Isaiah says: "What do I care for the multitude of your sacrifices? says the Lord. I have had enough of whole-burnt rams and the fat of fatlings; in the blood of calves, lambs, and goats I find no pleasure. When you come to appear before me, who asks these things of you? Trample my courts no more! To bring offerings is useless; incense is an abomination to me. New moon and Sabbath, calling assemblies—these I cannot bear. Your new moons and festivals I detest; they weigh me down, I tire of the load. When you spread out your hands, I will close my eyes to you; though you pray the more, I will not listen. Your hands are full of blood! Wash yourselves clean! Put away your misdeeds from before my eyes; cease doing evil; learn to do good. Make justice your aim; redress the wronged, hear the orphans' plea, defend the widow" (Isaiah 1:11–17).

A good many Catholics today don't understand the real meaning of Catholicism. They think Catholicism is just making it to Sunday Mass and maybe receiving one or two other sacraments once in a while. If they don't want to forgive or mend the broken relationships or get over misunderstandings, compromise on opinions, or just be humble enough to make the first move so that broken links fall into place again, their worship is worthless, and the Eucharist is of no use to them. When the prophet Isaiah speaks about fasting, he says, "See you fast only to quarrel and fight and to strike with a wicked fist! Do not fast as you do today to make your voice heard on high" (Isaiah 58:4). If you put the Eucharist in place of fasting, the Lord may be telling us, "See, you go to church on Sundays only to leave with the same bad attitudes, to quarrel and to fight with your family members, to eat and to drink, to watch sports and movies, and, some of you, to browse through ugly Internet sites. After celebrating the Eucharist, which is the sacrifice of my Son for the reconciliation of the world, which is the memory of His Passion, Death and Resurrection, for all these years, you seem to remain in the same place. You don't progress an inch forward!"

The true spirit of what we celebrate is well reflected in what Isaiah tells us when he speaks about the authentic fasting that leads to blessing. Here again, try to replace fasting with the Eucharist to get a better understanding. Have a look at what he says in chapter 58, verses from 6 to 12: "Is this not, rather, the fast that I choose: releasing those bound unjustly, untying the thongs of the yoke; setting free the oppressed, breaking off every yoke? Is it not sharing your bread with the hungry, bringing the afflicted and the homeless into your house; clothing the naked when you see them, and not turning your back on your own flesh? Then your light shall break forth like the dawn, and your wound shall quickly be healed; your vindication shall go before you, and the glory of the Lord shall be your rear guard. Then you shall call, and the Lord will answer, you shall cry for help, and he will say: 'Here I am!'" (Isaiah 58:6–9).

When Eucharistic people go home, they become a Eucharistic family. A Eucharistic family is a family where the members live the kind of lives the Eucharist demands of them. The Eucharist demands more love and understanding between husbands and wives or parents and children. The Eucharist demands more sacrifice from husbands and wives; it demands more respect for each other, demands more awareness of the needs of the other; one or the other may have to make more adjustments or more room for the other. That is a big challenge.

A Eucharistic family is the family that kneels before the Lord in prayer, especially in the evenings, which is the extension of the Eucharistic celebration; it is the family that sits down around one table for family dinnertime, which should be the extension of the bread broken at the altar of sacrifice, from which everyone received the body and blood of the Lord, the food of eternal life. A Eucharistic family will not see the Eucharist and family life as two separate entities, but as one: the former enriching the latter! In other words, the life of a Eucharistic family should be an extension of the Eucharist.

When a family is able to reshape its life according to the invitations of the Eucharist, then that family becomes a Eucharistic family, where everyone is ready to sacrifice his/her time and talent for the other, where the needs of the other come first. That is the kind of family the Lord is looking for; that is the kind of family the Lord would like to use as the canvas for His "artwork." When every family becomes a Eucharistic family, a parish becomes a Eucharistic parish, a Eucharistic community. When children are born to such a family, which is modeled after the challenges of the sacrament of the Eucharist, those children will certainly grow in holiness and in the favor of God and other people, as the Lord Jesus grew up in the home of Mary and Joseph.

Some Practical Ways of Spreading the Gospel

As an associate pastor, I am very happy to be part of a parish where so many families understand the significance of this challenge. There are many families and people who really strive to make what they celebrate come alive by being involved in parish life and ministry. Actually, those are the families who make my parish a truly great parish. There is a general understanding that such a parish is a wonderful one. It is true. But the greatness of the parish comes from those families who strive all the time to meet the needs of the parish. There are many who serve at food banks; many people work with the St. Vincent de Paul Society; many men and women work with St. Martha's Guild; many men and women volunteer at various nursing homes around the parish; many men, even more than women, witness at the abortion clinic or Planned Parenthood on a regular basis. They do it both in summer and winter, day in and day out. Some of them do it even as early as four in the morning! *These* are the people who really "die" for the Lord. And I believe that living for the Lord is dying for the Lord today. We need men and women who would *live* for the Lord today, not just those who would die for Him.

I always was happy to see in my former parish a group of older men who, after the 8:00 a.m. Mass on Mondays, would gather around to discuss what they were going to do at the St. Nicholas food bank. Afterward, some of them would drive to McDonald's to have coffee and to chat further. Later, they would drive over to the food bank. They serve food to people who are less fortunate. They bring joy and satisfaction to the lives of many every week. As they bring joy into the lives of other people, the service they do brings joy and satisfaction into their lives too. As I was driving back with a friend after helping at the food bank, he said to me, "This is one of the best things I've ever done. As I fall on my knees today, I can be happy that I did something worthwhile for someone else." This should be the thought of each and every one of those who serve with great enthusiasm. They do it without expecting anything in return. It is a selfless service. This is an outstanding way of "breaking" themselves for others. They are contributing their time, energy, and even money. They do it as part of their mission.

When I was serving a parish in India, there were a few women operating a charity shop for the less fortunate, while a few others went to an orphanage and to an old-age home and helped serve food and to do laundry for them. Young men and women gave haircuts to the inmates; some helped those who could not take a shower without assistance. I saw a few young people going from door to door literally begging for food and clothing for these homes. They all were much happier people when they returned after Sunday Mass, because they were breaking themselves in the service of others.

These are times when we need men and women who will become the voice of the Lord to proclaim what He came to proclaim; they become His hands and feet to walk the ways He walked and to do what He did. When one joins the March for Life in Washington DC, one is announcing the message of the Gospel of Life. When we sign "roses for life," as we do in some parishes, we are leaving our signatures where there will bloom a little life that will bear our signature of love and life.

Being "broken and shared" by being a lector, cantor, extraordinary minister of Holy Communion, singer in the parish choir; dedicating time and energy to the upkeep and maintenance of your parish; belonging to some pious organization in the parish such as St. Vincent De Paul, Legion of Mary, Knights of Columbus; or volunteering to work with food banks, visiting and helping those in nursing homes or the homebound to pray, spending time every day praying for various intentions; or anything like that—any of these will be a simple but practical way of being at the service of the Gospel. That is how we try to personalize the invitation of the Lord. The Eucharist becomes personally meaningful when we try to spread our charity for others, and thus we grow in love for the Lord.

Go Further

We said earlier that since we have been offered up and transformed with the bread and wine, we also have been "broken" with the Lord. The final invitation is to be broken in the context of our entire lives. And there are many radical ways to be broken, and many are possible in each life situation.

How About Being a Blood Donor?

Being a blood donor is a very simple and easy way to shed your blood, yet it is one of the most meaningful ways. Sr. Tessa, who prepared me for First Holy Communion, used to tell us of breaking and shedding oneself. She would always suggest donating blood as one of the noblest means of shedding our blood for others. And when I was old enough to donate blood, she told me, "Jesus was shedding his blood for us. Blood means life, and donating blood for a needy person would mean that we are giving life to that person." For many years I donated blood, not once, but on many occasions. I was a student earning a master's in social work in a college that was close to a medical center. When anyone needed blood, someone would come to my college looking for the blood they needed, since there were many young students who were willing to donate. When I was in a blood donation counter, reclining on a couch and looking with a faint smile at my own blood dripping into the bag, which was pulsating as blood oozed into it, Sr. Tessa came, now a woman close to seventy; she smiled at me and said, "Now, you are truly a follower of Christ." The Lord gave us life by shedding his blood, I thought, and I too can be part of His creative and healing work in this world in my own way. But most of us don't do this because of various reasons.

According to the statistics of Red Cross USA, every two seconds, someone in the United States needs blood, and more than 41,000 blood donations are needed every day. A total of 30 million blood components are transfused each year in the United States. The need for blood in our hospitals is ever on the increase. Sickle-cell anemia affects more than 70,000 people in the United States. About 1,000 babies are born with the disease each year. Sickle cell patients can require frequent blood transfusions throughout their lives. More than 1.6 million people were diagnosed with cancer last year alone. Many of them will need blood, sometimes daily, during chemotherapy treatments. A single car accident victim can require as many as 100 pints of blood. The blood type most often requested by hospitals is Type O.

In my parish, the Knights of Columbus organize a blood drive every six months. I make it a point to donate every time the Red Cross comes for the blood drive. I am proud to say that I've donated around thirty-six times to this program to this point. Most often, they draw two pints from me. I am glad to give because I know one donation can help save the lives of as many as three people. If one began donating blood at age 17 and donated every 56 days until he/she reached 76, he/she would have donated 48 gallons of blood, potentially helping save more than 1,000 lives! That inspires me to donate blood every time the opportunity presents itself.

Each time I walk into our gym, where the blood drive takes place, I notice that people who donate blood mostly are older people; younger ones are very few. The two most common reasons cited by people who don't give blood, according to the Red Cross, are the following: "Never thought about it" and "I don't like needles." Organizations like the Knights of Columbus are there to remind people to donate blood. Though they advertise in the parish bulletin for many weeks, they get only forty to sixty people from three thousand families, which is great but certainly not enough. The second reason, "I don't like needles," is a very poor excuse. For example, when one is in need of blood due to a car accident, thousands of needles might poke the person! If one person can save 1,000 lives, how many could have been saved if every one of us were willing to donate blood? Although an estimated 38 percent of the US population is eligible to donate, less than 10 percent actually do so each year, says Red Cross. Remember, Jesus saved us by shedding His blood.

Be an Organ Donor

Another practical way of "breaking ourselves" is to donate our organs when life has ended, if not while we are alive. Once I happened to watch a two-minute video ad, a very touching one, for being an organ donor: a blind boy was sitting at a train station, listening to the trains running by. A young man sitting across from him was reading a book and was laughing at something funny in the book. The boy asks, "Why? What's so funny?" The man says, "I beg your pardon?"

"You were laughing."

"Oh, it's something I read in the book."

"What's that?"

"Well, a man sees another man limping toward him and asks, 'Why are you limping?' The limping man replies, 'Because I have a toothache.'"

They both laugh. The boy seems to laugh longer than the man. Then slowly, the laughter fades away on the face of the boy. He asks, "When you are done, can you give it to me?" "The book?" the man was amazed. "No. The eyes." The ad ended by saying, "Once your eyes have finished seeing, pass them on. There is always someone waiting." The Lord said, "You are the light of the world" (Matthew 5:14). He also said, "The lamp of the body is your eye" (Matthew 6:22). If we are willing, we certainly can be a light to someone; we can light up the life of someone by donating our eyes, our lamps.

On Calvary, the Lord physically broke His body for us. In today's vocabulary, He freely was donating His body for us so that we might have life. There are many people who part with their vital organs while alive so that someone else can have a normal life. Well, if you think that is asking too much, what about donating organs after death? What is a body once the spirit is gone? We call it a dead body. We don't even say the name of the deceased; we say "sprinkle the body," "incense the body," "move the body," "lower the body," "cremate the body," "bury the body," and so on; the basic identity is lost. We can use our bodies for noble causes, not only while we live, but after death also. I personally do not want a place on earth; I don't want you only to pray for me after my death; please do it now, while I live, if you can. No headstone and no inscriptions; let me not be remembered by my place of burial or by a tombstone and inscription; I would rather love to live in the memories of people; let me live only in the hearts of others.

We Turn the Day of the Lord "Unholy"

Though the Sacrament of the Eucharist is holy, there are many problems in the way we celebrate the sacrament. It is not a problem of the sacrament; the problem is with us, the participants. Maybe we have forgotten the value and worth of this sacrament. Maybe it has been reduced to a mere ritual. That is a big danger.

The people who attend Mass, especially the younger generation, don't do so with full conviction or enthusiasm. Maybe they don't get the point. That is one problem today. I came to this conclusion by observing the actions and reactions of people. The way most people attend Mass indicates that many have no basic respect for what they are celebrating; the Mass does not interest them. There are many reasons to say that. First of all, look at all those people who come late; look at all those who leave church before Mass ends. If they were truly serious about Mass, they won't regularly be late or leave the church before Mass ends. Most people try to arrive early, or at least on time, for a movie or a theatrical performance; why do they seem to be relaxed or casual for Mass? Why this dichotomy? Perhaps something is wrong!

Look at all those people who sit or stand at the back of our churches, or around the corners, while there are seats available! Does it not mean that they are not really interested in the Mass? Are they there due to some pressure, like knowing that missing Mass is a sin, or did someone (parents or spouses) "pressure" them to come? Does anyone go to a movie and stand in a corner and watch it? For movies, people hurry to take a seat. People even reserve seats in advance to make sure they get seats. Why is it different when it comes to Mass?

Think about all those who are irreverent during Mass: people who all the time are playing with their cell phones or sending text messages. I do understand that there are people who follow the Mass on their smart phones. But there are people who play computer games, or text, during Mass. They do so even at the consecration. What irreverent behavior!

Consider how people sit in church: some sit with their legs crossed, while leaning back to place their hands on the backrest. Some people sit rubbing the back or thigh of their beloved. Some people chew gum; they keep chewing even when receiving Communion!

Look at the dress style of some people, especially in summertime. They seem to enjoy exposing all parts of their bodies; maybe nothing is secret anymore! Young and old alike go to church as if they were going to a park or a beach—for walking, jogging, or for golf. Or look at the middle-aged lady coming to Communion dressed for tennis. If some young ladies cause temptations with their style of dress, please remember your wife or daughter may be doing the same to other people.

Look at the large numbers who receive Communion first needing the sacrament of Reconciliation. Approximately 20 percent celebrate the sacrament of Reconciliation, but nearly 100 percent receive Communion! Does this not mean that many people no longer give any serious thought to this practice? We tend to treat this precious gift so casually and with such disrespect that we seem not to know the worth of the gift. Are the many modern Catholics losing sight of the worth of the Eucharist, so much so that they tend to misuse the great gift or fail to see its true worth?

Personal reconciliation is making room for the Lord. Try to recall the preaching of John the Baptist. He came to prepare the way for the Lord. He asked the people of His day to make preparations. This is what He said: "Prepare the way of the Lord, make straight his paths. Every valley shall be filled and every mountain and hill shall be made low. The winding roads shall be made straight and the rough ways made smooth" (Luke 3:4–5). The content of the preaching was repentance. St. Luke says that John the Baptist "went throughout [the] whole region of the Jordan, proclaiming a baptism of repentance for the forgiveness of sins" (Luke 3:3). When we make a good confession before we go to Mass, we are preparing our hearts for the Lord; we are making the paths straight; we are filling in the valleys of life; we are making rough areas of life smooth. Thus we welcome the Lord into our hearts. The self-preparation we undergo shows how important the gift is to us. The many preparations we make to receive a guest show how important that person is to us. Lack of preparation means we don't care about the person coming to us.

Do you think these are appropriate ways of celebrating the Eucharist? Can you recall the day of your First Holy Communion, that very first day you received the Lord in the Eucharist? How far away are you today from that point? With that immaculate and beautiful dress or suit, you were in the front of the church. You arrived there before Mass started. You sat, knelt, and stood before the Lord with folded hands, with devotion. What is happening today? Our immaculate dress or suit has disappeared; we are almost regularly late for Mass; we stand or sit at the back of church; most often we show no reverence for what is taking place. Maybe we are very far from the day of our First Holy Communion. Try to relive those memories of the past. Try to walk back to those days of innocent childhood. The Lord said, "Unless you turn and become like children, you will not enter the kingdom of heaven" (Matthew 18:3).

CHAPTER 5

An Invitation to Live According to the Spirit

And I will ask the Father, and He will give you another Advocate to be with you always, the Spirit of Truth.
—John 14:16–17

The Lord conceived me in His mind before I was formed in the womb. He carved me on the palms of His divine hands. He fashioned me wonderfully, like an artist, in the womb of my mother. He portrayed me on the canvas of matrimony and chose my parents as His coartists. He called me by name through the sacrament of Baptism and planted me by the waters of grace. He washed me with the waters of repentance in the sacrament of Reconciliation and made me ready for His great gift of Eucharist, in which He gave Himself totally for me. Now He is going to anoint me with the Holy Spirit in the sacrament of Confirmation to strengthen me to do my mission in the world: to glorify Him by living a life witnessing to the Gospel, to announce the goodness of the Lord till I take my last breath. I am waiting for the anointing of the Spirit with bowed head.

One of the promises the Lord gave us was the Holy Spirit that the Father would send in His name and would teach us everything and remind us of all that he told us (cf. John 14:26). This promise was fulfilled in the life of the Church on the day of Pentecost, when He sent forth the Spirit upon the apostles. But this promise was fulfilled in our lives personally when He gave us the fullness of the Spirit on the day of the sacrament of Confirmation, which we received as adults. We should humbly thank the Lord for this great sacrament, which confirms us in His Spirit.

Jesus told us, "It is the spirit that gives life, while the flesh is of no avail" (John 6:63). On the day we received this marvelous sacrament, He invited us to be confirmed and to be reestablished in the Holy Spirit, to be deeply rooted in the Spirit. As I grew older, since my Baptism, at certain points in life, I became a worldly man, even without being conscious of this tendency. The Spirit breathed on me on the day of Baptism became inactive; His voice became very thin. I moved from spiritual paths to worldly ways. As spirit and flesh fought fiercely within me, more often my flesh won the battle. I needed the assistance of a higher power from above. And on the day of Confirmation, You poured on me Your power that will, thereafter, help me fight a good fight and to win over the desires of my flesh and the world.

Lord, I praise You for bringing me to that day to receive Your Son's promise: the Counselor, the Advocate, and the Spirit of Truth. Yes, He was a true counselor. A counselor is one who helps others to make right choices. I was making wrong decisions in life. Even so, there was always the presence of the Spirit that gave me timely counsel to make right choices. At the crossroads, I heard His voice saying, "Go this way." And that was the right turn; I know it now. The presence of the Counselor you promised, Lord, helps me reject the false ways and follies of life. He assists me to keep focused in my spiritual life. When I am wearied and worn out, He encourages me with His gentle promptings to go on and on. He is the voice of truth; He is the armor of courage; He is the spring of my life. He makes my heart glow even during the coldest winter of life, when everything stands frozen; when nature is without color and life, He makes my life colorful and lively.

The sacrament of Confirmation is Your second seal of permanent ownership on my soul; it made me Your holy dwelling place and made me mature in my spiritual life. I received this sacrament at a time when my body was going through major changes. People said I was maturing. That maturity was not always good. I also began to move along wrong directions of life. My body craved for things that it did not crave for before. I had thoughts about people and things I never had before. I had feelings and emotions that gave me a kind of physical pleasure. I began to look at people and things with a different eye. People and things that had never caught my attention before began to draw my attention. I began to be inquisitive about certain things I never cared about before. I tried doing things that I never even tried before, things that embarrassed me later on. It was a stormy time. I needed a friend, a counselor, a guide.

God Fans into Flames the Spiritual Person within You

Sr. Tessa, who prepared me for the sacrament of Confirmation, told me that this sacrament marks maturity of life, both physical and spiritual. She told me that it was the time God fans into flames all the graces I received at the time of Baptism, but were dormant within me: the graces I was not really aware of; the powers that were asleep in me until then. She told me there was a better man, a more powerful man within me, the spiritual man, and it was time for me to awaken that new me. That was the *real* me. She told me that the life I would lead from the time of the reception of the sacrament of Confirmation would be qualitatively far better than the life I led until then.

Later on, I understood the meaning of what that venerable nun told me. I understood that the "real person" is the spiritual person inside of me. And my duty—and the duty of everyone—is to wake up "that real" person and stir it into action. The saddest thing on earth would be to not realize the power that lies within us, not to fan into flames the spiritual side of life. The biggest loss in life would be to miss that "real person." As a person grows up, the spiritual side should be able to outgrow the physical or material side of life and defeat the worldly person, the undue cravings of the flesh, that bestial side of life. Confirmation is the time God gives us the weapons to fight against the bestial side of a person. We should polish the spiritual side of life, because we know that what endures is the Spirit; the flesh is corruptible. St. Paul said that our life is a constant warfare between Spirit and flesh; one stands opposed to the other. The Spirit is clean, contrary to the flesh (cf. Galatians 5:16–17).

Look at your life. What do you see there? You labor to meet the needs of the flesh, mostly at the expense of the Spirit. You labor day in and day out to satisfy the flesh! How many times do you wash your hands a day? Perhaps many times. Most people take a shower at least once a day. How often do you polish your shoes and press your dress? What do you do to sharpen your spiritual side of life? How much do you labor to nourish that "real you"? Humanity has reversed God's creation. It thinks that the flesh is the real person, and it feeds the flesh. If you continue to starve your spiritual side and nourish the flesh-related side of life, it will be like feeding a cobra that will turn back and sting the same hands that fed it. The world is too "flesh mongering" because it feeds the flesh, not the spirit.

> It is the spirit that gives life, while the flesh
> is of no avail. (John 6:63)

Sr. Tessa told me that what makes the real person are spiritual elements. She quoted the letter of St. Paul to the Galatians, in which he speaks about the fruits of the Holy Spirit, to prove her theory. The fruits of the Spirit were "love, joy, peace, patience, kindness, generosity, faithfulness, gentleness, self-control" (Galatians 5:16). It was easier for me to understand what she said about being a spiritual person. She herself was a personification of these divine qualities. She was an angel! We loved to be around her all the time. It was not surprising that I thought about how the world would be if everyone was like Sr. Tessa.

She said God's invitation to me and to all who are baptized was to be a spiritual people. (Maybe like her, I thought.) We should rise above the cravings of flesh to look for nobler things in life; we should consider more important things that really matter; we need to look beyond the boundaries of this passing world; we must bring out the fruits of the Spirit. She also told us that saints are the people who fully aroused the spiritual powers within them, which in turn conquered their physical side of life.

God Is Giving Us the Greatest Spiritual Gifts

The sacrament of Confirmation is the time when God gives us his superior gifts. When I grew older, and when I fell in love with the Scripture, which I read at least four times from the beginning till the end, that is, from the book of Genesis to the Revelation, I came across those superior gifts that Sr. Tessa mentioned many years ago. St. Paul in his first letter to the Corinthians says, "There are different kinds of spiritual gifts; there are different forms of services but the same Lord; there are different workings but the same God who produces all of them in everyone. To each individual the manifestation of the Spirit is given to some benefit. To one is given through the Spirit the expression of wisdom; to another the expression of knowledge according to the same Spirit; to another faith by the same Spirit; to another gifts of healing by the one spirit; to another mighty deeds; to another prophecy; to another discernment of spirits; to another varieties of tongues; to another interpretation of tongues. But one and the same Spirit produces all of these, distributing them individually to each person as he wishes" (1 Corinthians 12:4–11). And in chapter 14, he tells us to "strive eagerly for the spiritual gifts" (14:1).

Traditionally, the Church believes that there are seven gifts of the Holy Spirit. They are the following: wisdom, understanding, counsel, fortitude, knowledge, piety, and fear of the Lord. I believe that these gifts of the Holy Spirit are gathered and are taken from the book of Isaiah, chapter eleven, in which he prophesies about the ideal Davidic king. The prophet says, "The spirit of the Lord shall rest upon him: a spirit of wisdom and of understanding, a spirit of counsel and strength, a spirit of knowledge and of fear of the Lord" (Isaiah 11:2–3).

Now if we go back once again to what we said earlier, about what makes the real person, it should be the *fruits* of the Spirit (Galatians 5:22), which are nine in number, and the *gifts* of the Spirit, which are seven in number. What is a person without the fruits of the Spirit? I cannot even think about a life without these ingredients that make our life worth living. Actually, life would become hellish without love, joy, peace, patience, kindness, generosity, faithfulness, gentleness, and self-control.

Spiritual progress, in my understanding, is furthering these precious qualities of life. There are many who cannot love anyone selflessly; there are many who feel they are not loved. There are so many in the world who have no joy in life, though they have everything they need in life. I have come across many people who are very religious and pious, but cannot even smile at another person, who go about with a long face! While I was in India, I met many Americans and Europeans, born and raised Christians and Catholics, who were visiting different Hindu,

Buddhist, or Jain monasteries in pursuit of "peace." Even now, you may find quite a few people wandering around Eastern parts of the world looking for peace.

There are people who are frustrated because they have no patience in life for anything or with anyone. They seem to burst out with fury for any little or minor thing. They seem to snap at people and hurt their feelings; they get irritated over any minor failures of other people. In my experience, it is lack of patience that most people struggle with. There are many families that are broken because the spouses lacked patience; impatience made them choose wrong choices. There are many who repent later of the imprudent and thoughtless decisions, which resulted from their impatience.

We all share the kindness of the Lord in various ways and times, maybe at every second of our lives. But yet, there are many who fail to show compassion and kindness to those who deserve it. On the contrary, humanity suffers from the cruelty of people around us. Sometimes when we see atrocities around us, we wonder if those who inflict such terrible sufferings upon the innocents of the world are human beings, or animals!

As a children's song goes, which I will include at the end of this chapter: "If goodness was a cherry, a yummy pie to all my neighbors I would carry." Our goodness or generosity can be a yummy pie, a comfort and pleasure to many who are less fortunate than we are. We can make a difference in the world. Like the five loaves the boy in Scripture shared with the Lord, who multiplied them for thousands; like the silver nickels of the poor old widow of Scripture, who contributed "more than all others"; if we are willing, our generosity can cause a big change in the world. We can feed the poor, clothe the naked, satisfy the thirsty, visit the sick; we can be the healing of the Lord in a wounded world. It all depends on our goodness and generosity. We need the Holy Spirit to move us to do all the good works, which, the Lord tells us, will bring us to the right side of our Heavenly Father (cf. Matthew 25:34–40).

Faithfulness is at the heart of our spiritual life and social life. In today's world, we see a lot of unfaithfulness. We see unfaithfulness in married life; unfaithfulness in religious life; unfaithfulness in social, political, and cultural commitments, which brings in many evils. If married people had been faithful in their commitment, faithful to each other, divorces would have been unheard-of in our societies; if we had the courage to be faithful to our religious commitments and the traditions of our fathers in faith, our nation would have been much more blessed and stable; if the citizens of our nation had been faithful to its rich value system, they would be building a stronger nation with moral fabric; if our national leaders had been faithful to their political promises and commitments, the world would enjoy more peace and security. But sadly, faithfulness has gone from our midst. "Help, Lord, for no one loyal remains; the faithful have vanished from the children of men. They tell lies to one another, they speak with deceiving lips and a double heart" (Psalm 12:1). We need the Holy Spirit to replenish us with faithfulness.

If only we could imitate the gentleness of the Lord! Jesus was a gentle lamb who came to conquer the heart of the humanity with His gentleness. This is what the prophet Isaiah says of the servant of the Lord: "Here is my servant whom I uphold, my chosen one with whom I am pleased. Upon him I have put my spirit; he shall bring forth justice to the nations. He will not cry out, nor shout, nor make his voice heard in the street. A bruised reed he will not break, and a dimly burning wick he will not quench" (Isaiah 42:1–3). "I gave my back to those who beat me, my cheeks to those who tore out my beard; my face I did not hide from insults and spitting" (Isaiah 50:6–7).

That was Jesus, who brought salvation and justice to us by His gentleness. How different was He from our present rulers, who try always to be heard by raising their voice, by making empty and insincere promises and stupid comments day and night. They live like lions, tigers, and wolves: ferocious animals who prey upon others who are weaker. When people think that being gentle is a sign of weakness, Jesus came "meek and humble" (cf. Matthew 11:29), like a little lamb, and proved by His life that being gentle means that you are stronger than your opponent. He said, "Offer no resistance to one who is evil. When someone strikes you on [your] right cheek, turn the other one to him as well. If anyone wants to go to law with you over your tunic, hand him your cloak as well. Should anyone press you into service for one mile, go with him for two miles" (Matthew 5:39:41). That was a different law in the sight of the world; that was the law of the gentlest man on earth.

Self-control is a sure recipe for spiritual and physical well-being. People with no self-control are the people who fall victims to temptations of life. Most body-related sins occur due to a lack of self-control; issues of anger, overeating, excessive drinking, and smoking are all related to this problem. One of the most common problems of both young and old today, as you may know, is sex-related. Pornography is something like cancer today. This terrifying sin seems to grin at a large number of people who fall victim to it over and over again. They find it hard to control themselves. Every time they try to decide against this sin, they fail miserably. This is also true for all other sins of the flesh.

One of the main health problems is obesity, which usually stems from overeating (obesity can also be caused by many other factors). People overeat and overdrink because they are not able to control themselves. They feel drawn to food and drink. Inordinate passion for anything is a result of lack of self-control. Self-control is a virtue by which you are able to attain mastery over yourself, that is, you get your body to obey what your mind commands. That is also called self-discipline. This means that you do not always follow the passions of your heart, but instead, you train yourself to do what should be done, not what is easy and appealing to you.

You might have seen many people who can control and navigate their life toward spiritual and physical well-being. They are strong like a rock, unshakeable. No one and nothing can tempt them. They have absolute mastery over their feelings and emotions. You have heard the phrase, "The spirit is willing, but the flesh is weak" (Matthew 26:41). But people with self-control are the people who control the spirit even when the body is noncooperative. St. Paul said, "I do not do the good I want, but I do the evil I do not want" (Romans 7:19). Then he goes on to speak about the wretchedness of human life: "Now if [I] do what I do not want, it is no longer I who do it, but sin that dwells in me" (7:20). It means that you are controlled by something else; self-control means you are able to control your life. Then he explains the duality of two principles: law of God and law of self, existing at the same time. "So, then, I discover the principle that when I want to do right, evil is at hand. For I take delight in the law of God, in my inner self, but I see in my members another principle at war with the law of my mind, taking captive to the law of sin that dwells in my members. Miserable one that I am! Who will deliver me from this mortal body? Thanks be to God through Jesus Christ our Lord. Therefore, I myself, with my mind, serve the law of God but, with my flesh, the law of sin" (7:21–25).

This statement of St. Paul shows two principles warring with each other in the same person; and the person, though in mind serving the law of God, unwillingly falls a victim to the flesh and serves the law of sin. This shows how difficult self-control is, how hard self-discipline is. But in order that our mind and body should serve God, we need to control the law of the flesh. St. Paul says, "I drive my body and train it" (1 Corinthians 9:27). We should learn to control ourselves by constant disciplining and training of our body and mind. If not, the end result will be self-destruction. We need the Holy Spirit to help us produce His fruit of self-control.

Confirmation Helps Us Do Extraordinary Things in Life

Sr. Tessa told us that the Holy Spirit allows us do extraordinary things in life, things that seem impossible to ordinary people.

She asked us if we knew the "greatest wonderment" of God. We blinked our little eyes. She said it was the Incarnation of Jesus. She quoted the words of the angel Gabriel to the Virgin Mary to prove her argument: "The Holy Spirit will come upon you, and the power of the Most High will overshadow you. Therefore the Child to be born will be called holy, the Son of God. And behold, Elizabeth, your relative, has also conceived a son in her old age, and this is the sixth month for her who was called barren; for nothing will be impossible for God" (Luke 1:35–36). That was, she said, something no person of this world would understand completely. Yet the Holy Spirit made that extraordinary thing possible to us. She asked me if I knew of any other miracle that was the work of the Holy Spirit. I blinked my little eyes twice. She said that it was the transubstantiation of bread and wine into the Body and Blood of the Lord. It is, she said, the Holy Spirit who makes that miracle before our eyes. I then remembered the prayer of invocation that is used in our Eucharistic prayers. If the Holy Spirit can make the Incarnation of Jesus possible and transubstantiate the bread and wine into the Body and Blood of the Lord, then anything is possible for Him! I was convinced.

She also told us that the Holy Spirit chose men and women to do miracles for the Lord in the world. When I say miracles, I mean great things for the Lord. When I saw for the very first time an ordination to the priesthood in my parish, I understood what the nun told us. There I saw the Bishop, with his hands outstretched and praying for the indwelling of the Spirit, as the candidate lay prostrate on the floor. The bishop laid his hands on him and anointed him to the priesthood. I then recalled what is written in the book of the Acts of the Apostles: "While they were worshipping the Lord and fasting, the Holy Spirit said, 'Set apart for me Barnabas and Saul for the work which I have called them.' Then, completing their fasting and prayer, they laid hands on them and sent them off" (Acts 13:2–3). Here, by the power of the Holy Spirit, the young man was made a priest; he was set apart from then on to do extraordinary things for the Lord in the world.

This brand-new priest did many extraordinary things for us: that same day he celebrated his first Holy Mass. There, the bread and wine were transubstantiated into the Body and Blood of the Lord by the Holy Spirit, but through his hands! It was exactly what Sr. Tessa had told us. That was indeed something miraculous. The new priest heard confessions and absolved sins in the confessionals. "Who but God alone can forgive sins?" (Mark 2:7). When the scribes doubted, Jesus said to them, "But that you may know that the Son of Man has authority to forgive sins on earth, I say to you, pick up your mat and go home" (Mark 2:10–11). Jesus passed on this authority to his apostles. He said to them, "Receive the Holy Spirit. Whose sins you forgive are forgiven them, whose sins you retain are retained" (John 20:23). Down through the centuries, men in Holy Orders perform extraordinary things in our lives.

Later on, I grew older and read about the saints, especially the martyrs, who were heroic in their lives. Their lives were extraordinary witnesses to the Lord! I often wondered how they could stand against such dreadful ordeals in life. Not much later, I came to know that they were given their strength by the Holy Spirit. They considered their life as trash, everything as loss. Their eyes were set heavenward. They did not heed the voice of the world and the murmurings of their flesh. The Spirit concealed them like arrows in the quiver of their Lord, protected them like the apple of His eye. The pains they underwent, though terrible, could not shake them. The power of the Most High gave them fortitude in the face of suffering. St. Paul, in his second letter to Timothy, reminded Timothy of the gifts he had received: "For this reason, I remind you to stir into flame the gift of God that you have through the imposition of my hands. For God did not give us a spirit of cowardice, but rather of power and love and self-control" (2 Timothy 1:6–7). Men and women did not flee from persecutions and sufferings; they were not cowards. They were courageous; they accepted their sufferings with the power of the Holy Spirit.

Confirmation Helps You Subdue the Beast Sleeping within You

That graceful woman, Sr. Tessa, told me that there was also a beast asleep in each of us, a beast that tries to wake up at any moment of our life. She said that beast was made up of everything that stands against Christ and His teachings. She quoted St. Paul to make us understand better: "Immorality, impurity, licentiousness, idolatry, sorcery, hatreds, rivalry, jealousy, outbursts of fury, acts of selfishness, dissensions, factions, occasions of envy, drinking bouts, orgies, and the like" (Galatians 5:19–21). She told me that when these get the better of a person, then animality within him/her takes control of the "real person." I understood clearly what she meant because I knew some of them already in my life, though not all of them.

I also had seen people who lived a very immoral life, people who are drunkards, especially one of my neighbors; I had seen men and women who were married and divorced many times; I knew people who were promiscuous, though at that time I did not know what *promiscuity* meant. I knew many men and women with rivalry and hatred for each other. There were people in my neighborhood who never spoke a word to each other; they lived many years that way and died that way. My parents had tried many times to reconcile them, but they refused to be reconciled. Actually, I myself was not happy with people who divorced and remarried many times; they seemed to change their spouses as I changed my clothes. I was afraid of drunkards, and I hated them. I had an uncle who died of alcoholism. He drank excessively. He found reasons to drink. When someone died, he drank for grief; when a child was born, he would drink for joy; when he was upset with his wife, my aunt, he would drink out of anger; when his kids were taking exams, he would drink due to "tension." He had reasons to drink. He drank and used all kinds of abusive words with his wife and children. His behavior was no better than that of an animal. As Sr. Tessa had told us, his animality got the better of him. Thank God, I thought to myself, that God called him early enough. The nun said that a person who is led by the elements of the flesh is a person of the flesh, not of the Spirit. Obviously, I did not want to be a man of the flesh; I did not want to wake up that bestial side of life.

She said that vices will raise their head like serpents from time to time if we are negligent in the spiritual life. Later on, they will coil up and suffocate us like an anaconda; we will be unable to escape from their power. The devil can turn such a person into one who is spiritually dead. Eventually, all traits of being a child of God diminish. Satan will claim such people for himself; they will be turned into people who bring out negative and destructive energy.

The nun asked us to consider our life as a tree; God is looking for fruit from us. What does He expect from us? As I rummaged through the pages of my favorite book, I came across the parable of the Barren Fig Tree (Luke 13:6–9). Let me mention it here once more. There, the landowner, God the Father, was looking for fruits from his tree, which he had planted and protected for many years. The fruits he was looking for were spiritual fruits like love, joy, peace, patience, kindness, generosity, faithfulness, gentleness, and self-control. The landowner wanted to cut down the tree that did not produce the fruits he expected. I think that the sacrament of Confirmation is the time that the gardener, Jesus, digs around the tree, cultivates the ground and fertilizes it so that the tree will bear spiritual fruits for the future. When every tree planted by God the Father produces spiritual fruits, then the world becomes an extension of God's kingdom on earth.

I have a feeling that most of us are worse than the barren fig tree. It was easier for the gardener to cultivate the ground and fertilize the fig tree and to make it yield. But the sad fact with us is that we, most often, produce wild fruits instead of sweet ones. Try to recall the "Song of the Vineyard" in the book of Isaiah, which I've already quoted once before when I spoke about the sacrament of Reconciliation. He is singing about the chosen people. It shows how much the Lord loved His people, considering all that He did for them: "Now let me sing of my friend, my beloved's song about his vineyard. My friend had a vineyard on a fertile hillside; he spaded it, cleared it of stones, and planted the choicest vines; within it he built a watch tower, and hewed out a wine press. Then he waited for the crop of grapes, but it yielded rotten grapes. Now, inhabitants of Jerusalem, people of Judah, judge between me and the vineyard; what more could be done for my vineyard that I did not do? Why, when I waited for the crop of grapes, did it yield rotten grapes? Now, I will let you know what I am going to do to my vineyard: take away its hedge, give it to grazing, break through its wall, let it be trampled! Yes, I will make it a ruin; it shall be not pruned or hoed, but will be overgrown with thorns and briars; I will command the clouds not to rain upon it. The vineyard of the Lord is the house of Israel, the people of Judah, his cherished plant; he waited for judgment, but see, bloodshed! For justice, but hark, the outcry!" (Isaiah 5:1–7).

Sr. Tessa once said that the sacrament of Confirmation confers on us the power to subdue the negative forces within us, those forces that always try to subjugate the positive energy of life. The sacrament of Confirmation is given to us to equip us with the spiritual weapons to battle against the enemies of the spiritual life. If the confirmed person lived according to the promptings of the Spirit, she said, no evil power could ever conquer that person.

One day she told the candidates to be confirmed that we are supposed to form a spiritual army for the Lord in the world in order to fight against the evil powers, which always try to destroy the kingdom of God. She exhorted us with these words from St. Paul: "Finally, draw your strength from the Lord and from his mighty power. Put on the armor of God so that you may be able to stand firm against the tactics of the devil. For our struggle is not with flesh and blood but with the principalities, with the powers, with the world rulers of this present darkness, with the evil spirits in the heavens. Therefore, put on the armor of God that you may be able to resist on the evil day and, having done everything, to hold your ground. So stand fast with your loins girded in truth, clothed with righteousness as a breastplate, and your feet shod in readiness for the gospel of peace. In all circumstances, hold faith as a shield, to quench all [the] flaming arrows of the evil one. And take the helmet of salvation and the sword of the Spirit, which is the word of God" (Ephesians 6:10–17). St. Peter warns us, saying that our "opponent the devil is prowling around like a roaring lion looking for [someone] to devour" (1 Peter 5:8). We need to stand up to him with the power that comes from the Holy Spirit, bestowed upon us on the day of Confirmation.

When carnal cravings drag me down, the Holy Spirit reminds me of the eternal bliss that lies beyond this transient world and its momentary pleasures. The Lord is challenging me and reminding me to live in the world, but not be of the world. The Lord is prompting me to live by the Spirit, and not to gratify the flesh (cf. Galatians 5:16). To fight a good fight, to be a man for the Lord, not for the world. To be a genuine human being, to be in the best shape the master artist designed in His mind, I had to receive the sacrament of Confirmation.

God Is Building You into a Spiritual Edifice

If life is considered a spiritual edifice, a building, the foundation was laid in the womb of our mother through the sacrament of Matrimony, as we discussed earlier. The Lord prepared us physically and spiritually through the sacraments of Baptism, Reconciliation, and the Eucharist. With the sacrament of Confirmation, the actual process of building, which began in the sacrament of Baptism into a spiritual edifice, takes its full mature course, because the Holy Spirit provides us with all needed "spiritual materials" in the form of the fruits and the gifts of the Holy Spirit. These are needed to complete the building.

Our call is to grow into the image of Christ, to grow into a sacred temple for the Lord, to be perfect like Him. This, of course, is a hard task. But it is also easy, as we have all the "materials" from the Spirit of God, who strengthens us to grow into a spiritual edifice. Every Christian is supposed to grow into the image of Christ. The image of Christ will be reflected in our lives when we are able to put forth the fruits of the Spirit. When we live in love, peace, joy, patience, kindness, generosity, faithfulness, gentleness, and self-control, we become reflectors of the face of the Lord. Basically, this is called life in the Spirit. This is the kind of life the Lord is looking for from us; this is the kind of life St. Paul asked us to lead for the praise of God's glory.

When the Lord told us to build our house on strong foundations (Matthew 7:24–25), was He not also telling us to be established in the Holy Spirit, who strengthens our life? A life founded in the Holy Spirit means a life filled with the gifts and fruits of the Holy Spirit. When I was confirmed, I was confirmed in all the good qualities of a human being: these qualities make me a child of God and make me a spiritual house for the Lord. These qualities make the life of an individual strong and stable. A person with these qualities is a person who builds his life on solid rock. "The rain fell, the floods came, and the winds blew and buffeted the house. But it did not collapse; it had been set solidly on rock" (Matthew 7:25). Therefore, Confirmation was an invitation to be founded on this solid rock of the Holy Spirit and to multiply on a daily basis the fruits of the Spirit.

To finish the building work, we need to work with the materials the Lord has given us through the sacraments of the Church through Confirmation. Just because we have all the materials unloaded in our worksite, the building is not going to become a reality if we don't actually start to build. That is *our* responsibility. So, too, is the sacrament of Confirmation. The Holy Spirit gives us all we need to turn our life into a spiritual building, to build our life on solid ground, to be firmly established and deeply rooted in the Lord. But if we don't try on our part, that is, if we don't fan them into flames, as St. Paul said to St. Timothy, then the fruits and gifts of the Spirit will go wasted. We will remain barren trees. Then the Lord will think of cutting us down because we are wasting the land; we are wasting the precious gifts of God we received on the day of our Confirmation, in the imposition of the bishop's hands.

We Become Temples of the Holy Spirit

Confirmation turns our bodies into mature temples of the Holy Spirit. Remember what I said about how my body was acting and reacting as I grew up physically; how I felt the urge to sin with my body; how my body was drawn to carnal pleasures. I was told that was "normal" for my age, that every man and woman goes through that stormy age. Yet deep within me, I heard a better and a sweeter voice inviting me to rise above the urges of my body and to consecrate my body to the Lord. I knew my body was sacred, as it was anointed with the oil of salvation on the day of my baptism. I knew I should glorify the Lord in my body. On the day of the sacrament of Confirmation, the Lord consecrated my body to be a temple of the Holy Spirit. Ever since then, I had to glorify the Lord in my body. St. Paul asks: "Do you not know that your body is a temple of the Holy Spirit within you, whom you have from God, and that you are not your own? For you have been purchased at a price. Therefore, glorify God in your body" (1 Corinthians 6:19–20).

Confirmation is a decisive awakening to God the Holy Spirit, the giver of all spiritual gifts, present in us.

A building becomes a temple, a sacred place, because of the presence of God in it. When the presence of God leaves the building, say a church, then it becomes just like any other building. If you roam around Europe, you will see so many abandoned churches, though not necessarily Catholic churches. Most of Europe, which gave birth to many saints and martyrs, is in utter darkness today. The United Kingdom is no longer Catholic, nor even Christian, in her practices. France has become almost a Muslim nation. Many of the churches in Spain and Italy are no longer crowded, as they used to be. If by chance you find a crowd in some churches in Rome, it is not the local people; they are tourists from around the world! Generally, Europe is like the loincloth of which the prophet Jeremiah spoke:

> The Lord said to me: Go, buy yourself a linen loincloth; wear it on your loins, but do not put it in water… A second time the word of the Lord came to me thus: Take the loincloth which you bought and are wearing, and go at once to the Perath; hide it in a cleft of the rock… After a long time, the Lord said to me: Go now to the Perath and fetch the loincloth which I told you to hide there. So I went to the Perath, looked for the loincloth and took it from the place I had hidden it. But it was rotted, good for nothing! Then the word came to me from the Lord: Thus says the Lord: so also I will allow the pride of Judah to rot, the great pride of Jerusalem. This wicked people who refuse to obey my words… will be like this loincloth, good for nothing. For, as the loincloth clings to a man's loins, so I made the whole house of Israel and the whole house of Judah cling to me—oracle of the Lord—to be my people, my fame, my praise, my glory. But they did not listen (cf. Jeremiah 13:1–11).

Europe gave birth to innumerable saints and martyrs. She was the birthplace of missionaries who evangelized practically the whole world. As you are aware, they brought the light of the Gospel also to the United States. But now, that same Europe seems to have forgotten God and religion. The presence of God has gone away from most men and women and from their church buildings. The Church stands baffled at the crossroads, not knowing which direction she should take. Wandering around with eyes wide open, no one would never miss the abandoned churches, which once upon a time reverberated with the praises of God. Now silence and gloom prevail around them. The courtyards of these churches, which bore the footprints of hundreds of thousands of worshippers and religious-minded people for centuries, are now covered with thorns and thistles. Huge stone pillars have cracks, into which grow the roots of nearby trees. Sometimes one can see boys and girls kissing passionately and even indulging in sex behind the pillars of these abandoned buildings.

If you peep through the broken windows, all you can see is darkness. You would be frightened by bats flying in the dark corners of these church buildings. The stuffy smell! The forgotten sanctuary where no priests stand anymore reminds one of the alienation of humanity from God. The altar upon which sacrifices and the prayers of the faithful were offered stands bare today. There is no one to stand between the altar and the sanctuary to raise their hands in prayer. No bread and wine to be offered on these holy altars. Beautiful pipe organs that sang incessantly the melodies of God are silent. Baptismal fonts that gave rebirth and a promise of salvation stand in a dark corner, wrapped in melancholy and gloomy silence. Pews that seated many people seem to be waiting for visitors. It would seem that the words of Azariah have come true, for he says, "For we are reduced, O Lord, beyond any other nation, brought low everywhere in the world this day because of our sins. We have in our day no prince, prophet, or leader, no burnt offering, sacrifice, oblation, or incense, no place to offer first fruits, to find favor with you" (Daniel 3:37–38).

The tombs of people who are buried around these churches lay desolate. Inscriptions on them are vague now. As the nation forgot God and religion, the people have also forgotten the generation that worked tirelessly for the growth of their nation, generations that lived religious values. The young ones do not even know the meaning of Christmas. They know that it is a time to give and receive gifts! Some of these nations today are like whitewashed tombs, which appear beautiful on the outside, but inside are full of men's bones and every kind of filth (cf. Matthew 23:27). These nations need to pause a while to listen to the stories their forefathers have to say about the manner of religious life they lead. Unvisited sanctuaries, stripped altars, silent pipe organs, baptismal fonts empty of cleansing waters, and desolate tombs: living signs of a generation that invariably lived a religious life, and striking signs of a secular generation that tries to keep God and religion as far away as possible from its life. These are living signs of the presence of God being removed from their midst.

Some churches are falling down, and the gates to these churches are locked up with huge iron chains with a warning sign: Dangerous Building, Keep Out. Some churches have been turned into restaurants and nightclubs, others into mosques. Why? Because the oil of God's presence from the lamps of human hearts has gone out. Therefore, the lives of these nations that forsook God smolder, having nothing to be proud of today. Loss of family life, lack of sense of God and religion, increasing divorce, men and women living together under the modern banner "cohabiting," and disregard for the institution of marriage all flourish. At the age of twenty-eight people becoming grandparents, eleven-year-old boys becoming fathers and ten-year-old girls walking around with signs of pregnancy, children being born to unmarried people and most of them living with single parents, rising unemployment, and economic crises crushing these nations, which once were known as lands of affluence and lands that do not see the sunset, are all they have to their credit now. The result of a culture forgetting God! When these nations decided to step away from the presence of God, God too must have decided to hide His face from them.

> Moab shall become like Sodom, the Ammonites like Gomorrah: A field of weeds, a salt pit, a waste forever. The remnant of my people shall plunder them, the survivors of my nation dispossess them. This will be the recompense for their pride, because they taunted and boasted against the people of the Lord of hosts. The Lord shall inspire them with terror when he makes all gods of earth waste away; then the distant shores of the nations, each from its own place, shall

bow down to him. You too, O Cushites, shall be slain by the sword of the Lord. He will stretch out his hand against the north, to destroy Assyria; He will make Nineveh a waste, dry as the desert. In her midst flocks shall lie down, all the wild life of the hollows; the screech owl and the desert owl shall roost in her columns; the owl shall hoot from the window, the raven croak from the doorway. Is this the exultant city that dwelt secure, that told itself, 'I and there is no one else'? How has it become a waste, a lair for wild animals? Those who pass by it hiss, and shake their fists (Zephaniah 2:9–15).

The people who go to church are older people. The young ones do not even know the names of the major religions. There, one who practices religion is mocked. I remembered reading in the paper that a nurse lost her job because she was wearing a cross! The students who go to church are bullied and made fun of in schools by their classmates who do not. Practicing religion and faith is considered mean and unbecoming to a "modern person." But at least some people who denied God and abandoned religion when young seek to die a Christian death and would like to have a Catholic, or at least a Christian, burial; in case there is a God and a heaven, they don't want to miss them!

Remember, what makes a building a sacred place, a temple, a church, is the presence of God. When we enter a church building, we genuflect, we bow down, and we behave with utmost respect because we know that there is the presence of the Lord, because there is the tabernacle. That is precisely the reason we do not misbehave in a church. We go in and out with a sense of the sacred. If anything terribly bad should happen, say a murder, then we should rededicate the building before we can use it. It is all because there was the presence of God in a very special way; the building was a temple of God.

This sacrament reconfirms our bodies, which God chose at the time of Baptism, a dwelling place, a temple of the Holy Spirit, says the Scripture. It means that this sacrament is an invitation to keep our bodies sacred and holy, just as we keep our churches sacred and holy. If a church is a static temple of God, our bodies are moving temples of God. So this sacrament also challenges us to avoid all bad materials in our bodies, to keep away from all that will desecrate our bodies as we keep away all bad materials from churches. Therefore, we are invited to avoid all immoralities with our bodies. St. Paul again asks, "Do you not know that you are temples of God, and that the Spirit of God dwells in you? If anyone destroys God's temple, God will destroy that person; for the temple of God, which you are, is holy" (1 Corinthians 3:16–17). So this sacrament poses a big challenge; a challenge to keep our bodies holy and pure for the Lord.

If we all considered our bodies as moving temples of God, of the Holy Spirit, we would have treated our bodies with more respect and love; we would have looked at every other person as a moving temple, and not as a commodity to be consumed. I am of the opinion that if we bow down or genuflect when we enter a church, we should also do it much more when we see a person. That is a more beautiful way of respecting God's wonderful creation. This would bring more tolerance and less violence committed against other persons. This would reduce murder and character assassination, or any other sort of violence against human bodies.

If we had known our bodies in the light of this theology, that is, that our bodies are temples of God, we would have kept away from all that would desecrate our bodies; I refer to all the sexual anarchy that we find in our society, especially in the Western world. St. Paul is very assertive when he says God will destroy the person who destroys God's temple. I am particularly sad when a Catholic considers abortion, which is destroying a temple in which God dwells. I personally feel that Catholics who indulge in sex, even with mutual consent, merely for pleasure, without any real commitment and responsibility, are intentionally violating and desecrating the temple of God. That is a grave sin; that is a sin against the Holy Spirit. The Lord said, "Amen, I say to you, all sins and blasphemies that people utter will be forgiven them. But whoever blasphemes against the Holy Spirit will never have forgiveness, but is guilty of an everlasting sin" (Mark 3:28–29). The Lord said this when people said that He was driving out demons with the help of Beelzebub, the prince of demons. They knew that the Lord was doing it by the finger of God, the Holy Spirit. But they did not want to acknowledge that. They rejected the working of the Spirit with knowledge. When we reject the Spirit present in us with knowledge, by desecrating the temple, our body, with body-related sins, even after knowing that we should consider our bodies as moving temples of God, we continue destroying the temple of God; then, God will destroy us!

The world is so bad maybe because it does not know the Holy Spirit; or people do not live by the demands of the Spirit; or the people who have received the Spirit do not "stir it into flames" (2 Timothy 1:6). Most people today receive this sacrament without full awareness of the implications; they do it for different reasons. When I observe our youngsters preparing for this great sacrament, I have a feeling that most of them are not even aware of what they are receiving; most of them are not serious enough; they very much lack formation. It is indeed sad. They get it anyway, because it is generally given to them when they reach eighth grade, regardless of their knowledge about the sacrament. I am not sure how many "wait" for the coming of the Spirit as the apostles waited for the indwelling of the Spirit. The Lord said to His disciples to "wait for the promise of the Father" (Acts 1:4).

Once, I was talking to some candidates for confirmation. I asked them if they knew the fruits of the Holy Spirit. One smart young man raised his hands and said, "Peaches, apples, grapes"! That is the knowledge of our youth. But he too was confirmed! When our youngsters receive this sacrament without basic knowledge of what they receive, what will be the manifestation of the Spirit in them? Our bodies no longer have any original sanctity of being temples of the Lord, because we do not want to live by the demands of the Spirit. As the people of the Lord's time traded in the temple areas, most of us "trade" with our bodies. Today's generation is mainly after pleasure, usually that of their bodies. This generation is an evil generation, as it glorifies sex for pleasure alone. That is why we have so many sex-related sins around us in the form of fornication, adultery, premarital sex, pornography. You name it. They are all immoralities, sins against the temple of the Holy Spirit. We reduce the body to a mass of flesh through rotten desires; we downgrade the creation of God. The masterpieces of God, the great artist, are far from their original make because the Spirit, the *soul* of the artwork, has been lost. We look entirely different now, far from what was designed in His mind. We are no more masterpieces now. We are like any other work of any other artist.

We are lukewarm people; we do not fan into flames the spiritual gifts the Lord bestowed upon us through the Holy Spirit. Maybe the Lord has spat us out of his mouth because we are neither hot nor cold, but are lukewarm (cf. Revelation 3:16). As that lazy servant did in the parable of the Talents (cf. Matthew 25:14–30), we buried our many spiritual gifts under the soil. Maybe many of us are no longer temples of the Holy Spirit though we received the sacrament of Confirmation, because the presence of the Lord has left the temple as we desecrated our bodies with shameful sins. We need to rededicate our bodies so that once again the presence of the Lord, the Spirit, will return to the temple of our bodies. The Lord gives us the help and grace of the sacraments so that we will outshine others in the world. We will live like lamps in darkness, like yeast and salt in the world.

What would our life have been like if God the Holy Spirit would *not* have come? Our life would have been like a heap of bones or a mass of flesh. The world is so bad because there are too many people living without the Spirit. They live by the flesh and its desires. But our call is to live by the Spirit, by the power that flows from the Holy Spirit. When the Spirit leaves us, or when we choose to leave the Spirit, we reduce ourselves into a mass of flesh. There begins all the problems in the world. The world is not guided by the Spirit; rather, it is guided by the flesh and its desires. People live to satisfy the flesh and its cravings. They run after the desires of the flesh. Most peoples' lives today revolve around the axis that is flesh; it is no more the axis of the Spirit. Maybe the biggest enemy of humanity is the flesh and its corrupt desires. Many men and women seem to live solely for the purpose of gratifying their flesh. But gladly, the Spirit teaches us to concentrate on the spiritual aspects of life and that our life is not for the body but for the Lord.

Helps You Proclaim the Message of the Gospel with Courage

One of the main reasons for the indwelling of the Spirit is to turn us into proclaimers of the message of the Lord, to become witnesses of the Gospel. We did not know what we were receiving at the time of Baptism. Our parents and godparents professed the faith for us on our behalf. They received the light of the burning candle, the light of the Lord, for us. Now we are old enough in the world to embrace all the nuances of our Baptism, to profess the faith with conviction, to accept the Word, to be made into mature witnesses for God in the world.

The Holy Spirit makes it possible for us do this mission with power. Actually, the mission that the Lord enjoins on us when we receive each sacrament cannot be done without the assistance of the Holy Spirit. The world remains somewhat visibly untouched at times by the reception of the sacraments because the recipients are afraid to proclaim the message. The apostles were afraid of their mission too; the Lord knew that. The Lord knew they would not be able to do anything until they received the power of the Spirit. That is why Jesus asked them to stay in the city until the coming of the Spirit. The Lord said, "I am sending the promise of my Father upon you; but stay in the city until you are clothed with the power from on high" (Luke 24:49). In the book of the Acts of the Apostles, we read what the Lord said to the Apostles just before his Ascension: "But you will receive power when the Holy Spirit comes upon you, and you will be my witnesses in Jerusalem, throughout Judea and Samaria, and to the ends of the earth" (1:8). The apostles were afraid of the outside world, which was inimical to them; after the Ascension of the Lord, they were shut up in a room for fear of the people, but they became courageous after receiving the Spirit.

We find the first speech of St. Peter just after the indwelling of the Holy Spirit upon the Apostles and disciples of the Lord. The Acts of the Apostles, chapter 2, verses 14–36, gives us the account of his speech. If you read through it, you will know how powerful and sharp his speech was. Verse 37 says that the people were "cut to the heart." St. Peter, who said, "I am going fishing" (John 21:3), maybe out of frustration and loss of a sense of purpose, because the master who had promised them "a kingdom" had suffered a terrible death, and now there was nothing much left to look forward to—this same man became an eloquent speaker. Since then, all of the apostles became agents of the Good News of the Gospel. Many of them had to stand before the Sanhedrin. This is what Peter said to those who questioned him and the other apostles: "We must obey God rather than men. The God of our ancestors raised Jesus, though you had him killed by hanging him on a tree. God exalted him at his right hand as leader and savior to grant Israel repentance and forgiveness of sins. We are witnesses of these things, as is the Holy Spirit that God has given to those who obey him" (Acts 5:29–32).

They stood unflinching before rulers and kings; the Spirit gave them strength to face even death. The Lord had told them of the coming trials of life: "However, they will seize and persecute you, they will hand you over to the synagogues and to prisons, and they will have you led before kings and governors because of my name. It will lead to giving testimony. Remember, you are not to prepare your defense beforehand, for I myself shall give you wisdom in speaking that all your adversaries will be powerless to resist or refute" (Luke 21:12–15). Later on, many of them became martyrs for the Lord.

The Church, down through the centuries, has met with oppositions and persecutions; much of it is still in the memories of the Church. The Church continues to be cornered by systems and people across the world. There are enemies who try to destroy the Church; they hunt down Christians just because they are Christians; even today, Christians in many parts of the world, especially in the Middle East, run from place to place for safety; they are displaced; people speak ill of the Church; they try to underestimate what she is all about; she is often misunderstood; the leaders are often misquoted and falsely accused; there are many behind bars for no reason. There are people and organizations trying to make money by accusing priests of terrible acts. When I see terrible persecutions around the world—anti-Christians and religious fundamentalists or fanatics waging war against the Church, against Jesus—and still the Church flourishes across the world, and the number of the Catholics rises, not dwindles, I think there is some secret to it.

I see people lined up, including innocent babies who, not knowing what is happening, smile at men who are armed with machine guns, to be shot to death. But still they are proud to hold on to their identity as Christians. They are like many martyrs of the Church, unflinching before the face of death. Where do they get that courage from? There are thousands who are even today hunted and displaced by Islamic terrorists. But they hold on to their faith even when they hear the footsteps of death every second. The Church holds her head high! She is unbeaten. As St. Paul says, "We are afflicted in every way, but not constrained; perplexed, but not driven to despair; persecuted, but not abandoned; struck down, but not destroyed" (2 Corinthians 4:8–9). People who try to destroy the Church fail every time, because she is not built on sand, but on a solid foundation; she is not built by any human, but by the power of the Holy Spirit.

We are afraid too, like the apostles. We shudder when the waves of the world rise high over us. We fear we will sink into the world. We are swept by the unkind tides of this unkind world. Sometimes some of us are ashamed to proclaim the Gospel; sometimes we are afraid of our religion. There may be Catholics who might feel awkward and out of place among their friends and colleagues who say they have no religion. There may be Catholics who are bullied in school, college, and workplaces because they are Catholics. In certain places and countries, people have to hide a crucifix under their garments. Sometimes they are sidelined; other times the world is unfair to them, all because they bear the name of Christ. There are people who jeer and mock us. We feel like giving up the title.

But deep down, in our innermost being, we hear another voice that murmurs to hold our heads high. There is a superior power that gives us strength. There is a higher force that propels our life forward. There is something within us that makes us find sense even when nothing around us makes sense. That is the Holy Spirit, the promised assistance from on high. He is the one who formed the Church; He is the one who guides the Church. He hovers over the Church like an eagle in the sky. He is our strength in weakness, our comfort in sorrows, our courage in fear, clarity and counselor in confusion, our perseverance in persecution, our sense in nonsense, our sword and shield in battle against the powers of darkness. He makes us smile at the odds of life. He helps us rise above the pains that the world can inflict upon us. He makes us stand before courts and trials. He puts His words into our mouths. He is the one who speaks for us before rulers and judges. With all the trials and tribulations, we remain Christians because the power of the Spirit sustains us! Lord, we are praying for a double portion of Your Spirit so that we will be as strong and fearless as Your apostles and the great men and women who laid down their lives for You and Your Church. Let us pray: Come, Holy Spirit, fill the hearts of

Your faithful and enkindle in them the fire of Your love. Send forth Your Spirit, and they shall be created, and You shall renew the face of the earth.

We thank You for the Holy Spirit, for pervading the world with Your Spirit, for the continued guidance of the Holy Spirit, for setting people apart by the Holy Spirit for the greater glory of Your name (cf. Acts 13:2); we thank You for all the saints who lived by the Spirit, for all the martyrs who laid down their lives because the Holy Spirit enabled them to do so, for all the evangelization that the Spirit achieved, for all the promptings that Your people continue to receive from the Holy Spirit, for making the Church holy in and through the unfailing presence of the Holy Spirit.

Now, allow me to conclude this humble session with—I hope it is—a children's song, which I promised earlier to put down here; it is a song that I discovered on WhatsApp:

> If love was a pomegranate, I'd want to grow
> so red, I would color the entire planet;
> If joy was a tangerine, I'd want my peel to be
> the orangiest you've ever seen;
> If peace was a pear, "Lord, make me juicy
> and delish" would be my prayer.
> Holy Spirit, grow your fruit in me.
> Your fruit is love, joy, peace, patience, kind-
> ness, goodness, faithfulness, gentleness and
> self-control.

If patience was a plum, I'd want to ripen
until purple I become;
If kindness was a banana, I'd want to be a
bunch as massive as Montana;
If goodness was a cherry, a yummy pie to all
my neighbors I would carry.
Holy Spirit, grow your fruit in me!
Your fruit is love, joy, peace, patience, kindness, goodness, faithfulness, gentleness and
self-control.

If faithfulness was a watermelon, I'd be so
luscious, juicy, green, and big enough to
dwell in;
If gentleness was a kiwi, the Lord would
peel my tough brown skin so I'd be squishy;
If self-control was an apple, I'd want to turn
all red and shiny in a Snapple.
Holy Spirit, grow your fruit in me.
Your fruit is love, joy, peace, patience, kindness, goodness, faithfulness, gentleness and
self-control.

As we wait for the coming of the Holy Spirit, through the
sacrament of Confirmation, our prayer should be, "Holy Spirit,
grow Your fruits in me."

CHAPTER 6

The Final Touch of God

It was good for me to be afflicted, in order to learn your statues.
—Psalm 19:71

The Mystery of Suffering
What Does the Bible Say?

"Is not life on earth a drudgery, its days like those of a hireling? Like a slave who longs for the shade, a hireling who waits for wages, so I have been assigned months of futility, and troubled nights have been counted off for me. When I lie down I say, 'When shall I arise?', then the night drags on; I am filled with restlessness until the dawn. My flesh is clothed with worms and scabs; my skin cracks and festers; my days are swifter than a weaver's shuttle; they come to an end without hope. Remember that my life is like the wind; my eye will not see happiness again" (Job 7:1–7). This passage shows the suffering of Job, who was a just man. One of the greatest dilemmas a faithful follower of God's precepts encounters is the question of suffering, especially the suffering of the innocent. Why do good people get bad things in life? There may be no satisfying answers to the question. All that we can do is to try to find meaning for suffering or try to find some answer to the question of the suffering of good people.

I say *good people* because no one will have any problem with so-called bad people suffering. We might say, "Well, they deserve that." But our faith shakes, and we seem to question God when we see good people, the innocent ones, in suffering. There are many who are baffled at the mystery of suffering; there are many who even turn away from God because of it.

Maybe suffering is the only question to which the Bible does not give any direct answer. Maybe it is Job, the just one, in the book of Job, who tried for the very first time in the Bible to probe into the great mystery of suffering. You may know that the book of Job is not a historical account, but a moral story, an exquisite treatment of the problem of the suffering of the innocent. This book, written between the seventh and fifth centuries BC, is not a solution to this mystery. It rather challenges its readers to come to their own understanding and conclusion.

Job tried to argue with the Lord for his "unjust" suffering. He tried to encounter the Lord using his case. He said, "But I would speak with the Almighty; I want to argue with God" (Job 13:3). "Slay me though he might, I will wait for him; I will defend my conduct before him" (13:15). "Behold, I have prepared my case, I know that I am in the right. If anyone can make a case against me, then I shall be silent and expire" (13:18–19). But Job did not get an answer. On the contrary, God silenced him by asking counterquestions. God said, "Gird up your loins now, like a man; I will question you, and you tell me the answers!" (38:3) Then God continued to arrow down His questions to Job. Chapters 38 and 39 contain God's questions to Job, for which poor Job had no answers. It would be so fascinating and intriguing to read those chapters. At the end, Job said, "Look, I am of little account; what can I answer you? I put my hand over my mouth. I have spoken once, I will not reply; twice, but I will do so no more" (40:4–5). Yet God did not leave him; God continued the interrogations in chapter 40:7–32. And in chapter 41, God tells Job how strong he is. But He did not answer the question of Job on suffering. God silenced Job with His might. Job said, "By hearsay I had heard of you, but now my eye has seen you. Therefore I disown what I have said, and repent in dust and ashes" (42:5–6).

I wonder why such a mighty God did not answer Job's question on suffering. Why did God silence Job? Why does He continue to silence you and me when it comes to the question of suffering? Why is there no clear answer to the question of suffering, especially that of good people? Why does this remain a mystery? We don't know. I have no answers; no one has any clear answers. I am sure that God has answers. Maybe God does not want us to know the answer; or He means to say that we as mere human beings—who are not able to find answers to ordinary questions, such as those God placed before Job—we must not try to delve into such a great mystery like suffering. Perhaps it is better for humanity that the issue of suffering remains a mystery forever.

When I visited a certain elderly lady in a nursing home who had been sick for a very long time, she told me, "I wish God would tell me why I suffer. It would have been easier for me to accept my sufferings. But I know God has a purpose for my suffering." I told her that suffering is part of being human, because we have a body. Human suffering is part of the deal. Both good and bad come to us in the same package of being human. Everything in this world has a rival; every positive has a negative: life has death, light has darkness, good has bad, virtue has vice, wealth has poverty, laughter has tears, up has down, joy has sufferings. We must not forget that Jesus came to the glory of the Resurrection after going through the agony of the Cross.

As human beings, can we ever expect to receive joys alone while here on earth? That is unfair! The fair deal is that we take both joys and sorrows equally. If we are looking for plea-sure alone, that would be selfishness. The best answer to the question of suffering is what Job said: "We accept good things from God; should we not accept evil?" (Job 2:10). That is what I mean by a "fair deal." The elderly lady whom I mentioned earlier would also tell me at the end of pouring out her frustra-tions: "But I had a very good life." That is the reality with most people. I don't believe that anyone has misfortune alone. There can be exceptions.

No Adequate Answers, Only Assumptions

Jesus is the second person we find in the Bible who asked the reason for suffering. On the cross we hear the heartrending cry, "My God, My God, why have you forsaken me?" (Matthew 27:46). But we don't hear an answer from God. God, who can solve every mystery, who has an answer to every question, a solution to every puzzle, a key to every lock, is silent, brutally silent! Does the silence of God say that He doesn't care? I am sure God must have wept himself to death watching His Son die on the cross. Yet God remains silent; maybe, as I said earlier, God likes to leave it a mystery forever; maybe He wants us to find an answer ourselves, an answer that is meaningful to each one who suffers.

At this point, we cannot say that there is no answer in the Bible to the question "Why do good people get bad things in life?", because there is an answer, and the answer is JESUS. Jesus was the best man who ever lived; there can be no better human being than Jesus in the future. Yet He suffered. We are nothing like Jesus. We are sinners. Remember what the prophet Micah says: "The faithful have vanished from the earth, no mortal is just!" (7:2) Human beings are basically sinful. God might allow the sufferings in our life to purify our life. As gold is purified in fire, our life is purified in the crucible of suffering. Jesus, though He was the perfect human being, suffered for the salvation of the world. Jesus suffered because suffering was the single easy path to glory. Jesus asks us to go through the narrow door to glory. "How narrow the gate and constricted the road that leads to life" (Matthew 7:14). Therefore, I think, suffering is good.

But you would tell me that the sufferings and the violent death of the Lord do not diminish our sufferings by one bit. You are very correct. In my humble understanding, the suffering and death of the Lord were neither to ease the physical sufferings of our present life nor to assure us that the followers of the Lord would not have to suffer. After all, we suffer physically because we have a body. At least some people are prone to think that God shouldn't permit any sufferings in their life because they believe in God and practice their faith. The reality is that as long as we live in the world, we will have physical suffering. That is a natural consequence of being human. It has nothing to do with God, except that He is the one who made us with a body. Jesus suffered and died for us so that eternal life would be possible for us. The Passion of the Lord simply shows us that no torments in the world can crush our spirit. It tells us that human beings have the inner capacity and strength to overcome pain and suffering in the light of faith, by looking at the Cross, Christ.

When we go through the Scripture, looking for a solid and satisfying answer to the problem of suffering, all that we get are some assumptions, which we can gather from the Scripture. The first assumption can be that suffering is vicarious, meaning in the place of and for the benefit of someone else. As Jesus suffered for us, we suffer for somebody else. A second assumption we get from this is that suffering leads us to future glory. A grain brings forth a harvest only when it falls to the ground and dies. "Unless a grain of wheat falls to the ground and dies, it remains just a grain of wheat; but if it dies, it produces much fruit" (John 12:24). The suffering and death of the Lord was a "falling down" for others. That brought everlasting life to us. If Christ had not suffered for us, we wouldn't have the joys of everlasting life. Consider this way: motherhood crowns womanhood. In other words, motherhood is a crown of glory for a woman. But a woman gets the crown of biological motherhood only when she goes through labor pain. Labor pain brings her the glory of being a mother. The sand of suffering that falls in our hearts today may be turned into a pearl of great value tomorrow. The sufferings of our present life may bring glory in the future!

A third assumption we can gather from the Scripture is that suffering exists to make us stronger in life. A person who has gone through the agony of cancer and survived would be much stronger than a person who hadn't gone through any trials in life. It is a fact that the tree that stands on the brow of a hill, that stands against all the wind and rain and other forces of nature, would be of a greater strength than a tree that stands in a valley, which doesn't have to resist any force of nature. Suffering makes us stronger.

Finally, suffering can also be occasions of experiencing God. Haven't you seen people who did not care for God and religion coming closer to the Lord through sufferings? One example is St. Paul. He who was "breathing murderous threats against the disciples of the Lord" (Acts 9:1) came to be the number one and the strongest supporter of the Lord in the postresurrection era through his sufferings. He "saw" the Lord not when he had sight, but when he was struck down, when he was blind (cf. Acts 9:1–19).

This is what I received on Facebook recently:

> Some time ago, a few ladies met to study the scriptures. While reading the third chapter of Malachi, they came upon a remarkable statement in the third verse: "He will sit refining and purifying silver" (Malachi 3:3). One lady decided to visit a silversmith, and

report to others what he said about the subject. She went accordingly, and without telling the silversmith the reason for her visit,
asked him to tell her about the process of
refining silver. After he had fully described
it to her, she asked, "Sir, do you watch while
the work of refining is going on?" "Oh, yes
ma'am," replied the silversmith. "I must sit
and watch the furnace constantly for if the
time necessary for refining is exceeded in the
slightest degree, the silver will be injured."
The lady at once saw the beauty and comfort of the statement, "He will sit refining
and purifying silver." God sees it as necessary to put His children into the furnace
but His eye is steadily intent on the work
of purifying, and His wisdom and love are
both engaged in the best manner for us.
Our trials do not come at random, and He
will not let us be tested beyond what we can
endure. Before she left, the lady asked one
final question, "How do you know when
the process is finished?" "Oh, that's quite
simple," replied the silversmith… "When I
can see my own image in the silver, the refining process is complete." What is the lesson?
God allows us to go through hard times so
that we may grow and become smooth and
shiny. His goal is for us to become a reflec-

tion of Him that not only He can see, but also so others can see Him in us.

We need wisdom to understand the mystery of suffering. The book of Wisdom, chapter 3:1–12, entitled "On Suffering," unfolds this great mystery of suffering:

> The souls of the just are in the hand of God, and no torment shall touch them. They seemed, in the eyes of the foolish, to be dead; and their passing away was thought an affliction and going forth from us, utter destruction. But they are in peace. For if to others, indeed, they seem punished, yet is their hope full of immortality; Chastised a little, they be greatly blessed, because God tried them and found them worthy of himself. As gold in the furnace, he proved them, and as sacrificial offerings he took them to himself. In the time of their judgment they shall shine and dart about as sparks through stubble. They shall judge nations and rule over peoples, and the Lord shall be their king forever. Those who trust in the Lord shall understand truth, and the faithful shall abide with him in love. (3:1–9)

Don't Fail the Test

If you, though innocent, suffer, that shows God's confidence in you. He thinks that you will still remain His best child, His best friend, regardless of suffering and pain. When God allowed Satan to inflict all kinds of physical pain on Job, He was sure and certain that Job would remain faithful to Him. It is good to listen to the conversation between God and Satan: "The Lord said to Satan, 'Have you noticed my servant Job? There is no one on earth like him, blameless and upright, fearing God and avoiding evil.' Then Satan answered the Lord and said, 'Is it for nothing that Job is God-fearing? Have you not surrounded him and his family and all that he has with your protection? You have blessed the works of his hands, and his livestock are spread over the land. But now put forth your hand and touch all that he has, and surely he will curse you to your face.' The Lord said to the Satan, 'Very well, all that he has is in your power; only do not lay a hand on him.'" (Job 1:8–12). Job won the test. Job made God proud before the wicked Satan. If Job had cursed God at the advice of his wife, he would have defeated God's challenge to Satan. But Job proved a real man, a real friend of God; thus, he stood at the side of God and defeated the wicked plan of Satan.

Therefore, sufferings are good for ourselves and for others. After all, did God ever promise to us that He will give us good times always? I don't think so. Actually, the Lord warned us of troubles and sufferings that await us in the world, especially for those who choose to follow him. Most often, those who are distressed over their sufferings are people who practice

255

their faith, who love God, faith, and religion. It is most hard for them to understand why they suffer even when they stay close to the Lord. I think it is wrong to think that we will not have any suffering if we love God, religion, and are practicing our faith. Actually, it is of these people that the Lord spoke of, those who would face terrible sufferings in life. Jesus said that those who choose to follow Him will have to suffer on account of Him. For He warned them, "You will hear of wars and reports of wars; see that you are not alarmed, for these things must happen, but it will not yet be the end. Nation will rise against nation, and kingdom against kingdom; there will be famines and earthquakes from place to place. All these are the beginning of the labor pains. Then they will hand you over to persecutions, and they will kill you. You will be hated by all nations because of my name. And then many will be led into sin; they will betray and hate one another. Many false prophets will rise and deceive many, the love of many will grow cold. But the one who perseveres to the end will be saved" (Matthew 24:6–12). Are these not proofs for sufferings in life, forewarned by the Lord? In the Gospel according to John, Jesus said, "In the world you will have trouble, but take courage, I have conquered the world" (John 16:33). What is important to remember in the face of suffering is not to be overwhelmed or distressed over suffering. It is very important to remember that our sufferings cannot defeat us or destroy us forever because the Lord has conquered suffering and the world that offers suffering.

So what should we do in the face of suffering? Should we become overwhelmed, distressed, disappointed, or frustrated? What use is there in cursing God, grumbling, complaining?

What good is there in being cranky and snappy with sufferings? That is not going to make your situation any better whatsoever; rather, it makes things more difficult for yourself and for others. You are creating a hell of your sufferings. People who watch you become sick over you with worry.

I have seen many who curse God and others for their sufferings, who grumble and complain all the time, who snap at doctors, nurses, and bystanders. In the next room, there may be one who smiles at the odds of life. They are the people who grin at their "fate." They are the people who conquer their sufferings with a smile. Haven't you seen people who inspire many others from their sickbed? They are the people who turn their sufferings into a salvific work for themselves and for others. They are the people who truly follow the Lord; they are the true friends of God, who prove to God that they can be trusted like Job. They are the people who make their sufferings a joy. I have met many who have created blogs to write about how they found meaning in their sufferings. There are people who have died without waiting to complete the journal of their journey through the single-lane road of suffering. Yet they deemed their suffering a blessing.

I don't mean to say that we need to seek to suffer. All that I want to tell you is that we should not be distressed over the fact that we have suffering in life. And if we have to suffer, suffer it willingly, uniting your sufferings with those of the Lord, who suffered for you and me. Then our "burdens become light, and our yoke becomes light." The Lord knew that suffering is a big issue of human life. That is why he spent much of His ministry curing the sick; that is why the Church continues the ministry of healing in natural and supernatural ways. With the sacrament of Anointing of the Sick, the Lord offers us the supernatural grace of healing. St. James says, "Is anyone among you sick? He should summon the presbyters of the Church and they should pray over him and anoint him with oil in the name of the Lord, and the prayers of faith will save the sick person, and the Lord will raise him up. If he has committed any sins, he will be forgiven" (James 5:13–15). The book of Psalms says, "Therefore, every loyal person should pray to you in time of distress. Though flood waters threaten, they will never reach him. You are my shelter; you guard me from distress; with joyful shouts of deliverance you surround me" (Psalm 32:6).

Anointing of the Sick: The Last Touch upon the Soul

The sacrament of the Anointing of the Sick is the last sacramental touch of God on our souls, by which the Lord makes our souls shine like gold. I wish to tell you that every bit of suffering in this world polishes our soul as well, turning us into the eighth sacrament of God for others. As the suffering of Jesus was for you and for me, our suffering can bring healing to someone elsewhere.

Whenever I officiate at a funeral, I tell people that a human being is a masterpiece of God. But since we were brought to being through the instrumentality of our parents, weak human beings, the human mold is not perfect. Over the years, through the sacraments of the Church, the Lord perfects us! The sacrament of the Anointing of the Sick—if it is administered as the last rite—is the last touch of the Lord; the master artist works upon his creation, upon the soul of a person here on earth, the touch that perfects the artwork that will enable the soul to present itself before its Creator.

The Lord has been touching the life of a Catholic with the sacraments of the Church, thus perfecting His creation. It is like an artist giving some final touches to his artwork; he seems not quite satisfied; or rather, he wants to make his work the best version of the design he had in his mind before he started to create. He wants to make us unique. Every person is a masterpiece to God. That is the reason the Lord constantly touches us with various sacraments from time to time. The Lord is shaping and reshaping us, as the potter did in the book of the prophet Jeremiah (cf. 18:1–5). He tried over and over again on the same pot until the shape pleased him. Even the sufferings of my life, I believe, are God's reshaping moments. He is refining me like gold in fire. He is making me the best version. We, as pots in the hands of the potter, refused to be the best versions of ourselves. Now, with the sacrament of the Anointing of the Sick, the Lord is making sure that our soul is immaculate to stand before the majesty of our Maker.

Healing for Both Body and Soul

The Anointing of the Sick is given for the healing of both body and soul. This healing takes place by the grace of this sacrament as it offers strength, peace, and courage to overcome the difficulties that go with the condition of serious illness or the old age. "This assistance from the Lord by the power of his Spirit is meant to lead the sick person healing of the soul, but also of the body if such is God's will" (*CCC* 1520). But this may be also given as a last rite or the extreme unction, which prepares the person to die a happy and peaceful death. Up until a few years ago, this sacrament was called last rites because it was given when the person was in danger of death. It was given just once. Most people were scared about receiving this sacrament because they thought that the reception of this sacrament meant that the person was going to die soon. They were right. As we said, this sacrament was administered only in danger of death. This would be the *last* rite for a living person; all that remains would be after-death rites. That is why this sacrament was called the last rites or the extreme unction.

But in recent years, there has been a new understanding of this sacrament. It is no longer called last rites, but instead the sacrament of the Anointing of the Sick. This became a sacrament that a Catholic could receive any number of times. The understanding of this sacrament changed from the point of view of death to one of health and healing. Sick people began to resort to this sacrament for various medical reasons like advanced age, minor or major surgery, in an extreme case of illness, or even when they felt generally weak. This became a sacrament not of the dying, but of the living. This came to be viewed as a sacrament that helps healing of both body and soul.

When I visit with people in hospitals, when the patient introduces me to nurses or doctors, I tell them, "Well, you treat his body. I came to treat the soul." Remember, a person is both body and soul. A healthy life means that we be healthy both bodily and spiritually. Therefore, the sacrament of the Anointing of the Sick is very important from a healing point of view as a person goes through medical treatment. This can certainly speed up the healing process. As a priest who has administered this sacrament to hundreds of sick people, I can say that most people were eager to receive this sacrament, as they knew this would speed up their recovery.

We must keep in mind that the healing ministry was one of the most important ministries that the Lord came to do. We see in the Scripture the Lord curing lepers, the deaf, the dumb, the lame, and the paralytic. This ministry was also entrusted to his apostles when the Lord sent them out to proclaim the Good News. In the Gospel according to Matthew, we see Jesus commissioning the apostles with the following words: "Do not go into pagan territory or enter a Samaritan town. Go rather to the lost sheep of the house of Israel. As you go, make this proclamation: 'The kingdom of heaven is at hand. 'Cure the sick, raise the dead, cleanse lepers, drive out demons" (Matthew 10:5–8). We understand that the apostles continued this mission in the life of the early Church. We see in the Acts of the Apostles St. Peter curing a crippled beggar with the following words: "I have neither silver nor gold, but what I do have I give you: in the name of Jesus Christ the Nazorean [rise and] walk" (3:6). In chapter 5, we read, "Many signs and wonders were done among the people at the hands of the apostles. They were all together in Solomon's portico. None of the others dared to join them, but the people esteemed them. Yet more than ever, believers in the Lord, great numbers of men and women, were added to them. Thus they even carried the sick out into the streets and laid them on cots and mats so that when Peter came by, at least his shadow might fall on one or another of them. A large number of people from the towns in the vicinity of Jerusalem also gathered, bringing the sick and those disturbed by unclean spirits, and they were all cured" (5:12–16). They handed this ministry down to the presbyters. That is why St. James in his letter said, "Is anyone among you sick? He should summon the presbyters of the Church and they should pray over him and anoint him with oil in the name of the Lord, and the prayers of faith will save the sick person, and the Lord will raise him up. If he has committed any sins, he will be forgiven" (James 5:13–15).

We can deduce two things from the statement of St. James: the anointing of the sick with oil heals the sick person, and the Lord will raise him/her up; also, the sins committed will be forgiven. That is why it is said that this sacrament has a dual function: healing of body and soul. Maybe it is the healing of the soul, that is, forgiveness of sins, that makes physical healing possible and faster. This agrees well with the Scripture. The Lord Jesus, before healing the paralytic, said, "Child, your sins are forgiven" (Mark 2:5). What does this mean? Spiritual healing comes prior to physical healing; in other words, spiritual healing helps physical healing. That is why we have the forgiveness of sins in the sacrament of the Anointing of the Sick.

This sacrament should be the best gift one could receive, along with good medical care. When we are sick, we might all be discouraged and disappointed at some point. This sacrament gives us the hope of healing, if that is the will of God. It gives us courage in the face of pain and suffering; it helps us unite our sufferings with the sufferings of the Lord. Thus, this sacrament enables us to go through the period of trial with the strength that comes from the Lord. Satan, whose intention is to drag people into disappointment and frustration, is defeated by the grace of this sacrament, because this sacrament is one of hope, peace, joy, and courage.

Today, this sacrament is administered to a Catholic who is sick, if he/she wishes to receive this sacrament. If the person is not in danger of death, this sacrament is administered in view of recovery by the grace of the sacrament. In this case, this sacrament is for both body and soul. The Lord raises up the person, as St. James says, by the merits of His Passion, Death and Resurrection, which is celebrated in the sacrament of the Anointing of the Sick.

A Bridge between Heaven and Earth

If the person is in danger of death for any reason, then this sacrament is the last rite or an extreme unction, preparing the person to meet the Lord; this sacrament then is not meant primarily for healing of the body, but for the soul. This sacrament, as the last rite or extreme unction, when received by a person with a true and sincere confession of his/her sins, anointing, and Viaticum (Communion) is a sure ticket to heaven. The *Catechism of the Catholic Church* (*CCC*) says that "if circumstances suggest it, the celebration of the sacrament can be preceded by the sacrament of Penance and followed by the sacrament of the Eucharist. As the sacrament of Christ's Passover, the Eucharist should always be the last sacrament of the earthly journey, the 'viaticum' for 'passing over' to eternal life" (1517). It is food for the journey. The Church does everything possible to help a person become the best version of himself or herself so that he/she can present himself or herself before the Lord without any fear.

When a person is sure of death, this sacrament fortifies the courage of that person to make that final journey, which can be frightening and difficult. This sacrament, then, assures the person of the nearness of Jesus, who will lead the person into the bosom of God. The final crossing from this world, to which the person was unduly attached, to the next world of everlasting peace and happiness can be hard as the person knew only the "joys" of this earthly life. Leaving behind the nest of family and friends, which the person wove over the years of life, becomes a struggle for many people. They get scared at the thought of death. Some people can be particularly frightened if they know they are not spiritually ready to make the final transition. I have seen many men and women who failed to lead a good life, admitting the fact that they failed to lead a just life and that their life was one of chaos. But the sacrament of the Anointing of the Sick, as the last rite, helps the person forget the world, helps him/her divest themselves of worldly garments and focus on a life of everlasting peace and joy, which will be his/hers very soon. This sacrament becomes a bridge that helps the person cross this world to the next, holding the hand of the Lord.

As a priest, I have anointed many people; but only a few times have I given extreme unction. One young man of thirty-three years old, who died shortly after receiving this sacrament, is worth mentioning here. I was on a home visit. It was almost sunset when the sacristan of my home parish called me on my home number. He said there was an emergency, and the pastor was out of town. He came to pick me up, and we went to the hospital. The man was in the cardiac ICU waiting for death. The medical team told me that there was nothing they could do at that time. His was a case of a massive heart attack, and all the cardiovascular arteries were damaged beyond repair. There was no hope even for a surgery. They said it was only a matter of time, at the most an hour. The only faint possibility was heart transplantation, but that was not practical, as there was no time to find a suitable heart. They told me that I could do whatever I needed to prepare him to face death.

He was from a good Catholic family; he practiced his faith and religion. He was married to a Catholic girl. But their marriage was a disaster. For some reason, he could not get along with his wife; people blamed him for his unhappy marriage. His wife lived in Dubai while their children stayed with him. He led a life estranged from others. When I entered the medical unit, he was conscious. I stood close to him. I saw a weak smile on his face. He knew his time was up! His feeble hand grabbed my white cassock and said he wished to see his wife. I said she had already been informed and that she was on her way. His second request was to give him the last rites. He said in a feeble voice that he was truly sorry for all the stupidities of life; how he wished to repair his life. There was no chance anymore. I anointed him and gave him the viaticum; I placed a tiny piece of sacred host in his partially open mouth. I was sure he was dying; his hands became loose on my garment. His breath became hard. I said the final prayer of commendation: "Go forth, Christian soul, from this world in the name of the

Almighty Father, who created you, in the name of Jesus Christ, Son of the living God, who suffered for you, in the name of the Holy Spirit, who was poured out upon you, go forth, faithful Christian. May you live in peace this day, may your home be with God in Zion, with Mary, the Virgin Mother of God, with Joseph, and all the angels and saints." He took just one more deep breath; his eyes rolled back; his hand fell off my garment. He was gone.

I am sure, as one who repented of the follies of his life, was anointed with the sacred oil, and fortified with Viaticum, he became the best version of himself. Though he failed to become the best version while he had time on earth, he became the best design God had in His mind when He created him in the womb of his mother, just before his death. I was glad that I could be there with him at the most crucial point of his death. I am sure he died a peaceful death; I believe that he felt reassured.

This is the time the Lord reassures us for the last time. He tells us: "Do not let your hearts be troubled. You have faith in God; have faith also in me. In my Father's house there are many dwelling places. If there were not, would I have told you that I am going to prepare a place for you? And if I go and prepare a place for you, I will come back again and take you to myself, so that where I am you also may be" (John 14:1–3). The Lord came back to take that young man with him to the mansion of God's kingdom. He walked into eternity holding the hand of the Lord.

The Final Defeat of Satan

With this sacrament, the Lord claims you and me for Himself. He defeats the power of Satan, who hoped to claim us to be his subjects. This sacrament snatches us away from the clutches of the enemy of God. Jesus carries us to the kingdom of God on His shoulders. In this sense, this sacrament also performs the function of the sacrament of Reconciliation, because this sacrament forgives our sins too. Recall what St. Peter says: "Your opponent the devil is prowling around like a roaring lion looking for someone to devour. Resist him, steadfast in faith" (1 Peter 5:8–9). This reminds me of the vultures that wait for their prey to fall dead so that they can feed on them. The wish of the prince of darkness is that we should die without repenting of our sins, that we should die in our sins so that he can claim us for his kingdom. As angels of God wait for us at our deathbed, to escort us to the mansion prepared by the Lord, there also is the devil prowling around our deathbed, wishing that we die without receiving the grace of the sacraments of the Church so that our souls might be lost to his power. When the Lord touches us for the very last time with the sacrament of the Anointing of the Sick, Satan is frustrated and defeated in his attempt. Therefore, we should make every effort to receive the last touch of the Lord, that touch which makes a world of difference here on earth, a touch that lets us behold the face of God and lets us inherit the kingdom prepared for us from the foundation of the world (cf. Matthew 25:34).

If we died in our sins, we would be defeating the purpose of the Lord. The Lord suffered and died a violent death for us so that we could have eternal life with Him. The very purpose of the Passion, Death and Resurrection, of the Lord was to save our souls, to claim us for God. If we are to die without receiving the graces that flow from the cross of the Lord through the sacraments of the Church, the one who is going to be happy is the devil, the enemy of God; he will grin at God. Even when we have the opportunity to receive the grace of the sacraments, if we turn our backs to the Lord, then we are siding with the devil; we are willfully choosing death; we are opting to be lost. When a person dies in his/her sins, there will be tears rolling down the cheeks of the Lord. On the contrary, even if a person led a sinful life, but decides to repent of his sins even at the point of death, that person will cause the Lord to breathe a sigh of relief. Definitely, that person will see the gates of paradise open and the Lord waiting for them with open arms to welcome him/her into the place of happiness.

While explaining the parable of the Lost Sheep, the Lord said, "It is not the will of your heavenly Father that one of these little ones be lost" (Matthew 18:14). He told us how eager he is in searching for the lost, how happy he becomes when he finds the lost sheep, how joyfully he carries it on his shoulders to the sheepfold. When the Lord spoke about the parable of the Prodigal Son, he pictured for us the anxieties of a father who awaits the return of his son. At the point of a person's death, the Lord becomes anxious, especially if that person led a wild life. The Lord wants us to repent, even at least on the deathbed. The desire of the Lord arises from His love for us and from His desire to claim our souls. The father in the parable rejoiced when his son came home after wandering for quite some time.

So does the Lord rejoice to see a person repenting of his past and closing his/her eyes in the bosom of the Lord. This is what the Lord speaks to us about through the prophet Ezekiel: "Do I find pleasure in the death of the wicked... ? Do I not rejoice when they turn from their evil way and live?" (18:23).

Frustration and Consolation

In the noontime of life I said, I must depart! To the gates of Sheol I have been consigned for the rest of my years. I said, I shall see the Lord no more in the land of the living. Nor look on any mortals among those who dwell in the world. My dwelling, like a shepherd's tent, is struck down and borne away from me; you have folded up my life, like a weaver who severs me from the last thread. From morning to night you make an end of me. Like a lion he breaks all my bones, from morning to night you make an end of me, like a swallow I chirp; I mourn like a dove. My eyes grow weary looking upward: Lord, I am overwhelmed; go security for me! What am I to say or tell him? He is the one who has done it! All my sleep has fled, because of the bitterness of my soul. Those live whom the Lord protects; yours is the life of my spirit. You have given me health and restored my life! Peace in place of bitterness! You have preserved my life from the pit of destruction; behind your back you cast all my sins. For it is not Sheol that gives you thanks, nor death that praises you; neither do those who go down into the pit await your kindness. The living, the living give you thanks, as I do today. Parents declare to their children, O God, your faithfulness. The Lord is there to save us. We shall play our music in the house of the Lord all the days of our life. (Isaiah 38:10–20).

I like to consider our life on earth as on a mission. When the Lord sent us to this world, He gave us a few years to live here on earth to complete the mission assigned to us. Maybe we spend too many years here, much more than we should have stayed. The additional years that we get are a bonus, a bounty of God. I think we sometimes forget that we are on a mission, on a project, and we should go back to the place where we belong. We try to stay on here on earth. All because we lose sight of our true home! We are expected to live here without getting attached to this world. As the Lord said, we are not of the world, we are not for the world. But we get ourselves entangled in the passing beauty of the world. The charm of this world sometimes blinds our vision of the glory of heaven. We never remember the Scripture: "Charm is deceptive and beauty is fleeting" (Proverbs 30:31). We run quite a while after the fleeting beauty of this world because the world God created is so beautiful. It is hard for us to resist temptations. I often wonder why the Lord created the world so beautiful!

It's not only my problem or your problem alone; it is the problem of the majority of people who are on vacation here on earth. They all get attached to this world below. They get attached so much to this world that they seem to replace their everlasting home with this passing world. That is why most of us are afraid to return; that is why most people are scared of death. If we had kept heaven as our only goal, we would have longed to die, because death is that medium through which God realizes heaven for us, through which God calls us to be with Him. Death is not a foe, he is a friend. The end of life here on earth is the actual beginning of real life, a life that will see no death.

Visiting people who are sick and old, especially the homebound, is a very humbling experience for me. Most people tell me how much they wish to die, how much they wished to go to heaven. Some of them would tell me of their frustrations in life: how they wished to walk back to repair their unsatisfactory past. Let me write down for you what a gentleman who died a few months ago told me: "Now I am old and weak, this passing world is of no interest to me anymore. I want to get to heaven. You know that there is nothing like heaven! I am lying in my sickbed now. I can feel my body breaking down. I feel my strength failing, my vision becomes blurred. I hear the footsteps of death around me. When I close my eyes, I see the dark shadows of someone I never saw before in my life looming around me. I am partially scared, partially relieved. The past episodes of my life flash in my memory like pages of a book I read, flipping in the wind. All the episodes are not very clean, that is why I am terrified of this inevitable moment. All the pages are not well written, I know. There is no way I can walk back now to rewrite the pages, though I truly wish to do so. I don't think I have enough time to rearrange every page I flipped by. I feel like hurrying back a few yards and ripping those shabby chapters out of the book of my life. But I know He will not wait that long now. Maybe I am too late."

"I was not a bad Catholic. Rather, I tried to be my best, though I failed miserably. Each time I failed, I resumed the remaining leg of my journey with renewed vigor and stronger resolutions. I am here now, almost at the end of the road. The last leg of my journey was no fun at all. Most of those who started out with me are no more with me. They have all preceded me in death. I wish to join them soon. I wish to walk with them once again in the Garden of Eden."

But we know that we don't have to strain too much, when we are old and sick, to walk back to our past to rectify the wrongs of life, because there is someone else the Lord is sending with some special power who can erase those illegible writings from the episode of life. He is the priest of God, who walks toward us with the last chance the Lord offers to us to put things right here, to prepare us to glide into another, far better region of life, like a migratory bird that flies to a more conducive place to live. His anointing is the last touch of the Lord. We don't remember the first touch the Lord gave us; perhaps we were too small to remember that. But we should be glad now, because we are conscious to remember His last touch upon our soul. As Isaiah made a poultice of figs and applied it to a boil for Hezekiah's recovery (cf. Isaiah 38:21), the priest applies the oil with which the Lord heals us spiritually.

Let us humbly thank the Lord for the sacrament of the Anointing of the Sick, which He instituted for the healing of our soul and body. Like all other sacraments, this one makes a profound difference in our life. Let us thank the Lord for viaticum, the food for our last journey. When we are struck with some mortal illness, this sacrament strengthens our life; it gives us hope and courage to fight the disease. At our moment of despair, this sacrament reminds us that the Lord is close to us, to lead us on. What a great comfort it brings to us when the priest anoints us! This sacrament is a reminder that death is not the end of the journey; rather, it is the beginning of a new journey to the Promised Land.

CHAPTER 7

Men Who Touch Your Soul

I will appoint for you shepherds after my own heart,
who will shepherd you wisely and prudently.
—Jeremiah 3:15

God said to Abraham, "Go forth from your land, your relatives, and from your father's house to a land that I will show you. I will make of you a great nation, and I will bless you; I will make your name great, so that you will be a blessing" (Genesis 12:1–2). This passage can be applied to Pope Francis. God called him from a place far from where he is now; he left behind his own diocese, people, relatives, and friends to go over to a new place. There he became—and still becomes—a blessing to the entire Church; God made his name great. This is also true in the case of every bishop, priest, and deacon, especially those who are sent as missionaries overseas. For example, I am a missionary here, in the United States. I came away from my own land, left behind my relatives and my parents; I came to an unknown place, far from my country. I don't know if I have become a blessing to many people, though that is certainly my intention!

But I am sure I touch the souls of at least a few people in my own way. God blesses the lives of the people that I serve; God blesses them through my priestly ministry.

God makes us the "eighth sacrament," an outward sign, a symbol of God's grace to others. Our call is to become a blessing to others. A person becomes the eighth sacrament by the reception of the sacraments of the Church, which are, as you know, the visible signs of God's invisible graces. The ordained ministers of God become coworkers of Jesus in making us the eighth sacrament of God. So the purpose of the sacrament of Holy Orders is to help us become the eighth sacrament of God in the world! Holy Orders consecrate men to administer the sacraments of the Church. Without the sacraments of the Church, a person cannot fully become what God intended in His eternal mind. Without the sacraments, there is no life for the Church. Therefore, without the sacrament of Holy Orders, there is no Church.

Ordained Ministers Are the Coworkers of God Who Touch the Soul

The ordained ministers of God are great because they help Him complete the final touch of His masterpiece on the soul of the human being! God brings forth you and me through our parents in the sacrament of Matrimony, the canvas on which God paints us (I am sure I have said this many times by now!). Once we are portrayed, I mean, once we are born, the care of souls is given over to the ordained ministers of God, who nurture them with the sacraments of the Church. They help us become the best we can be, a masterpiece of God through the grace of the sacraments.

Ministers of Holy Orders are the coartists (not exactly like our parents, who had a different role) with God because they can help actualize the idea or the design that existed in His mind through the sacraments of the Church. It is they who work with and for the souls. The sacrament of Holy Orders makes possible the other sacraments, which touch souls. It is through their hands, through the hands of men in Holy Orders, that the soul of a masterpiece of God, a human being, becomes holy and immaculate enough to stand before the Creator. They give the final touch to the artworks of God. Therefore, the sacrament of Holy Orders is of utmost importance because Holy Orders directly deals with the souls of individuals. The Lord said, "It is the spirit that gives life, while the flesh is of no avail" (John 6:63). It would seem then that the works of the ordained ministers of God are more significant than those of other people serving in different walks of life, because while other people, like doctors, deal with the "flesh" side of life, the ministers of Holy Orders deal with the soul.

The Lord said that it is the soul, the spirit, that gives life. Yes, it is so true. When we look at some artistic work, we feel it comes alive because it has a "soul." We don't experience this feeling with every artwork, but only those with a soul. In a similar way, we become alive because we have a soul. We are dead when the soul, the spirit, leaves our body. Therefore, it seems that we should admit that the work of those who work with the body and the soul is more important than that of those who work only with the body. I am trying to emphasize how important the sacrament of Holy Orders is to the Catholic population; how lucky we are because we have men who can touch souls. It is an amazing touch; it is a healing touch; it is a perfecting touch; it is a divine touch.

Priests: The Visible Presence of an Invisible God

When we spoke about the sacrament of Baptism, we said that the Lord planted us by the streams of running waters, the Church, which is the fountain of everlasting grace. The hands that planted you were the hands of a priest or deacon. The Lord worked through his ordained men. He was using their hands to give us the very first touch of life in our souls. It was their hands that made the very first sign of the cross on your forehead; it was their hands that anointed your supple forehead and soft breast with the oil of salvation; it was their hands that poured water over your head; it was their hands that anointed you with the sacred chrism; it was their hands that clothed you with a white garment; it was their hands that gave you the lighted candle that represented Christ the light; it was their hands that touched your ears to hear the word of God and your mouth to proclaim what you hear. They did these actions in the name of Christ. Their hands, indeed, were the hands of God!

The unseen hands of God follow us all through our life, though various sacraments administered to us by the ministers. Perhaps you are old enough to know the significance of a priest in the life of a Catholic, and hopefully you go to Church at least on Sundays as a committed Catholic. What makes Sunday so very special to a Catholic is the Eucharist. Who makes it, then, so very special? Is it not a priest, through whom God gives us the sacred Body and Blood? Yes, it is. As long as you live, and as long as the Church exists, there will be a priest for you, because you need the Eucharist; because without the Eucharist, there is no Church. Sundays are special not only to you, but also to many other people who practice their faith. The priest is instrumental in making Sunday special. He makes the lives of hundreds of thousands of people very special. He is instrumental in making the lives of Catholics joyful and meaningful by the celebration of the Eucharist.

Every morning as I go to church, I see a crowd waiting for me. They are waiting for the Eucharist, and only I, the priest, can bring it to them: no one else! There are very many people who have told me that they feel incomplete and missing something if they don't attend Holy Mass every day. Who helps them feel complete every morning? Is it not a priest? Who helps them start their day with the most sublime act of worship? It is a priest.

As you take part in the Eucharist, you see him at the altar raising his hands in prayer. He is pleading with God, with his hands raised for you at the altar of the Lord; he is pleading with God to have mercy on us. Standing between the altar and the sanctuary, he is mediating between God and the faithful. God receives the sacrifice that we offer on the altar through the instrumentality of that priest. He proclaims the Word of God to us; he explains the many nuances of the Word, perhaps ones we hadn't even realized. He inspires us and motivates us—

sometimes corrects us and, at other times, guides us with his words of wisdom. How would we receive the Word of God if he did not proclaim it for us?

Haven't you seen the priest at the altar doing extraordinary things? I have seen, and I do see it every time I attend Mass. The Lord makes Himself present in the Eucharist, the symbol of His everlasting love, through the instrumentality of that priest. The bread and wine that is offered up on the altar is transubstantiated into the Body and Blood of the Lord by the working of the Holy Spirit through the hands of the priest at the altar. He continues to perform this extraordinary thing every time he celebrates Mass. As long as you go to church, you will see the wonderment of God in the form of the Body and Blood of the Lord, the miracle that the Holy Spirit performs through the hands of a priest. When it is time for Communion, it is the priest who gives you the Body and Blood of the Lord, the very life of Christ. He is the agent of God who infuses the divine life into a mortal being. At the end of the Mass, he who gave you the life of the Lord also imparts the choicest blessing of God upon you so that your onward journey may be heavenward.

Later on, we will visit a place called the confessional, where we should receive often the grace of the sacrament of Reconciliation. There in the confessional, as we humbly and with tears unload the burden of our life filled with the filth of sin, our failures, and pitfalls, and we plead for forgiveness, the very same priest taps us on our shoulders with reassurance. As we fumble before him, he bends down and draws with his finger on the floor, as the Lord did in the Bible (cf. John 8:1–11); then he straightens up to pour on us his words of consolation, with the love and mercy of the Good Shepherd, and tells us that a restart is possible. At the end of it all, he tells us that our sins are forgiven. As in the parable of the Lost Sheep (Luke 15:1–7), he carries us back to the fold of God's flock by being in the confessional, sometimes for many long hours. Though it is Christ who carries us back, the shoulder Jesus uses is that of his priest. As in the parable of the Good Samaritan, he binds up our wounds caused by sins; he pours over our wounds the oil of healing; he carries us back to the inn, the Church (cf. Luke 10:29–37).

In the parable of the Prodigal Son (Luke 15:11–32), we see the father waiting for the son to return; when he comes back, he embraces him and welcomes him back into his household. This is what happens when a penitent comes into the confessional. God the Father waits for him/her. But today, it is done by the priest on behalf of the Lord. You are accepted back into the warmth of the family of God by the priest. He is the one who is the instrument of God's forgiveness. God showers his forgiveness and mercy in the sacrament of Reconciliation through a priest (cf. John 20:23). How blessed are we to know that we are forgiven for our great and small sins alike. If the Lord hadn't instituted the sacrament of Holy Orders and appointed the priest to forgive our sins, what would have become of our life?

We can certainly see all the other sacraments in the same manner. God gives you the sacrament of Confirmation, a bishop ordains one to Holy Orders, an ordained minister becomes a witness to the sacrament of Matrimony, and he anoints the sick, the final touch of God on the soul of an individual. In short, an ordained minister helps you become the best version of yourself in this world for the Lord. In that sense, the ministers of Holy Orders are men who reshape our life; they give you and me, the artworks of God, the perfecting touches, so that the design that existed in the mind of God, even before our birth, may be realized. The design that God had in His mind, of course, was of a masterpiece. But as human beings, fashioned in the image of God but brought into life by human instrumentality, we are not perfect. That is why the Lord makes use of ministers through the sacrament of Holy Orders to perfect us by the sacraments of the Church and turn us into His masterpieces; thus, we realize the design that He had in his mind before our birth. We cannot become the best versions of ourselves without the aid of the sacraments. Therefore, the Lord instituted Holy Orders so that He could have men who are dedicated to perfecting God's work in the world.

Men in Holy Orders Are Prophets Who Announce the Word of God

In the book of Deuteronomy, Moses spoke to the people: "A prophet like me will the Lord, your God, raise up for you from among your own kindred; that is the one to whom you shall listen. This is exactly what you requested of the Lord, your God, at Horeb on the day of the assembly, when you said, 'Let me not again hear the voice of the Lord, my God, nor see this great fire anymore, or I will die.' And the Lord said to me, what they have said is good. I will raise up for them a prophet like you from among their kindred, and will put my words into the mouth of the prophet; the prophet shall tell them all what I command. Anyone who will not listen to my words which the prophet speaks in my name, I myself will hold accountable for it." (Deuteronomy 18:15–19).

This passage, later on, came to be understood in a quasi-Messianic sense in the New Testament. When Jesus comes as the fulfillment of all the prophets and prophecies, we see Him proclaiming the Word of God with authority; Jesus can be understood as fulfilling what Moses foretold in the book of Deuteronomy. God raised up Jesus, who brings the Good News of the kingdom of God. And Jesus, in turn, selected his apostles from among the people to forward His mission, to continue to proclaim the Gospel in name of the Lord.

After the Resurrection, we see the Lord commissioning the apostles: "All power in heaven and on earth has been given to me. Go, therefore, and make disciples of all nations, baptizing them in the name of the Father, and of the Son, and of the Holy Spirit, teaching them to observe all that I have commanded you. And behold, I am with you always, until the end of the ages" (Matthew 28:18–20). They spoke for the Lord; they spoke to the world what the Lord commanded them to speak. They, in turn, chose men to succeed their ministry (cf. Acts. 14:23). Thus we have the Pope, bishops, priests, and deacons, who announce the word of the Lord directly to the people. They do it by teaching, governing, and sanctifying.

The Lord said to the prophet Jeremiah, "Today I appoint you over nations and kingdoms, to uproot and to tear down, to destroy and to demolish, to build and to plant" (Jeremiah 1:10). This is the basic call of everyone within Holy Orders.

They are called, chosen, and appointed by the Lord for two complementary missions. The first one is a negative mission, to uproot and to tear down, to destroy and to demolish. But this negative mission is geared toward a positive one, to build and to plant, which is the second mission. As we know, the men in Holy Orders are called to serve the Lord in his vineyard, to cultivate and to grow the kingdom of God by announcing the Gospel message. This cultivation will not take place—this "building and planting" will not be fruitful—without first preparing the ground. So when the Lord appoints them over nations and kingdoms, "uproot and to tear down, to destroy and to demolish," the ultimate and the more desired commission is to build and to plant. But to build and to plant, they first have to tear things down; they may have to demolish or destroy the existing corrupt systems. If they try to build and plant without first demolishing corrupt practices, which are against the mind of the Lord, then their work will not bear fruit. Before they can sow the seeds, they need to cultivate the ground. So uprooting, tearing down, destroying, and demolishing are all part of cultivating the ground in view of sowing the seed, that is, building and planting.

This is no easy task. This calls for real courage on the part of the clergy. Preaching is the tool that the clergy most often use to uproot and to tear down, to destroy and to demolish. Down through the centuries, the Church uses this means to call people to correct their ways. One of the reasons the Church became unpopular and the clergy became so intimidated is because the world fears the truth that the Church tries to proclaim. The actual context of laying the groundwork can be tough, since most people don't like to be challenged. In today's context, most people don't like to be corrected. They are rebellious toward correction. Even so-called practicing Catholics can become hostile toward clergy who tell the truth, because they don't practice what they should.

For example: one day, at the end of the 8:45 a.m. Mass, to which many people came late (a habit of many people of many parishes), I said with a smile as I always do, "Remember, eighty forty-five Mass starts at eight forty-five." I did not add to or cut anything from what I said. After the Mass, as I was greeting people at the door, two ladies, one in her late seventies and the other in her late fifties, were greatly upset by what I said. The older lady said that people have all sorts of reasons to be late for Mass and that the Lord does not care about their being late. I tried to explain to her that I did not mean anyone in particular, but that it was only a friendly reminder. However, she still was not happy! The other lady said she likes to think it is "better late than never," a cliché! She disagreed with what I said. Remember, I was only reminding, not accusing. She said, "Father, there are many, many people who go to Sunday Mass in very short shorts, and I am very upset with it. Why don't you tell them about that?" She did not like to hear about being on time for Mass because it challenged her. She prefers to hear about being modestly dressed or well dressed for Mass because she doesn't struggle with that. This is called a double standard. That is what I mean when I say people don't like to hear anything that challenges them.

Today, unfortunately, the homilies of a good many priests remain up in the air; they don't directly touch the life of anyone. Their homilies are no longer sharp, to the point. They don't challenge the life of the faithful because people don't like it when that happens. If the priest preached about the moral fabric of society, which, as you know, is the single most important issue of our culture, he would be in trouble. If he talks against the practice of contraceptives among the faithful, people who practice it become upset; if he preaches on the ill effects of divorce, people get upset, because there are a number of people who are divorced; if he preaches against cohabitation, people become upset, because there are many young people who live together; if he preaches against premarital sex, almost everyone is upset, because today, so many do it. What else should a priest preach about? People like to hear statements like "God is love, God is merciful, God forgives" statements that pleases everyone. But this does not address the actual spiritual dilemma of our times. This is an example of how priests have to fulfil their prophetic role of uprooting and tearing down, destroying and demolishing, *before* they can begin to build and plant.

Whether people like to hear it or not, the priests have the duty to tell them. That is the nature of the prophetic role. They have to speak what the Lord wants them to speak, not what people like to hear. One weakness of the Church in the Western world, and a reason people have lost all sense of right and wrong in their practicing the faith, is that the clergy no longer bother to correct the people; they no longer take the trouble to challenge the practices. They are afraid of the reactions of the people. Therefore, our churches have become hubs where anyone can simply hang out. People are so sensitive to any issue, the clergy seem not to take the trouble. They wonder why they should take the risk and be in trouble. It is all because the people, the beneficiaries of the sacrificial lives of the clergy, are not willing to be obedient to the spiritual authority of the Church. The rebellious attitude of the people has caused our clergy to be very cautious and wary in teaching and preaching the truth.

There are many other issues that are not right in the Western Catholic world, which are also reflected in the practicing of faith. But very seldom do we find any directives from the part of the Church, not even a reminder to the people. Today there aren't many priests who have the courage and interest to exercise the spiritual authority, which has been given to them by the Lord. Your priest is a prophet! He should fulfil his prophetic role. A prophet is one who becomes the voice of God whom God calls to announce His will. Prophets are expected to make structures and so-called conservatives nervous. They challenge the status quo and try to incite people to change and correct their way of life. This is what every priest should do in his homilies, by relating the Word of God to our life situations, which may be sinful, unholy, and unbecoming. As we saw in the book of Jeremiah, every priest is ordained to uproot and to tear down, to destroy and to demolish, to build and to plant. If the people were willing to take corrections in a good spirit, our Church could be much stronger. The clergy, along with the people, could build a spiritual edifice for the Lord; they could plant a beautiful vineyard for the Lord.

Priests Have Authority over You

The authority of men in Holy Orders is not a physical authority; we saw that earlier. You have to remember that your pastor
is your father, as you call him "Fr. Joe" or "Fr. Bill" etc. As a
father, he has the authority and right to correct you. It seems
he should be given that freedom. Doesn't he have the right to
point out weakness, with love and compassion? When that
lady was upset with me about my reminder on the time Mass
begins, I asked her if I had the freedom to even remind them.
If your priest does not have even that basic freedom to remind
you of the basic disciplinary matters in parish life, it seems he
should not be called *Father*. When someone, be it your priest
or another, challenges you about something you do that you
should not, or something you don't do what you are expected
to do, don't consider that person your enemy, whom you should
avoid in the future; take it as an opportunity to correct yourself,
a God-sent opportunity for growth in your spiritual life. That is
an example of mature spirituality.

The authority of the Church comes from the authority of
Christ (cf. Matthew 28:16–20). If Christ had no authority, the
Church wouldn't have any authority. It is to be noted that the
authority of Christ was not a physical authority (cf. John 18:36),
but a moral and spiritual authority. Therefore, the authority of
the Church also is moral and spiritual. The authority of the
Church today is exercised by the magisterium of the Church, by
means of teaching, governing, and sanctifying. When the magisterium teaches, we, as faithful followers of the Lord, have the
duty to follow the teaching. We cannot say that we love Jesus

but don't want to obey His teachings that come through the Church. Christ and the Church are not different, but one and the same. If we say we love Christ, we have to obey the commandments of the Church; the commandments of the Church are the commandments of Jesus. The Lord said, "If you love me, you will keep my commandments" (John 14:15).

When couples come to arrange their weddings, I first ask them if they are Catholics. Today we cannot presume that all are Catholics. They may say, "Oh, yes, we are baptized. We received our First Holy Communion." I would ask them, "Well, are you *practicing* Catholics?" Unfortunately, we cannot presume today that people are practicing. They often say, "You know, Father, I love God, I love Jesus, I love the Church, I love my faith." "You did not answer my question. Are you *practicing* your faith?" "Well, Father, my parents are really involved with Church." "*No.* My question is: are *you* practicing your faith?" They avoid the question because, as you can imagine, the answer would be "Not as much as I would like to." In short, they are not practicing their faith. They say they love God, Christ, Church, their faith. But if they don't practice their faith, this is a contradictory statement. If they love God, they will keep His commandments. So if they don't keep the commandments of Christ and the Church, it means they don't have any real love for Christ or the Church.

This is true when people come to arrange someone's funeral as well. People will say, "You know Father, my dad was a good person. He loved God, loved his faith, and loved the Church. But for some reason, he did not practice his faith." That, too, is a lie. If he cared about his faith or if he had any love for the Lord and the Church, he would have kept the commandments; he would have practiced his faith at least by going to Sunday Mass and by receiving the grace of the sacraments.

As you can see then, loving the Lord means keeping His commandments. The commandments of the Church come to us after much prayer and reflection, discernment, and study by the college of Bishops, with the Pope as the head. Therefore, when a teaching becomes a dogma, we cannot simply rule it out or disregard it. If we do so, the Lord will hold us accountable. The Lord said if "anyone who will not listen to my words which the prophet speaks in my name, I myself will hold accountable for it" (Deuteronomy 18:19). Before we disregard a teaching of the Church, which came, as we stated already, as the result of long prayerful reflection, serious study, consultation, and discernment by the college of bishops, we must have the humility to ask ourselves what credential or qualification we have to challenge or ignore that teaching.

The Lord governs the life of the faithful through the Church. To be more specific, today the Lord continues to sanctify our life through men who are in Holy Orders. They are, as we saw in the book of Deuteronomy, chosen from ourselves by the Lord to teach, to govern, and to sanctify. Since they are chosen from among us, they are, of course, weak as we all are. Just because the Lord called them to be men of Holy Orders, their human nature does not change. So they can make mistakes. But that is no excuse for us to disregard what they say or command. If we obey them, we obey the Lord; if we reject them, we reject the Lord, because they are the people appointed by the Lord to bring his will and preach his word. If we obey them, we will live; if we reject them, the Lord will hold us accountable, as we saw in the book of Deuteronomy.

A priest is also your leader; you should allow him to lead you. He is certainly your shepherd, and no good shepherd would ever lead the flock to dangerous places, as a father or mother wouldn't want a son or daughter to go a bad direction in life. So allow him to lead you to good pastures (cf. Psalm 23).

The priests must certainly lead, guide, shepherd, inspire, and motivate, but they should also correct people. They should correct the people under their care with love and compassion, not like a tyrant. See the advice of St. Peter to presbyters: "Tend the flock of God in your midst, [overseeing] not by constraint but willingly, as God would have it, not for shameful profit but eagerly. Do not lord it over those assigned to you, but be examples to the flock" (1 Peter 5:2–3). If they don't do it, they fail in their duty. I have seen many priests permitting everything in their parishes; people call them great priests when in fact those priests are not building up the people of God; they rather destroy the parish by letting people do whatever they want. Those priests who don't bother to say no to people are "people pleasers." They are merely looking for a "good conduct certificate" from people. But that is not for what they are appointed.

Priests are God's soldiers or guards whose job is to stand and keep watch and to inform the people of imminent attacks. In the Old Testament, the prophet Ezekiel was called a sentinel, a guard. A sentinel's duty was to watch for any enemy coming to their land. He had to warn the people of possible attack from their enemies. If people heard a sentinel's warning but did not take timely action and thereby died, it would be their mistake;

the sentinel would be free of blame because he warned them, but they did not take his warning. But if the sentinel saw the sword coming and did not blow the trumpet, and as a result, the sword killed the people, the sentinel would be held responsible. Hear what the Lord said to Ezekiel: "You, son of man—I have appointed you as a sentinel for the house of Israel; when you hear a word from my mouth, you must warn them for me. When I say to the wicked, 'You wicked, you must die,' and you do not speak up to warn the wicked about their ways, they shall die in their sins, but I will hold you responsible for their blood. If, however, you warn the wicked to turn from their ways, but they do not, then they shall die in their sins, but you shall save your life" (Ezekiel 33:7–9). If the priests do not say what they should, God will hold them accountable like the sentinel.

The basic call of every priest is to build God's kingdom by announcing the Gospel. Remember the call of the prophet Jeremiah: "Today I appoint you over nations and over kingdoms, to uproot and to tear down, to destroy and to demolish, to build and to plant" (1:9–10). The Lord places the Word in the mouth of priests who stand at the pulpit to preach. They sometimes will have to demolish, destroy, tear down, and uproot so that they can build and plant. It may be hard for us to go through the demolition process, but it is essential to true conversion. Therefore, please don't get upset when your priests preach a homily that might hurt your feelings. Take it as an opportunity to renew your life.

One Man Dies for Many

"Amen, amen, I say to you, unless a grain of wheat falls to the ground and dies, it remains just a grain of wheat; but if it dies, it produces much fruit. Whoever loves his life loses it, and whoever hates his life in this world will preserve it for eternal life" (John 12:24–25). This quote is true particularly in the case of priests. Priests are people who sacrifice their life for many. They leave behind their family and things that are very personal and dear to them to take up the challenge of the Lord to follow Him. They leave behind their "boats and nets" to follow the Lord to be "fishers of men." The price that they pay is not cheap. The cost of that discipleship is immeasurable. But I think each and every priest—at least most of them—are happy in their vocation; they are happy to give up everything that is dear to them because they know that their "dying" produces life for many; their losing is saying yes to gain for many. When they die, like a grain of wheat, they produce much harvest. From each grain there come forth many grains to the glory of God. Each priest dies in his vocation; but he touches the souls of many, and the impact he creates in the life of the faithful is beyond compare. Each of them produces fruits that cannot be measured.

We read in the Scripture what Caiaphas, the high priest, said regarding the death of Jesus: "It is better for you that one man should die instead of the people, so that the whole nation may not perish" (John 11:50). Caiaphas was prophesying the death of Jesus. Though he said it maliciously to get rid of the "troublemaker," what he spoke revealed the very purpose of the life, death, and resurrection of the Lord. Jesus died so that we could have life. Like one single grain, Jesus fell down and died, and the world as a whole received salvation. This is applicable to the life of priests too. Each priest is like a grain that falls down when they decide to accept the call to priesthood. When they sacrifice their life for the service of people and the Lord, the prophecy of Caiaphas comes true. Their struggles and sacrifices, often unnoticed by the public, bear many spiritual and material fruits that certainly outweigh their struggles and sacrifices. Thus, their life becomes a blessing to many. For example, what if I became sad or lonely so you could be happy in life? What if I go hungry or thirsty so you are fed with the Bread of Life? When I, a single man, fall to the ground through many sacrifices, there is an entire parish that benefits from my sacrifices. I, for one, agree with what Caiaphas said. What would become of the spiritual life of the faithful if no one followed the invitation of the Lord to priesthood, because they did not want to make any sacrifices? The life of a priest is fulfilling when the spiritual life of the faithful is fulfilled.

Every morning as I step out of my bed, I have a smile on my face because I know there is a group of people, however small it may be, waiting for me. What they are waiting for can be done only by a priest. The picture of people waiting for me inspires me. I forget everything else that might stand in my way.

I received a card on the day of my ordination to priesthood from a middle-aged nun. I don't exactly remember the wording, but the content of the card was something like this: "If you are on time, people will say your watch is fast; if you are late by a few minutes, they will say you are holding up the people; if you are well-dressed, they will say that you are stylish; if you don't care about your dressing style, they will say you are not culture-conscious; if your homily is short, they will say you are not well prepared; if you go long, they will say you are windy; if you decorate the church, they will say you are over-spending; if you don't, they will say you don't care. But, when you die, no one else can do what you do except another priest."

The life of a priest is one of many sacrifices. They give up everything that the world considers important. The Lord chooses men for himself and appoints them for the lives of the faithful so that through their sacrificial life, they can produce much fruit, fruit that will last. I think the fruits that last are the fruits of the Spirit of which we spoke earlier, in the section on Confirmation. The Lord said, "I chose you and appointed you to go and bear fruit that will remain" (John 15:16). The labor of priests brings out the best for the Lord: the salvation of souls.

Lord, we thank You from the depth of our hearts for the sacrament of Holy Orders, with which You continue to sanctify our life; You impart grace to our life; You lead our life on the path of holiness. The existence of Your Church is centered on the Holy Eucharist, and the Holy Eucharist is possible only if there is priesthood. I cannot imagine any life for the Church without the Eucharist, and the Eucharist can be enacted only through the priesthood. You told us, "I will give you shepherds after my own heart who will feed them with finest wheat" (Jeremiah 3:15). How true! Every priest is a shepherd who feeds us with the finest wheat, the Eucharist. Actually, we are nourished by the Bread, which the life of a priest makes possible.

Being a Priest Is Not Easy; Please Try to Understand Them

Remember what the Lord spoke through the prophet: I will raise up for them a prophet like you from among their kindred. This means that your priest is your relative, from your own family; he belongs to you! He is like you, not very much different from you. He has all the traits and characteristics that you and your children have. In other words, he has all the strengths and weaknesses that every one of us has. It seems that most people forget this general human nature. We must remember that our priests have been chosen from among ourselves to serve us. Therefore, we need to consider them normal human beings. If you think that you have many weaknesses of your own, then your priest also will have many weaknesses. It would be unfair to say that priests should be above all weaknesses.

Sometimes I become frustrated over the fact that people are insensitive to the life of priests. They don't grasp the pressure and stress of being a priest. They expect priests to be iron men. Whatever may be said, the life of a priest is not a "normal" life. Ordinary life is what laypeople lead, life in a family setting. The ordinary call of a person, I believe, is to married life—to be husband, wife, and parents. Therefore, at some point, the emotional life of some priests might manifest itself. I know people don't expect it to be so, but it is quite possible. The majority of priests contain their emotions well, not because they don't have feelings or emotions; but on the contrary, they, through constant practice, learn to discipline their mind and body so that they can serve the Lord by being at the service of people.

That is a big sacrifice. Try to recall what we spoke about: one man dying for many. Therefore, if something should go wrong, people should stand by the priest, because it is for them that they have taken up their life's challenge. Don't try to magnify the problem; try to understand them with compassion.

I have seen many priests, whom people loved, who were said to be great priests, who later experienced very sad, unexpected turns of events. I begin to realize that it doesn't take much for the people to forget the many hardships and sacrifices of a priest. One small failure can be enough for all the many good things a priest does to be forgotten. When they are accused of something by people, be it child abuse or financial issues or authority-related issues, the vast majority of the crowd believes what is said of them; those priests become strangers to the very people whom they served. People seem to forget all the many sacrifices and hardships the priests underwent and the many services they received from those great priests. In some cases, even the diocese may refuse to stand by them. Most often they are left by themselves to fight for justice. If their reputation is tarnished unjustly, they become a laughing stock and a byword even among other priests; if they are laicized due to any reason—sometimes even due to false accusations, since anyone can accuse any priest, and it is the duty of the accused to prove his innocence; it kills his reputation—they become helpless out in the world since they are not trained or qualified for any other job. There, no one cares about the life and the future of those men who served the Church, perhaps for many years. They become misfits, like fish out of water.

As a priest, I am constantly under pressure and stress, especially at a time when anyone can falsely accuse a priest, even many years after his death. When a child steps into the confessional and closes the door, my heart begins to pound faster. Sometimes, especially if the child is new to the sacrament, he/she is tense; he/she might even cry in the confessional. When I see them cry, I get scared, because when the child steps out of the confessional, I am not sure what the child is going to tell the parents, because they may not understand the situation. They might think that their child is crying because the priest inside the confessional did or said something wrong. I can be vulnerable; so much so that I encourage the little ones to leave the door open as they step into the confessional so that I may be safe. When I go to other parishes to hear confessions, especially of schoolkids, if there is a choice, I take an open confessional. When a child runs into me to hug me, I act a bit cold; I try not to touch, even the so-called safe touch. I wish to detach from the embrace as soon as possible for fear of consequences. I sometimes feel that I am losing my warmth; I become artificial. These are some of the stresses of a priest. It is hard to understand what a priest is going through.

There are many priests around the world who often feel bored, dejected, unwanted, uncared for, misunderstood, and unfairly criticized. People often do not notice their hard work, but magnify their weaknesses. Sometimes they are singled out for the mistakes or weaknesses of someone else. There are people who say priests are pedophiles, an unfair statement. My heart aches and breaks when people seem to think that priests must be beyond all human weakness, when people forget that priests are like themselves. I feel sad when people expect me to be without feelings and emotions, as though I must be a man with a stone heart!

This is what a priest friend of mine who serves in the United Kingdom told me: "At the end of the day, when I return to the rectory on certain winter days, a gloom descends on me. After all the hard work and stress of the day, who is there to wait for me or to care for me, comfort me and console me! Sitting in the half-cold or unheated room, I stare at the setting sun. As the sun disappears behind the horizon, I have asked myself many times, what was it all for? Or for whom did I labor?"

"On certain holidays like Christmas and Easter, while people all celebrate and make merry with their family and friends, I am here in my rectory without even a good dinner. A priest like me whose family is far away has to be happy with a drink and leftovers from the previous day. Who cares to understand the lonely life of a priest? While people all give and receive gifts, I think most people take it for granted giving a gift to their priests, who wear out in their service."

One Christmas is still vivid in my memory. I was a resident priest at a parish when I was completing my master's degree. The pastor was a seventy-three-year-old man. The parish was attached to a convent where there were around forty nuns. The parish church belonged to the nuns; it was their oratory. The diocese was making use of their oratory since it had no building of its own. Nobody sent any cards to the pastor or to me; no one brought any cake to the rectory (it is much better here in this part of the world. Out of three thousand families that I serve, I usually get some sixty to seventy cards. Some people bring some cookies, chocolates, or cakes). It was Christmas night. After the midnight Mass, people all hurried back to their homes for celebrations. We came to the rectory around two in the morning. We had two Masses to say the following morning, within a few hours. After the morning Masses, there was no breakfast for us! The pastor cut the cake, and we greeted each other. I went down to a small restaurant and got some breakfast for the pastor and myself. We were all by ourselves for lunch and dinner, which were bought from the same restaurant. I was shocked over the fact that even the nuns did not think to bring some food over to the rectory. I tell this story here just to show how priests can be forgotten by the people they serve all their lives.

As for now, I am young. After Masses on Sundays, there are a few people who come up and say, "Good job, Father," "Thank you for the Mass," "Awesome job," or "You are the best." But my heart does not leap at these compliments, for I know they will soon forget me. As I grow older, they will look for younger priests. I will eventually be forgotten. When I retire, I will be confined to a home for the retired clergy, where no one will come to see me. People who said "You are the best ever" will not even send me a postcard. This I have heard from many retired clergy. I have also learned it from my own experience as I reflect on the life of a retired priest who did a lot for the people of the parish that I serve now. No one ever speaks of him now. One day I asked my people: "How many of you think of Father so-and-so?" Only a few raised their hands. "How many of you ever have taken him out to a lunch or a dinner after he moved from here?" There were no hands. "How many of you send a postcard to him?" None! I know this may be my lot too. After having spent my whole life at the service of people, I am going to be forgotten by them.

Once I asked a priest, who has been in his present assignment for more than twelve years, if he thinks everyone who goes to his church has said hello to him at least once. He said he didn't think so. As you know, most people go to church only on Sundays. That is the only time you and your priest get a chance to meet. It will not be possible for your priest to go to each person every Sunday since there may be hundreds of people, and he may have multiple Masses. But if you try, you can go to him at least after Mass as you go out of the church. That simple gesture shows your appreciation for your priest who spends his entire life in your service.

Let me ask you a few more questions. This is not to embarrass you, but to make you think. How many of you invite your priest over to your house or take him to a restaurant for a meal? How many of you send him a greeting card on his birthday or his ordination anniversary? How many of you give him a gift for Christmas? How many of you tell him that you appreciate what he does for the parish? There may be a few; of course, not many. Remember the sole reason he is there is you. He is spending his life for you. If you think that he is paid for the job, well, I tell you, no one can pay enough to a priest for his life. If your present priest has been in the parish for twelve years, and you have never met him except for your spiritual needs—how sad!

Well, if you think that priests should be perfect, let me ask you a personal question: Do you have a perfect marriage? Do you have a perfect husband or wife? Do you have a perfect family? Do you have a perfect job? I think there is nothing perfect. We learn to live with the imperfections of life. We learn to put up with weaknesses and limitations of people. You love your spouse with his/her weaknesses; you love your children regardless of what they do. It should be the same with your priests too. Love your priests, just because their life is a life of many sacrifices.

No One Follows You as Does a Priest

How can we thank the Lord enough for the gift of Holy Orders, especially priesthood, because there is nobody on earth that touches the life of a Catholic as does a priest—not even the parents can do as priests. In this culture especially, grown-up children leave home to be on their own. But if they are still practicing their faith, they continue to be touched by a priest. In one sense, the influence of a priest in the life of a practicing Catholic is much more than that of his/her parents, as far as their spiritual life is concerned.

From the moment of birth until death—even after death—there is a priest behind every Catholic. Actually, the influence of a priest on a person begins even before the birth of a baby. In some cultures, the priest is asked to pray over the belly of a pregnant woman for the safe birth of the baby. Once the baby is born, it is a priest—or sometimes a deacon—who initiates the child into the Church by the sacrament of Baptism, then into Reconciliation and Holy Communion. I do not know if anyone could keep track of how many times a person who practices his/her faith seriously goes to a priest for just the sacrament of Reconciliation in their lifetime, or receives Holy Communion from a priest or a deacon. When the person grows to be an adult, the bishop confers on him/her the sacrament of Confirmation. Later on, when the person is old enough to get married, there is a man again of Holy Orders to lead him/her into the sacrament of Matrimony. He prepares the couple for a happy married life; he prepares them to accept and welcome their future children. You and I have been touched by clergy that way even before we were born. They prepared our parents to welcome us with prayers and longing.

When one becomes ill, the priest anoints him/her and prays for healing; when the person is in danger of death, a priest prepares the person for the final journey by being at his/her bedside. As the person takes in the last breath and closes his eyes, never to open again in this world, the soul glides into the arms of the Lord. If the soul is able to stand before the presence of the Lord confidently, know that it is all because there was an anointed hand that followed the soul from the moment of conception until it separated from the body. At the time of a funeral, there is a man of Holy Orders who accompanies him/her to the grave. After death, even after many years, a priest prays for the person, mostly by offering Masses. Who else is there with a Catholic who does as much as a priest? They follow you wherever you go. Priests make visible the invisible graces of God through the sacraments of the Church. They are not ordinary people!

A Happy Priest

On the other side of the coin, I am content even though my life is not always full. There are days of gloom, feelings of insufficiency, worries, and frustrations; I might feel I labored in vain. But there is an unexplainable joy and a sense of fulfillment deep down within my heart, because I know no one else can replace me, except another priest. When people say that my homily is boring and one or two minutes too long, or I am not punctual, or not active, or not understanding, or not up to the expectations of people, or anything like that, I am consoled because I know only a priest can do the sort of ministry that I do, and no one else. As I said earlier, who else follows a Catholic as a priest does?

As I sit in the confessional for hours listening to the stories of stumbling, falls, and failures and to the sobs and gasps of people who try to recount their sins, fighting tears, and when they walk out of the confessional strengthened and reassured, I feel God's greatness in me; I feel I am a superman. Who else could do that? They came into the confessional with heavy hearts, with their many burdens of sins. But there I was, waiting to be the shoulder of the Lord to take their burdens away, to be the tongue of the Lord to speak tenderly to them, to be the hands of the Lord to bind up their wounds. So many times have the penitents told me "Thank you for your vocation" just before leaving the confessional. I feel great, and I know my life has a nobler purpose.

When I celebrate the Holy Eucharist, when I make God's presence live once again, when He works the miracle through me, I know I am no ordinary man, because an ordinary person cannot do this. That thought makes me feel humble; how blessed I am to be chosen to perform such a sublime act for the rest of the people. Why me, and not anyone else? There were fifty students with me in high school, but I am the only priest! There were forty-two seminarians with me in the first year of seminary; only three of us became priests!

I do not like to brag, but here are a few examples of how people appreciate my vocation and ministry. There are a few who give me cards and gifts for Christmas. Though the number of people who think of me will never equal those who forget me even around Christmastime, I am happy, because those who think of me are people who really love and care for me. At least they appreciate my dedication. That is enough for me to be happy. When I preach a homily, there are many who tell me that my homily made them think, but there are at least a few people who e-mail me about how they felt about my homily. I appreciate people who write to me more than those who simply say, "Great homily, Father." This is what a woman wrote to me a few months back:

Hi Fr. Mathew,

I just want to thank you for that terrific homily you gave today on authority. My two teenage sons were there to hear it as well, which was so gratifying. You presented it so logically and simply that everyone could follow it to its natural conclusion. We want to follow Church teaching because it is directly from Christ. Your humor and joy help to keep the young ones engaged. Have a happy Sunday!

Here is what an eighth-grade student wrote to me:

Dear Fr. Mathew,

I am sorry for failing to respond in Mass. I am a privileged kid, who is able to freely worship Jesus and I am so lucky to have that freedom. My silence in responding today showed that I didn't have the passion or courage that shows that I love Jesus with all my heart. I sat in silence as you tried to make us happy and get us involved in our faith, and I am so sorry for that. I will smile and praise the Lord for all that is good and I will try my best to be passionate and involved in Christ.

God bless,
An 8th grade student

I can give you hundreds of such examples. I hope every priest will have stories and examples of such kind. It means that people appreciate the ministry the men in Holy Orders do, though there are people, as I said earlier, who try unceasingly to find fault with clergy. I think we can simply forgive them and concentrate on people who understand the value of the sacrament of Holy Orders.

When I am called to anoint a dying person, even in the middle of night, I, though unworthy, feel the greatness of my call. As I sit by the dying person, gently preparing him/her to make that final journey into the home God has prepared for us, I see the calm, serene, peaceful look in the face of the person. I become Christ for him/her, and the person feels reassured. As I walk into a hospital room, I most often see joy in the eyes of the patient, a twinkle in his/her eyes, especially if the person is a practicing Catholic. My presence makes a world of difference in the life of that person. Who else can do that? Even if they get the best medical care, I am sure they care more for the spiritual side of life.

I was visiting an older lady who was in a hospital for over two weeks. She was not in any danger of death, but she requested that I anoint her since she was about to undergo a complicated procedure. As I was preparing to anoint her, her cell phone rang. She took the call and said, "Vince, call me back after ten minutes"; then she hung up. Vince was her husband. I anointed her and gave her Communion. After exactly ten minutes, he called her again. She said, "Vince, when you called me, Fr. Mathew was here to anoint me and to give me Communion. You know, honey, the Lord is so much better than you!"

The sacrament of Holy Orders, which makes God's presence tangible in our life, is wonderful. I am not able to express in writing the significance of this sacrament. But I am sure of one thing: a man in Holy Orders makes the Lord present in the world in a very special way. I wish to thank the Lord for the supreme gift of this sacrament. I also wish to thank all priests, and all those who are in Holy Orders, who spend their lives in God's service and in the service of others. I wish to thank the Lord for calling me to the priesthood. I thank the Lord for making me an instrument of His many graces to His people. I thank the Lord for sanctifying the lives of His people through my humble life. If I could choose again, I would want to be a priest.

I have been a priest for fourteen years now! Time flies. It seems like not even twelve months. I can still picture the day of my ordination and all the celebrations right in front of my eyes. Not only the ordination-day celebrations; I can also remember well the day I left home for the seminary, which was not very far from my home. I was just sixteen. I still remember walking with my father to the nearest bus stop with a suitcase in my hand. I can still feel the warm tears rolling down my cheeks as I waved good-bye to my mother, who with tears in her eyes stood at the door to see me off.

From that day, home became a stranger to me. I left behind my parents, home, music of my home, my siblings, my favorite friends, food, comforts, hobbies, and many other things. Since then, a formerly unknown place became my home. As I recall that day, and as I write this, there are tears in the corners of my eyes. Leaving behind all that I loved for the Lord reminds me of the disciples who left behind their fishing trade, boats and nets, and their father to follow the Lord. I went through a rigorous seminary program for twelve years before I was ordained a priest; it was similar to a military training. Within the walls of the monastic seminary, I learned both good and bad. I molded many natural talents and spontaneities to adapt myself into a fitting candidate for priesthood. I developed certain talents and powers that I never knew I had within me. Now here I am, a priest of the Most High God; a priest for the Lord and his people.

People ask me about my vocation, my call to the priesthood. They ask me when I decided to become a priest; they ask me how that call from God happened. I tell them, partially jokingly, that I don't know if I have yet decided! I take one day at a time. I tell them there was no stereotypical call from God as they might think, as in the case of the young boy Samuel (cf. 1 Samuel 3:1–18). I honestly feel that it was nothing but an immature feeling of a young lad who was formed into a decision over a twelve-year period in monastic cloisters. That decision of an immature lad was later labeled a vocation.

By no means was it a well-thought-out decision, a premeditated or prayerfully considered choice. The initial decision to enter the monastery was not the result of any discernment over a long time, although my decision to become a priest was the result of prayerful discernment. For me it was just a feeling. I felt like entering a monastery, just as some of my friends felt like entering a school of medicine, teaching, or engineering. Some called *my feeling* a vocation while the feelings of my friends were labeled a profession. It's all a game of words. One of them serves as a doctor in a hospital; one of them is a teacher at a school in my hometown; the other is an engineer in England, working for a company; I serve as a priest in a church. The only difference is this: they do not deal directly with the soul, whereas I do; they are all married, I am not!

My parents were religious and God-oriented; they attended church almost daily, and I was an altar server. My family had family prayer every day, and my parents were close to priests and nuns. In short, I grew up in a family who was open to "possibilities." I was an altar server too. That didn't mean anything to me or my parents. I myself never thought I would ever become a priest; neither did my family or friends. I was a happy-go-lucky guy, seemingly never meant for priesthood. No one would say I had any priestly make about me. I had all the features of a carefree guy; I had all the fantasies of youth; I had my dreams and hopes about my future life, even had clear ideas about how my future wife should be! Of course, now I am very, very far from those fantasies. I was never too prayerful or even too religious-minded.

When I went into seminary, people were sad; my school-mates, especially girls, asked, "Really?" They could not believe that I would take such a drastic step. Many thought I would return once my initial enthusiasm died out. Actually, my original motive was to return after a few years of great formation, which would open up a better chance to other professions. At the end of the first year of formation, I went home for a visit. People thought I would not go back, but I did go back to the monastery. This continued for three years, and then the fourth year was novitiate. This occurred at a different place, where all those who were with me for the very first year came together again. Those who had not seen me since the first year were surprised even more. One of them bluntly said that he thought I would have left already.

At the end of the novitiate, I made my temporary profession, which was for a year, and received my white religious habit. I went on a home visit for fifteen days two years later. People who thought I would have left started asking me, "How many years more now?" But I never promised anyone I would get ordained. Actually, I told my parents that they must never conclude that their son was going to be a priest, that I would return even on the day before my ordination if I didn't like it. I did not want them to build any castles in the air around their son's priesthood. Nevertheless, I returned to seminary after the vacation.

Eventually, it was time for me to renew my vows for another year. The implication is that one is allowed to leave the monastery if he does not wish to renew vows for the next year. At the end of each year, the senior members who had the voting and decision-making power would evaluate each monk in temporary vows, based on the report presented to them by the rector. If the report was bad, they wouldn't let him renew his vows; he would have to leave the monastery. The custom was that the rector would tell the monk the summary of the report he would be submitting to the family chapter (decision-making meeting) before he presented it. The rector said my report was excellent.

The day before I was supposed to renew my vows, the prior called me to his room. He was a young man then, a very friendly man, exceptionally good and pleasant. But that day, he appeared very restless. With great difficulty, he said, "I am sorry, Mathew, the family chapter did not promote you because your report was not promising, it was bad." I was stunned. I told him that the summary of the report the rector read to me was a good one; at least, he told me it was. He silently looked into my eyes and said, "But I am promoting you at my own risk. You must reverse the report for next year." So I renewed my vows for another year. I renewed my vows for the next six years before I made my solemn vows. I was ordained in 2003. Perhaps it was the risk that the prior took that day that made all the difference.

Since the day of my ordination, my life has been a mixture of happiness and sadness, laughter and tears, frustrations and fulfillments, joys and sorrows, ups and downs, as in any other life; and I know that my life will continue to be a mixture of all of these. That will always be so; it will never change, and I don't want it to either. It is because the Lord chose me from the world, which is a mixture of all good and bad, happiness and sadness, laughter and tears, joys and sorrows, and so on. He said, "I have chosen you out of the world" (John 15:19). Just because I was chosen out of the world does not mean that the external world ceases to exist around me. I know I continue to live in the world, which is not perfect. Therefore, my life will have all the limitations that everyone else might have. But that does not bother me. The one who chose me to "follow him" is also one who knows the limitations of being a human being. He is able to make me strong; he is able to make me a channel of blessings to other people. I praise Him for his faithfulness and love.

CHAPTER 8

Arise and Shine

Nations shall walk by your light, kings by
the radiance of your dawning.
—Isaiah 60:3

Know What You Are

The Lord has made a masterpiece of you; arise and shine now. You are God's choicest creation, a masterpiece! He has made you the eighth sacrament for the rest of humanity. The Lord has "adorned you with jewelry, putting bracelets on your arms, a necklace about your neck, a ring in your nose, earrings in your ears, and a beautiful crown on your head. Thus you were adorned with gold and silver; your garments made of fine linen, silk and embroidered cloth. Fine flour, honey, and olive oil were your food. You were very, very beautiful, fit for royalty. You were renowned among the nations for your beauty, perfected by the splendor I showered on you" (Ezekiel 16:11–14). Remember that you are wonderfully made.

The prophet Isaiah says, "You shall be a glorious crown in the hand of the Lord, a royal diadem in the hand of your God" (Isaiah 62:3). We should always remember that it is the hand of God that shaped us and that we have a divine make. I often feel that we miss the point that we are conceived in the mind of God even before we were conceived in the womb of our mother. Most people do not remember and do not know that our names are written upon the palm of our God, that we are precious and honored in the sight of God, that God calls us by our name. This is a forgetting of our basic identity, and that is a shame.

How many of us remember, in our consumeristic world, that we are created in the image and likeness of God and to give Him glory through our life? How many of us have the basic desire to be perfected, by the sacraments of the Church, into the image God designed for us? We bring honor and glory to the Lord and make Him happy when we lead an authentic Christian life. Leading an authentic Christian life will certainly lead many more people to the Lord. Then we become the signboards that direct people to God and the channels of blessing to others.

God wants us to become a visible symbol of His many invisible graces to others. This is the purpose of our existence. I wish we understood the worth and importance of our call. As I try to conclude my thoughts on how God makes us a masterpiece and a symbol of His graces and blessings to other people, I wish to remind you just once more that our call is to become, by grace, what Jesus is by nature. Try to recall what the Lord said: "Before I formed you in the womb I knew you, before you were born, I dedicated you, a prophet to the nations I appointed you" (Jeremiah 1:5). Again, "See, upon the palms of my hands I have engraved you" (Isaiah 49:15–16). And again, "I have called you by name: you are mine" (Isaiah 43:1).

Remember: We Have a Mission to Fulfill

The Lord formed us so wonderfully in our mother's womb, adorned us with all heavenly beauty, and made us His masterpiece. He gave us a name, and He engraved that name upon the palms of His hands so that He will never forget us! He keeps us as the apple of His eye. He fortifies us with all the sacraments of the Church so that we will be a sacrament in this world. Now the Lord is asking us, "Whom shall I send? Who will go for us?" (Isaiah 6:8).

Be Like Salt, Be a Lamp

As a sacrament of the Lord, we are reflections of the Lord's goodness to others. Do people see the face of God when they look at us? Do we glorify the Lord by our lives? The Scripture tells us that we are created for God's glory. "All who are called by my name, whom I created for my glory, I formed them, made them" (Isaiah 43:7). Do we become a blessing to others, like Abraham was? Is there any quality difference between our life and that of a non-Catholic or a non-Christian? If there is none, is not our religious practice a waste of time?

The Lord said, "You are the salt of the earth. But, if salt loses its taste, with what can it be seasoned? It is no longer good for anything but to be thrown out and trampled underfoot. You are the light of the world. A city set on a mountain cannot be hidden. Nor do they light a lamp and then put it under a bushel basket; it is set on a lampstand, where it gives light to all in the house. Just so, your light must shine before others, that they may see your good deeds and glorify your heavenly Father" (Matthew 5:13–16). Does our life make any difference in the life of our brothers and sisters, as does salt? Does their life become tastier, lighter, and happier because of my being here with them?

A city on a mountaintop cannot be hidden; rather, it is visible to all. It stands tall as the pride of a particular place. The popularity of the city attracts people to it. The Lord means that Christians and Catholics are people to be seen by all. Let all people know who we are. Let us attract people, as a city attracts people, to the Lord. A flower attracts bees and other insects because it has sweet honey and fragrance. We attract people to the Lord through us, through our good deeds. That is why the Lord said, "That they may see your good deeds and glorify your heavenly Father" (Matthew 5:16). God gives a form to a life for His glory, as any painting declares the glory and skill of the artist.

The Lord said that we are the light of the world. Remember the burning candle that was given to us on the day of our baptism. The Lord showed us the path by being our light; now we must show others that same path by being a light in the path of their life. We received the light; now we have to *become* the light

315

in the world. In the sacrament of Baptism, God was turning us into a lighthouse that would throw light around it so that others may see their way clearly. That was an invitation not only to live and move in Christ, the light, but also to burn like a candle.

Have you ever thought about why the world, at times, is so dark and gruesome? What makes the world so bad? It is the evil things people do. The Lord wants us to dispel darkness by our good deeds: by our disciplined life, by our sacrifices, by our humanitarian works, by being messengers of God's goodness. Don't forget that it is the good deeds of people across the world that make the world somewhat livable.

The Christian life is one of receiving and celebrating the kindness and mercy of God. Every sacrament of the Church is a direct proclamation of God's favorable time to humanity. God wants us to proclaim the favor that we receive through the sacraments to the rest of the world. Recall what Jesus told the man whom he freed from the power of demons, "Go home to your family and announce to them all that the Lord in his pity has done for you" (Mark 5:19). The man goes and begins to proclaim everywhere what Jesus has done for him. That man became a signboard that directed people to Jesus.

The thought that we have been created in the image and likeness of God should lead us to consider and treat life with the utmost respect. This should lead us to live a life worthy of God's call, worthy of being children of God. Today, respect for life is gone because humanity has forgotten God himself, the author of life. When I say respect for life, I not only mean fighting abortion; generally speaking, we have degraded ourselves to a mere commodity to be exposed, used, reused, and disposed of.

That is belittling the handiwork of God; that is losing the value of being made by the divine hand of God. In short, we forget that we have a noble make.

God should be the ultimate value behind every other value. But the fact that so many are eager to do away with God in the present day points to the fact that any other value can be compromised easily because the concept of God, the supreme value itself, is lost. If people can forget God, the most important value of life, then what else can't be forgotten? One of the tragedies of present-day life is that the world consciously tries to forget God. This conscious negation of God leads to every sin in the world.

One way to bring back the lost value of life is to bring back God back into our life, into our culture, and into the world. As Christians, this sense of God in our life should be expressed by sincerely practicing our faith. As Catholics, we do this by being obedient to the teachings of the Church. If all Catholics adhere to the teachings of the Church, there will be more order in our society. Once God is set as the center of our life, everything becomes more meaningful. Nowadays, there is a kind of confusion even among Catholics because there are many people in the community who don't practice their faith and religion. This brings lack of order in our faith life, and eventually a lack of order in our society. As a consequence, important values and priorities of life are lost. Most men and women today are not able to distinguish between right and wrong. As a result, we who are created by God to glorify Him actually insult Him; we are spitting in His face.

I ask you: consider life a bit more seriously. Please bear in mind all the time that we have been created by God to glorify Him in this world. Consider this world a garden and yourself as a beautiful flower. The presence of all of us, the masterpieces, would make the world a lovely garden. God created us so wonderfully (cf. Psalm 139:14) in order to make this world a better place, a more beautiful garden. You will be glorifying God when you become a responsible parent who shapes and reshapes the life of your children. I know that is hard work. But that is something you chose on your own. As coartists with God, it is not enough that you accidently bring forth a life. You should do it intentionally with love. And then try to nurture that life that you have procreated, the artwork that you have produced, into a masterpiece by constantly shaping that life.

I wish we would become a bit more modest before our teenage children around our house, pools, parks, and beaches. Maybe in our present culture, at least some of us become a cause for stumbling. Kindly excuse me for saying that. I know there are many great men and women who try day and night to be a role model to their children. A big salute to all of them. Remember what the Lord said: "Things that cause sin will inevitably occur, but woe to the person through whom they occur. It would be better for him if a millstone were put around his neck and he be thrown into the sea than for him to cause one of these little ones to sin" (Luke 17:1–2). Our children are the "little ones." Let us not inject elements of sin into immature minds by our immodesty. Sometimes we don't feed them with the best and the healthiest. Sometimes we feed them with things that are not appropriate for their age, of course, not knowing their negative impact later in their life. What is the point in regretting parental mistakes once they are out of our control? I wish that parents could walk with their children a bit longer, even when the children are grown up. Maybe our children are eager to break away from their parents. I think it is partly because of their age, but also because the parents do not provide an environment that is inviting for their children.

How many parents are eager to take their children to church at least on Sundays and to religion classes? How many of you take them regularly to the sacrament of Reconciliation and other sacraments? How many of you find time to pray with your children? How many parents are somewhat grounded in a basic Catholic faith that they can pass on to their children? I sometimes feel that there are many people who do a job for which they are not qualified. I believe that parenting is an art; an art that requires professionalism and commitment. How many of you think you correct your children when you see them doing things that are not appropriate? How many of you become great role models for your children? How many of you can honestly tell your children, as St. Paul said, "Be imitators of me, as I am of Christ" (1 Corinthians 11:1)? Do you really think that you are a trustworthy coartist of God? Or a good caretaker of the treasures God placed under your care?

How many of you really wish that your children should grow up morally grounded and disciplined because you want them to excel in their studies or jobs? If you do, what do you do to accomplish that? How many of you really teach, inspire, motivate, and guide your children to swim against the currents and the trends of the time? How many of you honestly work for their spiritual well-being as hard as you do for their physical well-being? I hope you understand that for many of us, our priorities are wrong. Most people are not contributing positively to make this world a better place. We are making this world a competitive field where we teach our children to fight and conquer "the other." Remember what I said earlier: You are the makers of the world!

What is all the money you have in the bank if your children fail morally and spiritually? I am sure God is going to hold parents accountable. God gave you talents, but you hid them under the earth. Do you think you will hear on the Last Judgment Day, "Well done, my good and faithful servant. Since you were faithful in small matters, I will give you great responsibilities. Come, share your master's joy" (Matthew 25:12)? How many parents can honestly say, as St. Paul said, "I have competed well; I have finished the race; I have kept the faith" (2 Timothy 4:7)? If we look at the present situation, there are many young parents who are not able to pass the faith onto their children because they themselves are not rooted in their faith.

I am sure the Lord is going to hold me, his priest, even more accountable because I was given more. The Lord said, "Much will be required of the person entrusted with much, and still more will be demanded of the person entrusted with more" (Luke 12:48). Though I strive each day to do more for the Lord, I know I could still do more. As a priest of the Lord, He has entrusted to me the care of souls and appointed me a dispenser of the sacraments of the Church. A priest, like parents, is a coartist with God in reshaping souls with the sacraments of the Church, according to what he says and does. In other words, he is a lighted lamp on a pedestal, a city built on a mountaintop. He is seen and watched by many. As the Lord marked you out to be a coartist with Him to portray your child physically, the Lord marked me out or set me apart to accomplish His dream for humanity.

Be a Builder for the Lord

"Today I appoint you over nations and over kingdoms, to uproot and to tear down, to destroy and to demolish, to build and to plant" (Jeremiah 1:10). This was my ordination motto that I printed on my souvenir. I thought this verse best explains the basic but challenging mission of a person who follows the Lord. Why did the Lord know us before He formed us in the womb? Why did He appoint us to be a prophet to the nations? This means our life has a purpose, a mission to fulfill. The Lord creates each of us with a mission; the Lord commissions you and me for a task.

If you look at the first part of Jeremiah 1:10, you will see that the prophet was asked to uproot and to tear down, to destroy and to demolish. That is tougher than building and planting. But the second part would not be effective without the first part. The first part is preparatory and is a must before starting to build and plant. Now we need to do this more than ever. We have a lot to uproot and to tear down, to destroy and to overthrow in our society. Try to recall all that we said as standing against marriage and family life: premarital sex, cohabiting, abortion, divorce, sexual anarchy, and pornography. Building and planting will not be easy without uprooting these evils from society. How can we build without first putting down strong foundations? How dedicated are we in addressing these sins?

Being a builder for the Lord is challenging. It demands courage. It takes time. It is like a farmer preparing the ground before he sows seeds. If we sow seeds without preparing the ground—uprooting, tearing down, destroying, and demolishing—most probably, weeds will choke the seeds. Our labor will be in vain.

What is my task? What is the purpose of my life? To what purpose did God dedicate you and me? Some to be prophets, some to be priests, some to be religious, some to be parents. Everyone has a task to fulfill in this world. As I thought of putting together my thoughts on the seven sacraments of the Church, I felt that the Lord was calling us to be the eighth sacrament in the world. I believe that is our general vocation. By receiving the sacraments of the Church, the grace of God, we are to become another sacrament, a sign of God's grace to others. In other words, we have to become a blessing to other people.

Every life born is a "sending forth." God sends us forth into the world from the mind of God to be a blessing to other people. God wants to bless the world through each life. I do not think that the Lord sends anyone forth from His eternal mind into the world without any purpose or mission. The Lord called Abraham to be the father of all the faithful. God made him a blessing to other people; or rather, God blessed all the nations of the world through Abraham. This is what the Lord told him: "Go forth from your father's house to a land that I will show you. I will make of you a great nation, and I will bless you; I will make your name great, so that you will be a blessing. I will bless those who bless you and curse those who curse you. All the families of the earth will find blessing in you" (Genesis 12:1–3). Indeed, God kept His promise; God blessed you and me through Abraham. As we go through the pages of the Bible, we see how Abraham became a blessing to all the nations. God chose a nation to be His own, first through Abraham, then through Jacob, then through David. And finally, God blessed all of humanity through Jesus!

Catholic life is an amazing life, because we have a sure hope of everlasting life. God gives us every spiritual nourishment through the Church so that His promised life will be ours. Parents watch their kids grow up, so too does God the Father. He gave us life; He planted us like His choicest vine in this world, His garden. He not only gave us birth, He also gives us all the nourishment we need to grow. He cultivates the soil from time to time so that we will yield a harvest. He watches us grow up and produce good fruits, fruits that will last.

My Prayer

Lord, I was born in Your mind before You created me in my mother's womb. You made use of the sacrament of Matrimony as a canvas to give shape to the design You had in Your mind for me. You chose my parents to cooperate with Your plan for me. Your first invisible touch on my life came through the instrumentality of my parents; then You brought me to light. As the psalmist says, "I was wonderfully created" (cf. Psalm 139:14)! All who looked at me said I was the best of Your creation; I believe so. Lord, give to every man and woman who would like to enter into the covenant of marriage the grace to see this sacrament as Your canvas for giving shape to Your designs.

Lord, Your first visible and divine touch on me was when You planted me by the waters of grace by the sacrament of Baptism. You planted me in the Church, which is the fountain of divine graces. I became Your beloved son, and You became my Father. Give to everyone who comes to that fountain of everlasting life the courage to stay by the waters of grace until that person takes his/her last breath.

I have known Your kindness in the sacrament of Reconciliation, not once, but hundreds of times. Before the end of my earthly pilgrimage, I do not know how many more times I will need it, because "woe is me, I am doomed! For I am a man of unclean lips" (Isaiah 6:5) and am a sinful man. I need this sacrament to strip myself of my corrupted self and to put on Christ. Lord, draw Your people to this ocean of mercy.

I encounter Your unfathomable love in the Sacrament of the Eucharist every day; this is the sacrament with which You nourish me with the food of life. That food becomes my strength for the rest of the journey. You woke up the prophet Elijah from his sleep and said, "Get up and eat or the journey will be too much for you" (1 Kings 19:7). You wake me up every morning to feed me with the divine bread. As the prophet walked forty days and forty nights, strengthened by that food, to the mountain of Horeb, where he met You, I continue to journey on to the Promised Land with the hope of meeting You. Strengthen me and Your chosen ones with this divine manna.

As I make my journey to You, I need Your never-ending guidance, because the paths are crooked and rugged; I am confused at the crossroads. I see many roads; some seem easier, smoother, and wider. I feel like taking the easier ones, smoother ones, the wider ones. But You direct me through the sacrament of Confirmation with the Holy Spirit, who helps me choose the right path, not the easy, smooth, or wide one. He helps me to become the kind of person You want me to be with all the fruits and gifts of the Holy Spirit. He awakens the real man within me. Lord, help me to keep the fire of Your love, the Holy Spirit, always alive in my life.

Your last touch on my soul is the sacrament of the Anointing of the Sick, with which You finish Your work to make me Your masterpiece. Let me not be afraid of Your last, perfecting touch. Rather, let me be eager to receive this sacrament that becomes a bridge I walk over to reach Your bosom.

Thank you, Lord, for the sacrament of Holy Orders, for men who show the courage to be Your special ministers. Your work on souls would not have been possible if You had not established the sacrament of Holy Orders, to which You invite men who would try to elevate souls so that they would become more pleasing to You here on earth, and that this will help us stand before Your divine presence without any fear or trembling. I now know that You made use of my parents and people in Holy Orders to make me what I am today.

I wish to conclude my thoughts by praying Psalm 145, which sings of the greatness and goodness of God. I hope you will join me:

> I will extol you, my God and king; I will bless your name forever. Every day I will bless you; I will praise your name forever and ever. Great is the Lord and worthy of much praise, whose grandeur is beyond understanding. One generation praises your deeds to the next and proclaims your mighty works. They speak of your splendor of your majestic glory, tell of your wonderful deeds. They speak of the power of your awesome acts and recount your great deeds. They celebrate your abounding goodness and joyfully sing of your justice. The Lord is gracious and merciful, slow to anger and abounding in mercy. The Lord is good to all, compassionate toward all His works. All your works give you thanks, Lord, and your faithful bless you. (Psalm 145:1–10)

Thank you!
With love,
Fr. Mathew C. John

Comments

"In this time of relativism... and hollow commitments, Fr. Mathew has found both the inspiration and courage to define who and what we are to be, based on our Creator's perfection of His masterpiece: *man*."

—Reinhard Schuster
Former Vice Chancellor, University of Missouri–St. Louis

"Fr. Mathew is able to see more clearly many of the problems and difficulties found in living the moral life due to living the Western lifestyle. Using the lens of the sacramental life, Fr. Mathew has done a masterful job of examining these problems and seeing solutions. This book simply and succinctly recommends a prayerful reassessment and renewal of Catholic life: one which will allow Catholics to better live out their chosen vocation, to live out their faith."

—David J. Keys, PhD
Catholic writer/speaker and author of
Exploring the Belief in the Real Presence

"Fr. Mathew has ministered in India, Wales, and the United States, and so he brings a distinctly global perspective to parish ministry. His concept that we are the 'eighth sacrament' is a wonderful reminder to us of how each human being is truly a work of art in God's hands."

—Fr. Scott Jones
Associate Pastor, Sacred Heart Parish, Valley Park, Missouri

About the Author

Fr. Mathew C. John, born and raised in Kerala, India, is a Catholic priest of the Archdiocese of St. Louis. He served the diocese of Menevia in the United Kingdom until moving to St. Louis in 2012. He is currently the associate pastor at St. Joseph's Church, Manchester, Missouri. He holds a master's degree in sociology, social work, and English.